Strategic Management Accounting, Volume III

Vassili Joannidès de Lautour

Strategic Management Accounting, Volume III

Aligning Ethics, Social Performance and Governance

palgrave
macmillan

Vassili Joannidès de Lautour
Grenoble École de Management
Grenoble, France

School of Accountancy
Queensland University of Technology
Brisbane, QLD, Australia

University of Parma
Parma, Italy

ISBN 978-3-030-20156-2 ISBN 978-3-030-20157-9 (eBook)
https://doi.org/10.1007/978-3-030-20157-9

Cover illustration: Monty Rakusen / Alamy Stock Photo

This Palgrave Macmillan imprint is published by the registered company Springer Nature Switzerland AG.
The registered company address is: Gewerbestrasse 11, 6330 Cham, Switzerland

Introduction

This volume was added to the Strategic Management Accounting volumes one and two, based upon observations that management accounting scholars address a series of issues, including accountability, but tend to leave ethical questions either aside or very implicit. It is quite unusual to find management accounting research explicitly addressing the ethical dimension or ground of the discipline. Rather than a stream of research per se, this seems to be an initiative from individual researchers (Joannidès & McKernan, 2015; McKernan, 2012; McKernan & Kosmala, 2004, 2007; McKernan & McPhail, 2012; McPhail, 2009; McPhail & Adams, 2016; McPhail & Ferguson, 2016).

Even though the paucity of management accounting research on the subject could have been a sufficient reason for developing this third volume, I must confess this was an explicit request from two of my Doctor of Business Administration (DBA) candidates and an indirect inspiration from another two.

Everything originated from one of them, Panida Chotiyanon from whose thesis a book on the changing role of the management accountants was derived (Chotiyanon & Joannidès de Lautour, 2018). Chotiyanon told me there is something yet to clarify on the ontological construct of management accountants. This discussion took place on the evening after her viva, as she was a new Doctor in Business Administration. She was suggesting that I should write a book on these ontological constructs, because they are not much addressed in research, although they are crucial to understand the essence of management accounting. Addressing its essence, she was convinced that issues in management accounting information reliability would be central, thereby opening for a discussion on ethics in management accounting. In fact, this discussion led me to consider what Chap. 4 addresses: management accounting and its ethics as ontological constructs. Thereby, I concur with Hannah Arendt's idea that ontology precedes anthropology (Arendt, 1961). Before considering cultural differences, which management accounting research has abundantly done to date (Baskerville, 2005; Joannidès de Lautour, Wickramasinghe, & Berland, forthcoming), it seems important to me that the origins of management accounting be understood.

The day before Chotiyanon's viva, we met with a new DBA candidate for the first time. Chotiyanon gave him some sound advice as to how to get started and apprehending working with me. Interestingly, this new doctoral candidate, Marcelo Barros, currently employed as the Esporte Clube Bahia football club CFO, worked for Andersen before the Enron affair occurred. He shared with me that there was a real need for a book discussing ethical issues in management accounting: I remember he told me each time a management accountant is asked to talk about ethics, nobody is really capable of giving an answer. The question of ethics in management accounting seems to be complex, complicated and at times embarrassing for practitioners. This is how I found myself confronted with this idea of writing Chap. 2 addressing issues in trust and confidence.

At the same time, another of my DBA candidate, Tim Hayes, a semi-retired CEO and former chartered accountant, whose work is addressing the reliance paradigm and tone at the top, gave me the intuition that this notion of reliability is indeed central to management accountant's work and professional identity. I found that most of the literature on management accountants' professional identity had been addressing a series of issues, such as how they are perceived by non-accountants (Beard, 1994; Carnegie & Napier, 2010; Dimnik & Felton, 2006; Haynes, 2006; Kaidonis, 2009; Morales & Lambert, 2013) and how they see their role within the organisation from a strategic viewpoint (Annisette & Trivedi, 2013; Gambling, 1985; Kamla, Gallhofer, & Haslam, 2012; Ramirez, 2009), but not rarely as the guardians of information reliability. And yet, when we read Anthony's work, it is central that management accountants are expected to produce and diffuse information pertinent to decision-making, therefore reliable information (Anthony, 1965, 1988; Anthony, Dearden, & Bedford, 1984). This is what enabled me to build this book's canvas.

It proceeded from this idea that management accountants' ethics would lie in a reliability imperative upon a reflection on whence such reliability can come and how it could be understood or assessed. The first answer that came to my mind was that business ethics education would be central. Thinking this took me to reconsider my first doctoral candidate's thesis on workplace spirituality. In her thesis, Dunia Harajli-Berry raised the question of whether business ethics courses are really needed. Is ethics innate or learnt? This is a question discussed in Chap. 5 and an extension of discussions we had together but also took me to the origins of management accounting in the book as a divine revelation (Aho, 2005; Joannidès de Lautour, 2016).

Having already three chapters in hand explicitly addressing questions at the intersection of ethics, ontology and management accounting, I thought something was missing to really understand these issues. In the first place, reconsidering the origins of management accounting, it came to me that accounting history research has long endeavoured to show these roots and highlight some ethical issues at stake (Carnegie, 2012; Carnegie & Napier, 2002, 2012; Miller, Hopper, & Laughlin, 1991). Rather than reinventing the wheel, I found that there was a common historical thread across these individual pieces of work: management accounting has emerged as a rationalisation tool serving all types of masters. Management accounting could serve social and economic progress just as it could serve oppression and genocide. This raised the question of how management accountants justify that they are serving good or evil. This is how Chap. 1 was conceived. In hindsight, I must confess that I by default found that I had not addressed a very timely and yet important issue: social and environmental reporting. None of the other two volumes had addressed this point. Because in this third volume, I was discussing management accounting's whence and whither, it became clear to me that corporate social responsibility was the most recent expression of these concerns. By extension, social and environmental reporting would be a critical issue enabling to make sense of everything else discussed along the three volumes. I decided to place it as Chap. 3, having discussed the ontology of management accounting ethics and before engaging in questions revolving around reliability.

This third volume is structured as follows. Chapter 1 exposes how management accounting was formed during the industrial revolution as a tool for economic and social progress and has since then served any types of masters from colonisation or emancipation but also military strategy or the most severe genocide ever: the Shoah. Chapter 2 explicitly discusses management accountants' ontological construction, starting from the issue of trust and confidence. Chapter 3 exposes issues in social and environmental reporting as the awareness that corporate activity generates externalities that need consideration. Even this consideration appears as an ethical question: what good or evil do we do to others? How can we decide this is good or evil? What can we do, based on this observation? Chapter 4 questions the innate or learnt nature of ethics. This chapter is as philosophical as Chap. 2 and sets out to open for discussion practical concerns outside research. Chapter 5 extends this questioning by discussing the (im)possibility of ethics, especially knowing how it has been conceived of in the business world and in management research.

Bibliography

Aho, J. (2005). *Confession and bookkeeping—The religious, moral, and rhetorical roots of modern accounting*. New York: State University of New York Press.

Annisette, M., & Trivedi, V. U. (2013). Globalization, paradox and the (un)making of identities: Immigrant Chartered Accountants of India in Canada. *Accounting, Organizations & Society, 38*(1), 1–29.

Anthony, R. N. (1965). *Planning and control systems: A framework for analysis*. Boston: Harvard Business School Publishing.

Anthony, R. N. (1988). *The management control function*. Boston: Harvard Business School Publishing.

Anthony, R. N., Dearden, J., & Bedford, N. M. (1984). *Management control systems*. Homewood, IL: Irwin.

Arendt, H. (1961). *The human condition*. Chicago: The University of Chicago Press.

Baskerville, R. F. (2005). A research note: The unfinished business of culture. *Accounting, Organizations and Society, 30*(4), 389–391.

Beard, V. (1994). Popular culture and professional identity: Accountants in the movies. *Accounting, Organizations and Society, 19*(3), 303–318.

Carnegie, G. D. (2012). The special issue: AAAJ and research innovation. *Accounting, Auditing & Accountability Journal, 25*(2), 216–227.

Carnegie, G. D., & Napier, C. (2002). Exploring comparative international accounting history. *Accounting, Auditing & Accountability Journal, 15*(5), 689–718.

Carnegie, G. D., & Napier, C. J. (2010). Traditional accountants and business professionals: Portraying the accounting profession after Enron. *Accounting, Organizations and Society, 35*(3), 360–376.

Carnegie, G. D., & Napier, C. (2012). Accounting's past, present and future: The unifying power of history. *Accounting, Auditing & Accountability Journal, 25*(2), 328–369.
Chotiyanon, P., & Joannidès de Lautour, V. (2018). *The changing role of the management accountants—Becoming a business partner*. London: Palgrave Macmillan.
Dimnik, T., & Felton, S. (2006). Accountant stereotypes in movies distributed in North America in the twentieth century. *Accounting, Organizations and Society, 31*(2), 129–155.
Gambling, T. (1985). The accountant's guide to the Galaxy, including the profession at the end of the Universe. *Accounting, Organizations & Society, 10*(4), 415–425.
Haynes, K. (2006). Linking narrative and identity construction: Using autobiography in accounting research. *Critical Perspectives on Accounting, 17*(4), 399–418.
Joannidès, V., & McKernan, J. (2015). Ethics: From negative regulations to fidelity to the event. In P. O'Sullivan, N. Allington, & M. Esposito (Eds.), *The philosophy, politics and economics of finance in the 21st century—From hubris to disgrace* (pp. 310–331). London: Routledge.
Joannidès de Lautour, V. (2016). *Capitalism, accounting and the revealed religions—A study of Judaism, Christianity and Islam*. London: Palgrave Macmillan.
Joannidès de Lautour, V., Wickramasinghe, D., & Berland, N. (forthcoming). From critical accounting to an account of critique—The case of cultural emancipators. *Accounting Forum*.
Kaidonis, M. (2009). Critical accounting as an epistemic community: Hegemony, resistance and identity. *Accounting Forum, 33*(4), 290–297.
Kamla, R., Gallhofer, S., & Haslam, J. (2012). Understanding Syrian accountants' perceptions of, and attitudes towards, social accounting. *Accounting, Auditing & Accountability Journal, 25*(7), 1170–1205.
McKernan, J. F. (2012). Accountability as aporia, testimony and gift. *Critical Perspectives on Accounting, 23*(3), 258–278.
McKernan, J. F., & Kosmala, K. (2004). Accounting, love and justice. *Accounting, Auditing & Accountability Journal, 17*(3), 327–360.
McKernan, J. F., & Kosmala, K. (2007). Doing the truth: Religion—Deconstruction—Justice, and accounting. *Accounting, Auditing & Accountability Journal, 20*(5), 729–764.
McKernan, J. F., & McPhail, K. (2012). Accountability and accounterability. *Critical Perspectives on Accounting, 23*(12), 177–182.
McPhail, K. (2009). Where is the ethical knowledge in the knowledge economy?: Power and potential in the emergence of ethical knowledge as a component of intellectual capital. *Critical Perspectives on Accounting, 20*(7), 804–822.

McPhail, K., & Adams, C. A. (2016). Corporate respect for human rights: Meaning, scope, and the shifting order of discourse. *Accounting, Auditing & Accountability Journal, 29*(6), 650–678.
McPhail, K., & Ferguson, J. (2016). The past, the present and the future of accounting for human rights. *Accounting, Auditing & Accountability Journal, 29*(4), 526–541.
Miller, P., Hopper, T., & Laughlin, R. (1991). The new accounting history: An introduction. *Accounting, Organizations and Society, 16*(5–6), 395–403.
Morales, J., & Lambert, C. (2013). Dirty work and the construction of identity. An ethnographic study of management accounting practices. *Accounting, Organizations & Society, 38*(3), 228–244.
Ramirez, C. (2009). Constructing the small local practitioner: The changing nature of professional bodies and the management of professional accountants' identities in the UK. *Accounting, Organizations & Society, 24*, 381–408.

Contents

List of Figures

List of Tables

CHAPTER 1

Historical Perspectives on Strategy, Ethics and Management Accounting

Management control systems too often are collapsed to management accounting, itself reduced to managerial accounting. Through this reductionism, management control finds itself narrowed down to mere cost accounting, budgeting and budgetary control, a.k.a. variance analysis. Thereby, management control is amalgamated with a fraction only of what it encompasses and appears as a dated vision of its reality. This reductionism amalgamates contemporary management control with twentieth-century manufacturing companies' concerns. Thereby, the underpinnings of both strategy and management accounting tend to be ignored or underestimated.

It is therefore necessary to understand management control's origins and journey across history. Accounting history research, namely New Accounting History, reveals that management control and accounting were born in Ancient Egypt and developed alongside Antiquity until they were systematic with the three monotheisms (Carnegie & Napier, 2002; Cordery, 2015; Merino, 1998; Miller, Hopper, & Laughlin, 1991). Over centuries, management accounting and control have evolved as new political or economic concerns. It is commonly accepted that most of the contemporary accounting and control concerns arose with the development of Capitalism as a response to a quest for economic rationality (Berland & Chiapello, 2009; Carruthers & Espeland, 1991). Even though Capitalism and economics are significant features of management control, history shows they are not unique and as central as often thought.

V. Joannidès de Lautour, *Strategic Management Accounting, Volume III*, https://doi.org/10.1007/978-3-030-20157-9_1

Considering strategic management accounting, history reveals that military science informs the notion of strategy and how accounting has appeared as a way of executing it: how to trace the way a war is conducted and won (or lost). It is too often neglected that strategy originated from military sciences in Ancient China (Tzu, 1078) and then by counsels to European Monarchs (Clausewitz (von), 1832; Machiavel, 1520). Strategy has been perceived as the art of putting procedures and people in place to win or to avoid losing in a conflictual situation. Similarly, management accounting's roots can be found in a variety of non-business contexts, generally religious in the Middle Ages (Joannidès de Lautour, 2016). Both have been tightly connected.

Therefore, this chapter addresses the history of management accounting and control without pretending to be exhaustive. The purpose is not to go too far in accounting history research but to give an overview of how management accounting and control have evolved over time. This is aimed at highlighting where management control systems' current concerns find their origins and form a consistent whole. To this end, this chapter is structured around three themes that cover three eras and areas of management accounting thinking. In the first place, the religious heritage of management accounting appears as the philosophical and ethical grounds of contemporary management control systems. As these have influenced our Judæo-Christian world for centuries, the Middle Ages and modern history have been deliberately neglected. The second period discussed is that covering the development of Capitalism from the second Industrial Revolution and until the middle of the twentieth century. Lastly, in its discussion of strategy, this chapter cannot avoid wartime, starting with World War I and finishing with decolonisation. World War I is the cut-off date for two reasons. Firstly, historians consider it a pivotal event in war history: it is the last conventional war and the first war of a new type. In itself, it reveals concerns expressed in centuries of military activity and announces the modern war. Secondly, World War I was the first time strategy and management accounting were colligated.

1.1 Management Accounting as Religious Heritage

Accounting was born almost concomitantly to writing technologies and reading. This occurred with the development of the first advanced languages, that is, in Ancient Palestine and Egypt with hieroglyphs, Aramean and Hebrew. At that time, accounting systems were aimed at reconciling world dualism and operated as drivers of faith and thereby the utmost form of ethics. Accounting as an expression of ethics lies in this double-entry mode of thinking that has characterised business accounting ever since. Whence the importance of understanding its deepest origins: in religions (Joannidès de Lautour, 2016).

1.1.1 World Dualism as Accounting's Grounds

What is central to the four religions, and consequently crucial to accounting, is how world dualism is solved through accounting in different contexts and why solutions may differ from one setting to another. Within the four religions studied, a form of accounting differing from one belief system to another exists. It transpires from the three religions that the Book itself is not understood in a uniform way: God is jealous in Judaism, punishes Original Sin in Roman Catholicism and is a synonym of justice in Islam. This means that reality is contingent upon subjective representation of the meaning attached to it. That is, ways of pleasing God and salvation differ accordingly: a jealous, repenting or just God does not save believers in the same way.

Concurring with the idea of world's dualism, we can see the reach of God and mankind for contemporary accounting. Traditionally, as with Roman Catholicism, the business world has been seen as divided into funders and managers. Their relationship has been said to be resting upon information asymmetry. This has given rise to agency theory as well as annual reports, interim reports and the need for auditing records as a way of reconciling these two parties (Power, 2003, 2009). As there is no standard for content and shape of annual reports, there is still room for making them operate as metaphors with icons, heroes, facts and stories readers can retain (Busco & Quattrone, 2014, 2018; Davison, 2004, 2010, 2011; Quattrone, 2009). The entire story of actions undertaken—mergers and acquisitions or new markets gained—provides organisational discourses with some coherence and consistency. These enable us to grasp the big picture of the path taken (McKernan & Kosmala, 2004). A form of objectification commences when, falling into the public domain, these accounts can be appropriated by anyone. The crossing of people's subjectivities reifies and makes records as well as stories the truth for everyone. Funders and managers can then be reconciled through the representation of organisational deeds and achievements in financial terms, following either rules or accepted principles that make the whole intelligible (McKernan, 2007; McKernan & Kosmala, 2007).

Over time, world dualism has been considered more complex as to divide economic and non-economic items (Bebbington & Gray, 2001;

Gray, 1992, 2006, 2010; Gray & Collison, 2002; Gray, Owen, & Maunders, 1988; Quattrone, 2004). At the non-economic end, social and environmental accounts have initially formed another dualism. This seems to have been solved through the merging of corporate social responsibility (CSR) disclosures as to give a consistent representation of the organisation's conduct (Cho, Guidry, Hageman, & Patten, 2012; Cho & Patten, 2013). Such reports make public achievements through photographic representation of orphanages built or evidence of depollution campaigns. Despite endeavours from the Global Reporting Initiative (GRI) or other international bodies at enforcing organisations to adhere to their standards, organisational reporting and disclosure seem to remain dual. Subsequently, there is to date no working representation of communion between economic and non-economic concerns. This teleoaffective structure could be found in current discussions around the making of integrated reporting reuniting financial and CSR disclosures through a single technology (Adams, 2015; Flower, 2015; Frías-Aceituno, Rodríguez-Ariza, & García-Sánchez, 2013; García-Sánchez, Rodríguez-Ariza, & Frías-Aceituno, 2013; Tregidga, Milne, & Kearins, 2014).

Irrespective of whether this dualism is solved or not, the traditional separation of financial accounting (disclosure) from management accounting constitutes another dualism that still exists. As textbooks usually prescribe, disclosure addresses the bottom line's constituencies and is aimed at showing how earnings are formed. Conversely, management accounting accounts for what counts as strategic and can serve for day-to-day management (Parker, 2002a, 2002b). Seemingly, as with integrated reporting, financial and management accounting has not yet been unified, although the XML-XBRL project is pursuing this teleoaffective structure. To date there does not appear to be any clear routines or rules that enable us to solve this dualism. Hence, the journey is unfathomable until rules so arise as to enable representation through fully integrated data (Alles & Debreceny, 2012; Dunne, Helliar, Lymer, & Mousa, 2013; Liu, Wang, & Yao, 2014; O'Riain, Curry, & Harth, 2012).

1.1.2 Religious Accounting's Influence on Business Accountability

In today's private companies, it is generally accepted that an account is given to one who entrusts his or her monies to an organisation. Although this latter is often presented as a principal, we prefer relating to the term

"Higher-Principal" (Laughlin, 1996). This label is less suggestive of any systematic temptations to sneak the principal on the grounds of information asymmetry. The Higher-Principal lies over the traditional principal and has the possibility to investigate the truth and so interrogate the agent as to get the amount of information he or she deems satisfactory. While the notion of principal places the account demander in a position of weakness *vis-à-vis* the agent, that of the Higher-Principal positions him or her in a situation of exerting the power of demanding information and sanctioning the agent if his or her requirements are not fulfilled (Joannidès, 2012; Laughlin, 1996).

In a private, listed company, it is commonly agreed in the literature that the principal, or the Higher-Principal, is the collection of stockholders and that their expectations are to be fulfilled. Yet, the notion of stockholder and their expectations may vary. For instance, in family businesses, stockholders, generally company founders, might expect to perpetuate their business and undertake projects aimed at this. In private equity, stockholders are considered investors with a limited time horizon, therefore favouring investments that give returns within their time frame; such investors might ignore long-term productive investments.

This allows us to understand why the contents of accounts and recording procedures differ from one religion to the other. The Higher-Principal is not construed in the same way, so that his or her requirements cannot be exactly the same. In Judaism, what matters to God is that the believer accounts for the performing of all duties as ordered. Salvation can be gained only through this. In Catholicism, God cannot be known in person, which legitimates the clergy to act as surrogate for Him in determining what He expects through sacrament and sin accounting. Lastly, Islam is constructed of both, so that two angels record how the Sharia's five pillars are honoured. In private companies, differentiated understandings of the agency relationship between managers and stockholders can lead to differentiated forms and contents for accounts. Some only disclose annual reports, whilst others also disclose CSR reports. Some disclose interim figures, whilst others do not.

1.1.3 Double-Entry Mode of Thinking and Accounting Systems

This chapter contributes to the literature studying the rise of double-entry bookkeeping. The literature ascribing the rise of double-entry bookkeeping to the birth of Capitalism (Bryer, 2000b, 2006a, 2006c; Miller &

Napier, 1993), be its roots religious or not (Sombart, 1916; Weber, 1922), shows how accountability has been pursuant to rationalising the balancing of debits and credits (Carruthers & Espeland, 1991; Derks, 2008; J. R. Edwards, Coombs, & Greener, 2002) through the constitution of the Capital account (Weber, 1922). In contrast, the literature dealing with the non-economic roots of accounting has considered that double-entry bookkeeping had sought to balance faith and religious conduct, *for example*, prayer and Bible reading (Jacobs & Walker, 2004), sin and indulgence (Quattrone, 2004) or soul and sacraments.

This chapter shows that world dualism is wider than debits and credits, sin and indulgence or soul and sacraments, and encompasses all these. To a greater or lesser extent, these prior works convey religion as a common denominator, generally Christianity. Therefore, the systematic study of the three religions of the Book conveys a common perception of world dualism. This understanding encompasses all those aspects mentioned above; dualism is that of God and mankind.

It appears that accounting systems are derived from a double-entry mode of thinking pursuant to one's understanding of world dualism. We thereby concur with prior research showing how accounting systems can be developed, established and advanced. Prior publications show how a rational economic mode of thinking has given birth to contemporary double-entry bookkeeping (Bryer, 1993, 2000a, 2000b, 2006b, 2006c; Carruthers & Espeland, 1991; Derks, 2008; Miller, 2008; Miller & Napier, 1993). Research dealing with the non-economic origins of accounting systems points to rational theological modes of thinking, leading to emerging forms of accounting (Ezzamel, 1994, 1997, 2009; Ezzamel & Hoskin, 2002; Jacobs & Walker, 2004; MacIntosh, Shearer, & Riccaboni, 2009; Quattrone, 2004; Schweiker, 1993; Shearer, 2002).

This shows a universal rationality explaining world dualism as God and mankind unified through an open double-entry mode of thinking, leading to metaphoric accounting thinking. While accounting thinking in Judaism remains metaphoric, Islam suggests the most advanced metaphor closest to contemporary accounting whereby records are systematically verified by external actors commissioned by the Higher-Principal (two angels appointed by God). This concurs with the view that Islamic accounting has been abundantly disseminated in the Muslim world for centuries through textbooks and doctrines regarding bookkeeping (Napier, 2009). Roman Catholicism remains in between, more formal than Judaism and less oriented towards direct accountability to God than Islam. In the three religions, we can see similarities in the double-entry mode of thinking aimed at unifying God and mankind. Accordingly, our contribution consists of showing that accounting technologies are driven by a metaphorical representation of a double-entry mode of thinking aimed at unifying our dual world. How this is achieved and why approaches differ can be understood through differentiated common understandings and teleoaffective structures.

1.2 Accounting and the Rise of Capitalism

It is commonly agreed that management accounting emerged with industrialisation and the birth of Capitalism, that is, by the second half of the nineteenth century. At that time, the first factories were established, using steam machines. These were fuelled with coal extracted from mines all over Europe in parallel. Since the middle of the nineteenth century, the first of the largest companies ever have been erected, thereby giving birth to the blue-collar, working class (Bryer, 1993, 2000a, 2000b, 2013; Catchpowle, Cooper, & Wright, 2004; Chiapello, 2007; Joannidès de Lautour, 2016; Martin, 2010).

1.2.1 Management Accounting and the Birth of Industrial Capitalism

With the discovery of the steam machine and the industrialisation of economic activities in the second half of the nineteenth century, large factories started to be established across the Atlantic. Manufacturing companies developed, accompanied with the first railway companies for freight and passenger transport (Bryer, 2000a, 2000b, 2006b). The coal industry also commenced with the discovery of mines and the first of the blue-collar workforce (Allsop & Calveley, 2009; Otley, 1990). As Capitalism was in its infancy, it was considered highly promising for those who could benefit from it or an oppression by those subjugated by it, the emerging working class (Bryer, 2006a; Carter & Tinker, 2006). This context raised a series of issues that enabled the birth of management control systems.

This emerging Capitalism was promising high profits for entrepreneurs. Political economy was still influenced by classical economics characterised by utilitarianism and marginalism. Consistent with the law of diminishing returns, this profit which entrepreneurs were seeking was expected to decrease, just as they would generate it. This economic assumption was the main grounds on which rested Marx' Capital: tendency of the rate of profit to fall. Entrepreneurs would all seek a profit whose vocation was to decline and vanish (Marx, 1894). Outside of class struggle and the pursuit of profit associated with Capitalism, this was the first conceptualisation of the idea that profit and money more generally are scarce resources and that they must be managed wisely.

Irrespective of the quest for profit per se, the second Industrial Revolution occurring in the nineteenth century was the beginning of hierarchies in factories and mines and stepwise within society. In factories and mines, blue-collar workers were at the grassroots, executing orders given by foremen receiving instructions from company owners (Badiou, 2006; Ezzamel, Willmott, & Worthington, 2004). At that time, the development of hierarchies was not associated as yet with the notion of bureaucracy or division of labour. These appeared later on, at the dawn of the twentieth century. At least, some professions and professional bodies could emerge and articulate the grounds of their collective identities. The constitution of social groups with different interests and means progressively led to the rise of trade unions in Germany and the United Kingdom (Gumbrell-McCormick & Hyman, 2013; Reid, 2005; Schain & Kesselman, 1998).

Owing to different interests and the difficulty of collective bargains, workers' unions as well as employers commenced to use metrics, facts and figures to substantiate their arguments in negotiations. In order to enable this, they could produce information acting as tentative management accounting figures (Owen & Lloyd, 1985). On the workers' side, figures would relate to work conditions, namely health and safety as well as working hours. At the employers' end, figures would relate to production at large. None of these figures were systematically produced and therefore could be disputed. However, they were the grounds for major discussions (Barney & Flesher, 1994).

As railway networks developed alongside factories and mines, it became progressively crucial that time should be managed and controlled, thereby opening for contemporary supply chain management (Kabinga, 2016). In the first instance, it was important to set reliable departure and arrival times for trains. Consequently, materials and products would be ready on time, so trains could be loaded and depart on time. This notion of time management was the origin of time zones and the setting of official time across Europe and the United States, hence it would be possible to control the railway (Wonning, 2018). Outside of simple train logistics, the setting of an official time in different countries was opening for time standards, applied everywhere in the same way. More generally, this was accompanied with the generalisation of the metric system across Continental Europe, as inherited from the French Revolution (Free, 1977; Icon_Group_International, 2009; Isakov, 2014). The development of common and standard units to count appeared as the condition of possibility for the advent of management accounting and control systems, whose core and *raison d'être* are calculability and readability (Miller, 1992). Such is the case, to a large extent, because of the idea that calculability is a condition of possibility or governmentality and controllability (Miller & O'Leary, 1987) and perfectly instances the common thought that one can manage what one can measure (Kaplan, 1984; Kaplan & Johnson, 1987).

1.2.2 Economic Rationality and the Rise of Bureaucracies

At the dawn of the early twentieth century, industrialisation accelerated, factories being greater in number and size. The rise of larger factories resulted in owners becoming consistently less able to manage through forms of direct supervision. Growing numbers of employees and increasing complexity of procedures revealed the need for systematic ways of organising and managing. This is how bureaucracies could develop, as responses to this need for clearer and stricter procedures, roles and duties (Sombart, 1916; Weber, 1922).

Bureaucracies have developed in response to the complexification of organisations and social activities. Prior to the second Industrial Revolution, small organisations were prevailing, thereby representing the utmost form of markets (Williamson, 1985, 1999). Economic activities were left to craftspeople working in isolation from all others and selling their production separately. This was the reign of independent artisans selling their own production by themselves. In the case of sophisticated products requiring multiple, different skills, independent craftspeople would sell their parts to a separate entity in charge of assembling them.

This situation could be instanced by rifle-manufacturing company Winchester. In the Winchester borough, each villager was crafting one specific rifle part at home, irrespective of others' activity. The Winchester company was purchasing these parts from their homes and assembling them on separate premises. This resulted in high coordination and transport costs for the company, including a lengthy time period needed to assemble one item (Houze, 2004). Conversely, at the same time, confronted with the same issues, the Colt company internalised all these activities. Rather than purchasing parts from independent producers located all over the village, the company gathered all of them on common premises and gave them clear instructions as to the parts' expected characteristics. This resulted in lower coordination and transport costs as well as faster production (Belden & Haven, 2011). Colt is often presented as the first economic bureaucracy established to manage transaction costs (Rosa, 2000).

The two examples above reveal that the development of bureaucracies was originally associated with economic rationality and aimed at efficiency. The rise of bureaucracies has accelerated, as technologies were becoming increasingly sophisticated and required higher command and proficiency. This is how the first wave of activities' insourcing commenced at the dawn of the twentieth century, thereby allowing large corporations to rise. Even though the notion of cost was at that time not really central to management, the environment was carrying an intuition that some ways of doing things were more efficient and therefore more lucrative than others. The Colt company revealed the make-or-buy dilemma confronting management. Interestingly, the economic decision was based upon intuitions and empirical observation that processes were sub-optimal and not on metrics or costing systems.

This concern regarding transaction costs and the associated quest for economic efficiency found an expression in the 1950s in the pursuit of economies of scale (Berland, 1998; Berland & Boyns, 2002). After World War II, European countries were to be rebuilt. Under the purview of providing households with all the necessary equipment and reconstructing public infrastructures, large companies were established (Fleischman, 2000). The post-war era was the large manufacturing companies' heyday: in order to respond to an increasing demand in manufactured goods, companies employed high numbers of blue-collar workers. Labour and overhead costs emerged as real concerns for companies. Within the context of European reconstruction, these large companies accelerated the development of management accounting systems. As they were converging towards the same objective and were cooperating with one another, they developed the early forms of inter-organisational controls and network coordination.

In order for this to be possible, commonly shared accounting systems were needed. This is how standard costing arose: engineers and accountants from these companies agreed together on a common way of accounting for costs, leading to standard costing. As standard costing does not stand alone, most contemporary management accounting technologies emerged concomitantly: budgeting and budgetary control, including breakeven analysis, variance analysis and Cost-Volume-Price analysis (Berland & Boyns, 2002; Boyns, Edwards, & Emmanuel, 1999; R. Edwards & Boyns, 2012; Fleischman & Boyns, 2008).

1.2.3 The Rise of Scientific Management

Since the dawn of the twentieth century and concomitant to the rise of bureaucracies, a major characteristic of Capitalism has been the division of labour. This started with class consciousness and position in society associated with the rise of bureaucracies (Durkheim, 1902). Each social group would have a specified role in society, because it is impossible to do everything and do it well. This is how professions started to be structured and forged their identity, such as medical doctors, barristers and solicitors or accountants (Pratt, Rockmann, & Kaufmann, 2006; Ramirez, 2009). In parallel to these professions, the working class, trade unions and Capitalists appeared as specialised social groups.

This division of labour in society, associated with the rise of bureaucracies, appeared as the prologue of the scientific and mechanist organisation (Burns & Stalker, 1961; Lawrence & Lorsch, 1967). The scientific organisation arose in 1880 when American engineer Frederick W. Taylor found a way of maximising profitability through process optimisation (Fleischman, 2000; Parker, 2016). Influenced by classical microeconomics and the development of algebra, Taylor was seeking for a model that would help optimise profit under multiple constraints, including time and cost. To this end, he suggested that every activity should be subsumed to micro-activities until the smallest task could be identified. In order to optimise processes, each gesture was to be strictly designed and timed. In order to make this possible, it would be necessary that each worker's role be clearly and strictly defined. Thereby, each worker would be assigned one task only and would repeatedly execute it. Scientific management could appear as the utmost division of labour in the organisation (Taylor, 1911).

The principles of scientific management were implemented by Henry Ford from 1908 with the launch of the Ford T model. These principles were augmented with the development of mechanical shop-floors, whereby workers would repeat a limited number of gestures (Doray, 1990). More and more sophisticated management accounting and control concerns could arise. Subsequent to the implementation of scientific management in companies, target costing and related costing systems emerged (Anthony, 1952, 1965). Classifications of costs still in use nowadays were coined in support to scientific management, such as product cost versus period cost, absorption costing versus variable costing and fixed costs versus variable costs . Specialised journals were first launched to share with the profession's new advances in management accounting, such as *The Cost Accountant* in 1921. The ideal of optimising processes and costs is borne by engineers capable of devising articulate and complex accounting systems.

Scientific management and control could focus on planning through budgeting, expressing anticipated needs for workers by task, necessary machinery and raw materials. Budgeting also enabled to predict the number of units produced and sold as well as compute production capacity and pace. Until the 1970s, financial flows were not mobile, hence the main constraint on organisations was access to equity and credit (Berland, Levant, & Joannidès, 2010). Therefore, measures of financial performance could develop, such as financial ratios and associated analysis (Horringan, 1968). The first ratios were developed by Du Pont De Nemours to measure operational performance, such as return on equity, profitability, operating sufficiency (a.k.a. asset utilisation) and leverage (Kline & Hessler, 1955). Over time, more new ratios were identified, provided financial concerns were at stake. This could be evidenced in a US Department Store concerned with stock-inventory rotation (Magee, 1915).

Other metrics could develop in association with capital budgeting. As capital had long been the scarce resource *par excellence*, organisations were to thoroughly budget it and control its use. Therefore, the first investment decision-making models developed in the 1950s and 1960s, where resource allocation could prove to be difficult (Gordon, Loeb, & Stark, 1990; Grinyer & Daing, 1993; Miller & O'Leary, 1997, 2007; Pfeiffer & Schneider, 2010). Capital budgeting models have further developed and diffused, as calculations could be automated through the use of computers. In particular, these have facilitated the utilisation of actuary methods in capital budgeting, such as the well-known Discounted Cash Flow method, which is very popular amongst investors (Jensen, 1986; Laswad & Baskerville, 2007). The rise of scientific management has enabled to bring mathematical tools into corporate finance and management accounting, initially borrowed from capital market finance and portfolio management (Fabozzi & Markowitz, 2011; Fabozzi, Markowitz, & Kostovetsky, 2004; Manne, Markowitz, & Yale University. Cowles Foundation for Research in Economics, 1963; Markowitz, Sharpe, & Miller, 1991).

Subsequent to the seminal paper devising a theory of investment (Modigliani & Miller, 1958), capital budgeting has borrowed increasingly from geometric series concepts and tools, such as discount rate (cost of capital), internal rate of return, discounted cash flows, net present value and other related notions (Jensen, 1986, 2001, 2003). Similarly, after the Modigliani-Miller theorems were devised, private companies engaged in systematic dividend policies, accounted for as the profit shared with stockholders. From then on, the remuneration of equity could appear as a reality outside the mere cost of capital and also be included in advanced costing systems, such as absorption costing (Anthony, 1965, 1988; Anthony, Dearden, & Bedford, 1984).

1.2.4 *Financial Capitalism and the End of Bureaucracies*

Large mechanist organisations structured as scientific bureaucracies started to be called into question in the mid-1970s, as three joint phenomena occurred.

Firstly, when two models for options pricing were initially devised (Black & Scholes, 1973; Merton, 1973), notions of risk, uncertainty and liquidity could spread across corporate finance technologies and practices, and thereby real options. In the mid-1970s, bureaucratic organisations began to be called into question, with management thinkers increasingly calling for organic and decentralised management (Chandler, 1977; Chandler & Deams, 1979). The M-Form emerged concomitantly to corporate financialisation, leading to Activity-Based Management and Activity-Based Costing (Jones & Dugdale, 2002; Triplett & Scheuman, 2000).

The introduction of real options into corporate finance and management resulted in finance becoming more central to management accounting and control (Carter & Mueller, 2006; Gleadle & Cornelius, 2008; Müller, 2014). All sorts of metrics could be developed to assess the profitability of any corporate activity, leading to an unprecedented move towards systematically outsourcing activities that are not central in the value chain. The make-or-buy decision initiated by the Colt Company found a different expression: economic efficiency would lie in outsourcing all non-core activities. In this respect, IBM appeared as the initiator of this outsourcing wave (Mederos, 2018, 2020). This started with the outsourcing of IT towards specialised businesses that had the necessary technology. Over time, this movement has included any non-strategic or non-lucrative activities, including marketing, HR, accounting, legal and so on (Duan, Grover, & Balakrishnan, 2009; Lamminmaki, 2008; Langfield-Smith & Smith, 2003).

This management model has led to designing joint controls aimed at coordinating all these various activities as in networks. Inter-organisational controls started developing (Carlsson-Wall, Kraus, & Lind, 2011; Kraus, 2012; Mouritsen & Thrane, 2006). These could mostly have two forms: open-book accounting on one hand and management accounting standards on the other (Thrane, 2007). In order to make these independent business units, some being part of the organisation and others being subcontractors, mutual adjustment has appeared as a necessity. Over time, as transactions became increasingly complex and required more accurate information, new computing technologies arose. Accountants and auditors were facing new challenges: the imperative of reconciling financial reporting and management accounting figures. This is what initiated the XBRL movement in the 1990s: the same computer language used to translate management accounting figures into financial reporting and vice versa (Alles & Debreceny, 2012; O'Riain et al., 2012; Srivastava & Kogan, 2010). Similarly, the willingness to have all accounting information homogeneous and integrated has led to the Integrated Reporting initiative, whereby financial reporting would be coupled with social and environmental reporting released in a unique document with common standards (Adams, 2015; Dragu & Tiron-Tudor, 2013).

Secondly, the 1970s were characterised by an emancipatory movement, whereby managers were denouncing the totalitarian nature of bureaucratic organisations as well as old-school management and accounting. Subsequent to a broader democratic thread in the political world after decolonisation and the advent of independent States, managers also expressed their willingness to act freely and independently, such as becoming their own bosses. This political thread resulted in contesting the benefits of budgeting and budgetary controls perceived as the main constraints on them (Berland et al., 2010). This is the context in which management accounting technologies departing from the industrial organisation developed as alternatives to traditional costing and performance management. The Cam-I was established to respond to actual managerial demands and needs, which eventually allowed for the development of Activity-Based

Costing and associated technologies first (Alcouffe, Berland, & Levant, 2008). These technologies would then be followed by alternatives to the traditional master budget, such as zero-base budgeting, activity-based budgeting, flexible budgeting and rolling forecasts, and this unto beyond budgeting (Abrahamsson, Oza, & Bunce, 2010; Hope & Fraser, 2001; Østergren & Stensaker, 2011; Player, 2003; Rickards, 2006).

Thirdly, financial crises have increased in number and in severity since the first oil crisis in 1973. Since then, managers have been confronted with an increasingly turbulent environment, as opposed to the relative stability characterising the second industrial revolution and the post-war era. Yesteryears, as the economy was to be rebuilt and households to be fully equipped, organisations could see the future as relatively predictable. Pursuant to this predictability and foreseen stability, traditional management accounting technologies such as costing systems, budgeting and budgetary control were especially appropriate (see Joannidès de Lautour, 2018a, Chap. 5). Conversely, in an essentially crisis situation, the environment is turbulent and cannot be modelled with long-term visibility. New competitors could enter the market and change its structure, especially with the fast development of Asian Tigers and Dragons. Historic competitors could be bankrupt, as General Motors in 2009 or Fiat Motors in 2011. New technologies would reduce product life cycle and make current technologies obsolete at any time. This is how RIM's Blackberry has become obsolete since the first-generation i-Phone was launched in November 2007, making smartphones the new technology standard on this market. Nowadays, management accounting rests upon forecasting models taking the environment into account, in particular technological changes. Thereby, management accounting no longer focuses on mere financials relating to past activities but acts as economic intelligence for organisations.

Changes in the environment may result in altering the value chain accordingly and amend how operations are conducted. Some activities can be suddenly interrupted, whilst others can be instantly launched, depending on what competitors do and technology allows. In other words, companies can outsource or backsource any type of activity, as imposed by the environment (Mederos, 2018). This is possible, because they can rest upon reliable management accounting technologies, such as highly detailed and accurate target costing (see Joannidès de Lautour, 2018b, Chap. 2). These do not just comprise of costing but cover the entire design of the value chain, as it needs to be structured. An iconic example of this instant value chain adjustment, as markets evolve, is Cargill. Historically, the company has been the world's leading grain trader (Broehl, 1992). As the company is not listed, all the surpluses generated through this lucrative activity have not been used to pay out dividends to stockholders but massively reinvested in other activities, especially capital markets. The company opens offices and invests where it is lucrative and unregulated. As soon as an activity attracts significant competitors and begins to be regulated, the company steps out and closes down these offices and activities. Accordingly, the company's value chain adapts and changes as the market itself evolves (Broehl, 2008).

Customers would no longer be fair on one brand or product but would be increasingly inclined to change as fashion goes. Some products can be especially popular amongst customers and suddenly are no longer. Product or brand popularity has become ephemeral since the first oil crisis. This is how Dr. Martens shoes, very popular in the early 1990s, suddenly lost teenagers' interest (Roach, 2003). In 1991, Dr. Martens launched a model of shoes inspired from security shoes worn by tradespeople. The sole was made from a special rubber with numerous virtues for the security of people wearing them. Compressed air inspired from Nike was to absorb any shocks when stepping on sharp items. A secret gel borrowed from Reebok was to shape the sole for the person's foot. An anti-twist technology borrowed from Adidas Torsion was to prevent any muscle or bone injury. Those shoes were strengthened on the top with a round metal hull capable of supporting a heavy load. Since after launch, Dr. Martens shoes have become very popular amongst youngsters and young adults. Notwithstanding a high selling cost, for three consecutive years, sales increased dramatically, with these new shoes becoming more popular than the historical Converse All Stars®. In 1993, a triple phenomenon undermined the company. Other manufacturers started mimicking its original shape, selling at a lower rate. At that time, Dr. Martens' sales were not too much affected by these new competitors. Customers no longer had any interest in these shoes, and preferred the new fashionable, lighter and colourful product from Palladium®. Leather suppliers terminated their contracts with Dr. Martens, which was perceived as potentially insolvent. Taking this major threat on their lead product seriously, in December 1995, the company endeavoured to overcome this situation by launching new models with different shapes and colours. It was already too late; customers were disinterested in this brand and its products, leading the company almost to bankruptcy. A revival occurred in 2007 when the original models with new shapes and colours became fashionable again.

Owing to fashion's ephemeral nature, companies operating in the clothing industry have no longer been able to rely on a single product. They have been urged to shift their business models from mono-product to multi-product. At least, they have been confronted with the imperative of having evolving and adaptive products. Nowadays, companies endeavour to sell an ecosystem of complementary products, thereby creating an ecosystem. In the cosmetic industry, the ecosystem can comprise of shower gel, shampoo, moisturiser and aftershave. Thereby, the focus of management control has evolved so as to embrace strategic concerns relating to the perception of a product's necessity outside its mere profitability. Given ecosystem-based business models, it occurs that some products are not profitable per se but necessary to justify the existence of all the others surrounding it, which are profitable. Management accounting now tends to scrutinise cross-subsidies from one product to another and approach the organisation as a whole (Jørgensen & Messner, 2010). Accordingly, management accounting systems have adapted and broadened their remit, deploying increasingly sophisticated technologies enabled by information technologies (Baraldi & Waluszewski, 2005; Dikolli & Vaysman, 2006).

Another phenomenon has influenced the shape of management accounting: customers' need for more and more personalised products. The standard product's heyday was in the 1960s, as households were to be fully equipped. Nowadays, as they are equipped, concerns have so evolved as to marking one's difference and identity as a customer. This shift in customer needs and expectations has been made possible concomitantly to the spread of lean production and management, as inspired by Toyota (Ahmad, Zakuan, Jusoh, & Takala, 2012; A. Anvari, Ismail, & Hojjati, 2011; A. Anvari, Sorooshian, & Moghimi, 2011; Wickramasinghe, Hopper, & Rathnasiri, 2004). As customer tastes have changed, the mode of production has adapted to these new requirements, enabling more customisation. With lean production, orders can be placed upon demand and thereby integrate all their requirements. Automakers, not just Toyota, nowadays offer customers the possibility of designing their vehicle, by choosing the parts and colours they want. Ultimately, there are no two identical vehicles, since each of them is assembled on demand. Management accounting nowadays is confronted with the imperative of assessing the extent of customisation profitability (Vaivio, 1999).

1.3 Strategy, Management Accounting and Wartime

Even though modern management control systems are undoubtedly inherited from the rise and development of Capitalism, it was revealed that accounting does not only consist of balancing debits and credits. It was also showed that these debits and credits could be expressed through any type of unit, not just financial measures. The intertwining of accounting and strategy appeared very explicitly during wartime, when military strategy was to be executed and controlled to win the war. Historians tend to consider three steps in this, commencing with World War I, extended with World War II and finalised with colonial history. These three bellicose episodes confirm that management control systems do not merely consist of financials and address more than just cost and quantities.

1.3.1 Accounting and World War I

It is acknowledged in accounting history that modern management control systems are inherited from French and British army officers whose unique concern was to win the war, and this at any cost (Funnell & Chwastiak, 2015). This is what World War I revealed, in its dual capacity as the last conventional war and the first modern war (Gallhofer & Haslam, 2006). World War I was the last war launched because of the game of European military alliances, mobilising countries associated with another one at war. When Austro-Hungarian Archduke Francis-Ferdinand was stabbed in Sarajevo by a Serbian terrorist seeking to establish a republic, the war was declared on Serbia. An ally of Serbia, France declared the war on Austria-Hungary. Germany declared war on Russia, an ally of Serbia and France. The United Kingdom, allied with France and Russia, declared war on Germany.

According to historians, World War I was a political as much as an economic war opposing colonial empires and resulting from previous wars for colonies in Africa and the Middle East (Marseille, 2001, 2005). In this respect, World War I is often presented as the last war for possession and imperial extension. Pursuant to this political agenda, economic concerns were secondary. French colonel Émile Rimailho is presented as the first person who understood the imperative of enabling and controlling strategy execution. In the first place, Rimailho intuited that it was imperative that commandment perfectly understands how a war can be won or lost.

Outwith mere military strategy and capabilities, clear procedures and effective logistics appeared central (Berland, 1998, 1999; Berland & Boyns, 2002). In the first place, he had the intuition that commandment should establish forecasts regarding the nature and possible length of the conflict for each battle. These forecasts would rest upon a deep understanding of the battlefield, including how the enemy is organised. In order to win a battle, it would not be possible to send fewer men. Therefore, forecasts would establish the number of men that should be sent to the battlefront.

Accounting for soldiers had major implications as Rimailho also considered. Firstly, soldiers needed weapons, ammunitions and equipment. Stock-inventory management was developed in order to ensure that soldiers would always have sufficient equipment and ammunition. Ammunitions would be anticipated in relation to the difficulty of defeating the enemy and not randomly supplied. To this end, knowledge of the battlefield toponymy, combined with intelligence as to the enemy's capacities, was used as insights into the modelling of how many resources are necessary (Bryer, 2006c; Chwastiak & Lehman, 2008; Clausewitz (von), 1832; Funnell, 2006; Sonja Gallhofer & Jim Haslam, 1991).

A battle is not set but constantly evolved. As soldiers killed enemies, died or were caught as prisoners, it was also necessary to know almost in real-time the currents of human resources. A system of casualty reporting was developed in order to know at the end of each day how many men were lost in either camp. By knowing this accurate number, commandment could decide to send new battalions and regiments (Bryer, 2006c; Chwastiak & Lehman, 2008; Clausewitz (von), 1832; Funnell, 2006; Sonja Gallhofer & Jim Haslam, 1991). In order to make this possible, officers were to count the number of soldiers they had at the beginning of the day and how many returned. Amidst those who returned, officers were to detail how many were still valid and how many were injured and should be sent to infirmary or back to civil life. Owing to technology advances and the use of more destructive machinery (*e.g.* aircrafts and bombs, tanks, flamethrowers and gas), the human resource became increasingly scarce. Accordingly, in order to respond to the growing needs articulated by military commandment, the Defence Ministry was to know exactly how many more men should be enrolled. Management accounting figures from the battlefield would serve as a basis for conscription policy.

Not only would war accounting allow to determine the number of soldiers, food, ammunition and equipment, it also became crucial to develop and control processes by which these could be delivered to the battlefront. War accounting has also included logistics and what is nowadays known as supply chain management: warehouse, stock-inventory management and train organisation. Roads for lorries, harbour facilities for ships and the whole railway for trains were requisitioned and placed under military control, hence it would be easier to manage (Leonhard & Camiller, 2018). For greater efficiency, military commandment fully integrated the various links in the war value chain: from production to repatriation.

In the meantime, what is known as the "war effort" was also placed under military control. As men were at war, women were replacing them on their jobs in farms and in factories. In this capacity, they were receiving orders directly from military commandment so as to produce the necessary equipment, clothing and food for them on the battlefront. For greater efficiency, all procedures were standardised and set by military authorities. Thence, all companies contributing to the war effort would account for resources and production in a united way consolidated by the Defence Ministry. In case a company was not able to deliver, the information could be reported instantly, so that a different company would take the task over and eventually do it.

Interestingly, World War I conveys in a very eloquent way that management accounting is not just about economic efficiency too often collapsed to cost and quantities. World War I evidences the fact that management control systems are foremost developed to enable strategy and control its execution. When finance is not a constraint, management control systems remain necessary to ensure at all times that the right and sufficient resources are utilised and result in the expected output. To this end, processes and procedures fall within the remit of control. All told, management accounting and control systems are at the service of the ultimate goal shared by all actors. In the case of World War I, this goal was unambiguously to win the war. In other circumstances, this goal can just be the common objectives set by the organisation (*e.g.* ranking first, gaining a particular contract).

War accounting did not terminate with the end of armed conflicts. In fact, the Peace Treaty's clauses were extensions from the war and would even set grounds for World War II (Keynes, 1919). When the armed conflicts ended, the winning camp—France, the United Kingdom, Russia and the United States—imposed repairs on Germany, as it was considered to be responsible and liable for all the demolitions. Germany was supposed to bear the responsibility of financing the French reconstruction and all other associated costs. In the post-war era, French authorities would account for the total cost of the war, using an extensive absorption costing system. Those costs that were not accounted for during wartime were ex post facto (Leonhard & Camiller, 2018). Article 231 in the Versailles Treaty stated:

> *Allied and associated governments declare and Germany acknowledges that Germany and its allies are liable, for having caused then, for all losses and all damages undergone by the allied and associated Governments and their citizens consequent to the war that was imposed on the by the aggression from Germany and its allies.*

In total, Germany was to pay to 269 billion Gold-equivalent Marks to France. Germany paid its last instalment in 2010, that is, after 91 years. This amount was including the direct cost of all destructions (infrastructures, cities, farms etc.), the direct cost of war (materials used, equipment, ammunitions, food etc.) and the indirect costs incurred (pensions to severely injured war veterans, pensions to war orphans etc.) For the first time, death and destruction were made visible and were accounted for (Funnell & Chwastiak, 2015).

1.3.2 Accounting and World War II

It is often presented in history textbooks that World War II found its causes in the excessive repairs the victorious French government imposed on defeated Germany (Kershaw, 2016). This appears as an actualisation of what President Wilson was fearing when the peace treaty was signed (Keynes, 1919). The amounts computed and demanded by the successive French governments were perceived as impossible to fulfil and prone to humiliate Germany. Based on those premises, World War II is often presented as a consequence of this unfair peace treaty (Shirrer & Rosenbaum, 2011).

The concerns expressed in World War I and their implications in terms of management accounting and controls remained somehow identical from a strictly military viewpoint. This said, World War II differed from World War I on one major account: for the first time since the Westphalian Treaty in 1648, war has no longer been just a military matter but has resulted in the death of millions of civilians (Shirrer & Rosenbaum, 2011). Not only conscripted soldiers but also foremost civilians who were supposedly not concerned by military issues were killed on the battlefront. One reason why World War II has been so impactful in Europe is precisely that it has reached the climax of what horror can be, beyond understanding. Management accounting and control appeared as technologies for the "Final Solution" (Funnell & Chwastiak, 2015), the climax of dehumanisation and totalitarianism (Arendt, 1963, 1968; Levi, 1991, 1995).

Apart from restoring the German people's dignity after the biggest humiliation ever, the Nazi regime's agenda was to erect the pure Aryan race by exterminating all those who would qualify. The "New Man" and the "superior race" Nazi Germany was intending to establish would not allow Jews and Gypsies to qualify. Likewise, all those who would not fall within the mould of traditional Christian life would not quality either, *for example*, homosexuals and anyone whose life would not conform to strict Christian principles (Shirrer & Rosenbaum, 2011). It is important to note that the Nazi regime would deny these categories of people any human status on the grounds of their origins or actual life (Arendt, 1961, 1963). Being born a human being was not enough to qualify as a human body deserving the same respect and consideration as any other.

The first dimension of how management accounting happened to serve the Shoah was in the definition of purported objective criteria to identify and count people who would not qualify as members of this "superior race". People's surnames would operate as the first criterion to determine whether they are Jewish. This was supplemented with a systematic examination of religious documents relating to one's Christian life: a history of the received sacraments recorded in local churches and reported to the Bishop (Joannidès de Lautour, 2016). People with no records of any sacraments would be assumed to be non-Christians. Over time, these purported "objective" criteria were supplemented with others clearly subjective: physiological criteria. In the 1930s and 1940s, racist and anti-Semitic propaganda stated that Jewish people have certain physical attributes making them recognisable. On these grounds, Nazi Germany and occupied countries, such as Poland and France, would issue specific identification documents for Jewish people (Marrus, Paxton, & Hoffmann, 1995; Semelin, 2019). Once the various groups of people who would not qualify were identified, they were assigned a different sign and colour they were obliged to permanently wear. Jewish people would wear a yellow Star of David, Gypsies a brown reverted triangle, homosexuals a pink reverted triangle and so on.

Until 1940, Jewish people, Gypsies and homosexuals would undergo major humiliations and their citizens' rights were dramatically reduced. In June 1940, when France was defeated and occupied, the regime took a turn, accelerated in June 1941 when Nazi Germany endeavoured to invade the USSR. At this time, the regime decided that all Jews should be hunted and exterminated (Kershaw, 2013). This was facilitated by the thorough records kept since 1935 of people's religious and cultural affiliation. SS (Schutzstaffel) troops in Germany and militia in occupied countries started to chase Jewish people. In France, 16 July 1942 remains a shame date, as 16,000 Jews were subjected to the biggest police raid ever (Marrus et al., 1995). Jews from all over Europe were sent by train to concentration camps. Those who were young, strong and healthy enough were sent to labour camps, where they would work to support Germany's war effort (Levi, 1991). This could consist of digging mines, working in farms or assembling parts for industries. All others, including women, infants and elderly people, were sent to extermination camps (Kershaw, 2016; Levi, 1995).

The generalisation of extermination camps led Nazi Germany to rationalise the Shoah and make management control systems a powerful technology in the service of the world's largest genocide (Funnell, 1998; Funnell & Chwastiak, 2015). In the first place, being denied their human condition, Jewish people were considered "units". This means that police forces, militia and officers in extermination or concentration camps were counting how many "units" they had fetched and that needed to be "treated". Each "unit" was assigned a registration number tattooed on their forearm and replacing their civil identity (Levi, 1991, 1995). This number would specify the person's origins, arrival time, barrack number and ID therein. Newcomers would receive a unique number and would be recorded as such, whilst dead people would be written off the books (Kershaw & Sandys, 2019).

Through this accounting for "units", the Shoah actually commenced, thereby raising management concerns that management control systems would overcome. In 1942, officers managing concentration camps were confronted with a major issue: trains transporting "units" to be exterminated arrived at a pace gas chambers could not follow. It appeared that the arresting of Jewish people and the managing of trains transporting them to extermination camps were not aligned with these camps' capacities. Too many trains and too many "units" were arriving at their destination. Concentration camp officers started complaining about disorder in their machinery and required a better coordination of trains and extermination pace (Arendt, 1963; Kershaw, 2016; Kershaw & Sandys, 2019; Littell, 2007). They were requiring that logistics should be better coordinated, which implied that detention centres be established as transitions from the time of arresting and ultimate sending to extermination camps. For their part, SS and militia officers were praised for their zeal and efficiency at arresting Jewish people. Feeling supported in their action, they would not work at a slower pace. Some archives state that extermination camps' officers were confronted with a "flow-problem", whilst SS, police forces and militia were reporting a "stock-problem" (Kershaw, 2016; Kershaw & Sandys, 2019).

In 1943, the Shoah took a turn, as the Nazi regime endeavoured to accelerate the pace of extermination. The lethal gas used in gas chambers, a.k.a. Zyklon B, was initially invented to remove bacteria from Wehrmacht soldiers' shoes and avert the spread of diseases in trenches and camps. It was found that its concentration could be lethal and would enable gas chambers to exterminate "units" with greater reliance. Dr. Walter Heerdt, who discovered this gas, was urged to produce it in large enough quantities to enable the extermination agenda. It was found that this gas was very volatile and unstable, hence it would operate if not concentrated enough (Browning, 2007). As gas Zyklon B was not supposed to be used for such a purpose, Dr. Heerdt faced an unexpected dilemma, but in no way an ethical dilemma (Arendt, 1963; Silving, 1961): producing the gas in the right quantity or with the right lethal properties. The problem confronting him related to the fact that the unexpected use of this gas was constraining him to produce it in larger quantities than possible. Therefore, he could fulfil orders regarding quantity, even if "units" in gas chambers would not all die, which would aggravate the "flow-problem". On the other hand, he would produce as much as lethal gas as possible, thereby aggravating the "stock-problem" (Browning, 2007). Either solution was equally problematic, since it was aggravating the management problem.

The case of World War II and more particularly the Shoah reveals that management accounting and control are all but neutral technologies per se. They are very powerful and potent, as they can serve any type of agenda, the most commendable ones as well as the most horrific ones. The history of Nazi Germany sheds light on the potentially totalitarian nature of management accounting and control when rationality is pushed too far. This human tragedy is the extreme case where the quest for efficiency and rationality serves the worst purposes and eventually leads to genocide and the alienation of those who survive (Funnell, 1998; Funnell & Chwastiak, 2015). Indeed, when those in charge of the Shoah were trialled in Nuremberg, they claimed they were just civil servants fearing for their relatives' lives and for themselves, and were therefore only executing orders they had received (Arendt, 1963).

1.3.3 Management Accounting as a Tool of Colonial Oppression

Management accounting also appeared as a powerful technology during colonisation and after decolonisation, highlighting different concerns and uses. In fact, colonisation did not appear as a uniform process but responded to different political agendas from colonial powers (Appadurai, 1996; Naipaul, 1961). The main colonists in history were France, Britain and the Netherlands, even though other European countries had colonies or endeavoured to build a colonial empire. These conflicting philosophies, in which management accounting eventually played a different role, are exacerbated in British Prime Minister Benjamin Disraeli's speech before the Commons on 24 June 1872 and French President of the Council Jules Ferry's speech on 28 July 1885. Both reflect radically different views of what a colonial empire should bring and how it should be structured and managed (Marseille, 2001, 2005).

The two main philosophies at play were the French and the British. The British Empire was built on the idea that colonies would be new markets for British industry. Accordingly, colonies were presented by Disraeli as trade opportunities requiring certain investments. These would include the formation and the education of a local élite tied to Britain: locals would be called to prestigious metropolitan universities, just as the British gentry. Education in Britain was to socialise them to British mercantile concerns. Thence, on returning to their home countries, they would lead local businesses and administration in a way consistent with Britain and enabling the development of trade. Ultimately, development of the colonies would contribute to that of Britain (Bauer, 2019; L. James, 1997; Marseille, 2005). Under this purview, colonies were presented as a financial and commercial promise for British trade and industry. Pursuantly, the British government could articulate types of forecasts for trade opportunities.

Unlike British colonial philosophy, France had an ambiguous relationship to its empire. The official reason articulated by Jules Ferry to defend colonisation in Indochina was the humanist imperative of civilising primate people (Marseille, 2005). Based on these universal humanistic principles, the Parliament allowed colonisation. In the colonies, reality was different: French settlers would exploit local resources and people, impoverishing entire regions and families. In order to avoid any social movements and protests, French authorities would only provide indigenous people with basic education, refusing to have a local élite established. Civil servants and businesspeople from the metropole would rule these colonies and build fortunes at the expense of locals (Marseille, 2001). Accounting figures in use related to the wealth created in the colonies and sent back to the metropole for national development. Colonies were presented not as business and trade opportunities for the metropole but as a source of income and wealth for the nation (Thomas, 2012).

Other colonial powers' philosophies have appeared somewhere in between these two opposed views. Interestingly, these two philosophies were articulated at a late stage of colonisation, about a century after the first settlers voyaged to Africa and the Caribbean. These two speeches spoken before the House of Parliament were ex post facto rationalising of long-standing colonial practices (Marseille, 2005). Historians would agree that this official position regarding colonisation and the use of accounting figures to support was necessary, as slavery had been abolished for about 40 years in both countries. That is, a clear and formal post-slavery colonial doctrine was needed (Marseille, 2001, 2005). Prior to this doctrine, accounting has operated as a tool of oppression and dispossession for Africans in Africa and in the Caribbean (Barney & Flesher, 1994; Fleischman, Oldroyd, & Tyson, 2011; Fleischman & Tyson, 2004; Oldroyd, Fleischman, & Tyson, 2008; Tyson, Fleischman, & Oldroyd, 2004).

Colonisation and slavery in the Caribbean were known as the Middle Passage, whereby ships would carry Black slaves captured in West Africa (Naipaul, 1999). The Middle Passage was tightly associated with the international trade of slaves and made their valuation and recording in books necessary (Fleischman & Tyson, 2004; Tyson et al., 2004). Once carried to the West Indies or the plantations in the US Southern states, slaves were sold to the masters of large farms. Once sold, they were accounted for on the farm's balance sheet as tangible fixed assets at the historical cost. The counterpart was added to liabilities as their actual performances recorded as equity. Their net income, after their living expenses were deducted (food, accommodation, management etc.), would increase or decrease the farm's total equity. The logic underlying this recording system for slaves was that they were assets or tradeable commodities capable of generating capital gains for the plantation in case they were sold. As with commodities, slaves' vocation was twofold: working for the farm and generating operating profit on one hand and generating capital gains on the other (Barney & Flesher, 1994; Fleischman & Tyson, 2004; Fleischman et al., 2011; Oldroyd et al., 2008; Tyson & Davie, 2009; Tyson et al., 2004). The examination of farm books made it possible to set a price for this tangible fixed asset.

Seconds to masters would record slaves' production on a daily basis. These were accounted for using their respective working units and were not expressed in monetary terms. The most common working units in farms were weights expressed in ounce, pound and so on depending on the slave's condition; the second would set daily production objectives expressed using the same units. To do so, the second would use as a benchmark the average performance of the ethnic group and the age group of those whither the slave belonged. Through this system, each slave was recoded qualitatively according to age and ethnicity, and was expected to reach the same performance levels as others in the same group. In the early nineteenth century, slaves were no longer accounted for at their historical cost but at the market value expressed as their capability of meeting production objectives (Fleischman & Tyson, 2004; Oldroyd et al., 2008). Interestingly, the trading of slaves was resting upon a value colligating past achievements and promises of future actualisations (Table 1.1).

Each slave's production was also recorded in an income statement. Care and supervision were accounted for as debit, whilst their actual production was recorded as credit. If actual performance was below standard, the master had two options. Firstly, he could record the slave at his or her actual value in the balance sheet. In this case, the slave's value would be lower. Secondly, the master could value the variance between objectives and results as retributions. These would be accounted as off-balance sheet values and would rebalance the whole account. Seemingly, masters tended to

Table 1.1 Accounting for slaves on the balance sheet

The slave		
Market value (fixed asset)	X	
Individual production (income)		X*
Accruals (anticipated production)		X**
Balance: X* + X** = X		

privilege the second option (Fleischman & Tyson, 2004; Fleischman et al., 2011; Oldroyd et al., 2008). Thereby, actual performance could remain unchanged on the income statement, whereas variance and retributions would be recorded off-balance sheet. The working unit for the employed to account for retributions was the number of whip hits. The sanction was accounted for as a debit expressing the variance between market value (objectives) and actual results, hence whip hits would be balanced and slave value maximised (see figure below) (Table 1.2).

The imperative of recording slaves at their market value and not at their historical cost owed to the price volatility caused by the unpredictability of their actual performance. In fact, slaves were considered like stock and certainly not machines. All this led to corrective actions that morals would disapprove and was recorded in parallel unofficial books of accounts. Just as off-balance sheet records were serving oppression, slaves started to protest about its lack of transparency, causing rebellions in a number of farms (Fleischman & Tyson, 2004, 2007; Oldroyd et al., 2008).

In general, outside of slavery, management accounting has been used as a tool for oppression and dispossession by European colonists, in the four continents where they settled. In the Caribbean, the United States, Canada and Australia, accounting was used to expropriate first nations (Annisette & Neu, 2004; Chew & Greer, 1997; Gibson, 2000; Neu, 2000a, 2000b; Neu & Graham, 2004, 2006; Neu & Heincke, 2004). Dispossession started with claims over land articulated by the first settlers. Through measures expressed in acres and geographical properties, all recorded at the land registry, European settlers could claim ownership over sections of land. In return, first nations, whose culture was not resting upon ownership but communion with land, could not protest and were thereby denied any rights (Alam, Lawrence, & Nandan, 2004; Chew & Greer, 1997; Davie, 2007; Greer & Patel, 2000).

Table 1.2 Off-balance sheet slave records

The slave		
Objectives		X
Actual results	X′	
Imbalance: Performance variance		
Accruals	Y	
Retribution (Y = X – X′)		
Balance: Compensated underperformance		

Accountants were to distinguish between ethnic groups and to rank them. For that purpose, they based their forecasts on ethnic stereotypes. European settlers categorised people by purported objective physical and physiological criteria, leading to the racialisation of colonisation (Upton & Arrington, 2012). That is, some groups or subgroups were to be assigned certain pretended characteristics, thereby enabling to rank them and grant them more or less rights. Ranking people on the grounds of pretended objective criteria would necessarily result in relying on stereotypes as scientific means to assess people. In anthropology and political science, such reliance is called racism or racialism (Fenton, 1999) with lingering effects 50 years after decolonisation (Annisette, 2003; Hammond, Clayton, & Arnold, 2012; K. L. James & Hill, 2009; K. L. James & Otsuka, 2009; Kim, 2004a, 2004b, 2008).

In a historical study of the accountancy profession in Trinidad and Tobago, Annisette (2003) outlines the process of integrating ethnic minorities. Prior to decolonisation, the accountancy profession was devoted only to Whites. As Trinidad and Tobago were colonised by France, Britain, the Netherlands and Spain, all these nationalities first represented the profession. After decolonisation, only White Anglo-Saxon Protestants were accountants. Indigenous peoples, *for example*, historical slaves, were excluded. Since the 1980s, racial laws have endeavoured to facilitate the integration of the Black *minority*. Although that ethnic group represented 80% of the population of the islands, it has long been considered a minority due to its slave history. In fact, Annisette recalls that the Black population had always been subjected to the White colonist and has never protested against the oppressor. Similarly, Maori women in New Zealand have undergone similar discriminations within the accountancy profession (McNicholas, Humphries, & Gallhofer, 2004).

Over time, the racial problem moved from the indigenous people to the migrants, who have experienced similar discriminations. The Chinese and the Pakistani minorities in Trinidad and Tobago have been allowed to do forensic accounting. In fact, they have become in charge of what the White and the Black historical ethnic groups had no longer wanted to take over. But none of the members of those minorities were offered partnership or managerial responsibilities. Nowadays, new racial laws uphold the hiring of migrant ethnic minorities to key positions. Notwithstanding, the latter still remain marginalised. Interestingly, Kim (2004b) makes similar observations regarding the Chinese minority in New Zealand. Informed with similar approaches, numerous studies have denounced the oppressive/repressive characteristics of accounting on indigenous peoples (Alam et al., 2004; Davie, 2005, 2007; Gallhofer & Chew, 2000; Kim, 2004a; McNicholas et al., 2004; Neu, 2000a; Neu & Graham, 2004) and slaves (Fleischman & Tyson, 2004; Tyson et al., 2004).

Protests against colonists and the oppression through colonial management accounting commenced in Domingo in the late eighteenth century (Bébel-Ghisler & Hurbon, 1997; Glissant, 1997; Tyson et al., 2004). Like Spartacus in Ancient Rome, Toussaint Louverture rose up against White domination in 1802 and undertook to expel the White colonist. Toussaint Louverture understood that slaves were considered resources for farms but were perceived as tradeable commodities. According to him, as slaves were contributing to the farm's wealth, they were to be considered a resource (equity) and not a fixed asset. The slave was not a wealth in himself-or-herself but the enabler of asset creation.

Toussaint Louverture also noticed that the potency of whip hits on slaves was dependent on their ethnicity, thereby revealing that some ethnic groups were preferred over others. As White people were unable to formally distinguish between various ethnicities, he understood that these preferences ought to be motivated by the role played and the performance achieved by each ethic group on farm premises and beyond. In fact, he understood the benchmark principle and the principle of retributions associated with variance from standards. In order to improve slave conditions in the farm where he was working, he suggested their collective performances should be lowered. In so doing, the elderly and the weakest could avoid severe sanctions. By construction, they would be in a capacity of meeting the objectives they were set: due to lower results, the benchmark value would mechanically decrease. This would have two consequences. Firstly, deviations from standards would be rarer. Secondly, records of balanced accounts would subsequently be fewer. For the first time, slaves understood the management accounting principles upon which farm management was resting and used them against those who devised them.

Progressively, slaves in farms and social protesters so appropriated the management accounting rhetoric as to using it for their own emancipation: they could claim that they were generating wealth more than they were a cost. They should be considered profit centres and no longer cost centres. This was the beginning of emancipatory accounting (Alawattage & Wickramasinghe, 2009b; Gallhofer & Haslam, 1996, 2003, 2004; Jacobs, 2011; McNicholas & Barrett, 2005; Molisa, 2011). Accordingly, they started demanding to be accounted for as equity, which would acknowledge their productive capacity and foremost their untradeable nature (Gallhofer & Chew, 2000; Gallhofer & Haslam, 1996). Whereas assets can be traded, equity cannot. By becoming part of equity, they could gain authority over their own fate, which being assets did not allow. This alternative recording of slaves would disconnect their value from the income, since this was accounted for as liability and could therefore no longer be their balanced counterpart. Similarly and consequently, the principle of retribution in case of low performance should become meaningless, since income was disconnected from the status as slave. In sum, this change in paradigm and transfer from assets to liabilities allowed to engage in a journey towards emancipation (Fleischman & Tyson, 2004; Tyson et al., 2004). In 1804, Haiti negotiated an independence treaty with France, pursuant to which it would pay in 1827 150 million gold-equivalent francs to reach independence, *namely* about 17 billion euros of today. This means that independence and the end of oppression were associated with a financial cost. The lump sum Haiti was to pay to the French government appeared as an estimated cost of opportunity if France relinquishes its colony. Nearly 60 years before Jules Ferry's explicit colonial doctrine, accounting appeared as a means of both dispossession and emancipation at the same time.

The emancipation process was enabled by the fact that slaves could also free themselves from their masters. After a certain number of years working on the farm, they could be freed, thereby receiving a livret stating they were free people and could not be enslaved anymore (Tyson & Davie, 2009). Liberation price was not the same as the market value or historical cost but a colligation of exchange value for members of that ethnic group and individual performance. What was important for the master was that the payment from the emancipated slave would be sufficient to purchase a new one. In other words, the price was revealing the slave's replacement value and cost of opportunity. When prices started to increase in the first half of the nineteenth century, slaves in the US Southern states protested against the opacity of the off-balance sheet records that would artificially increase prices and prevent them from gaining emancipation. The actual performance recorded on the income statement would not appear in the same terms on the balance sheet. Through off-balance sheet records, such imbalances could occur and be detected. Therefore, slaves were demanding that the details of these records should be unveiled. Refusal to inform them was perceived as the confirmation that masters' accounts were opaque and thereby unfair. Accounting was serving not just White masters but also provided Black slaves with means of rebellion against the oppressor who was obliged to smooth their performance through unrecorded coercion and retributions. Protests lasted until the twentieth century but were systematically repressed, such as the July 1830 riots, the 1848 revolution, the Commune de Paris in 1870 or the Spartakist movement. These protests reached Europe, where revolutionary socialists were using factories' accounts to denounce the spoliation and oppression of the working class by Capital (Gallhofer & Chew, 2000; Gallhofer & Haslam, 1996).

Protests became more and more severe after World War II, as colonised peoples could not only understand accounting but also practise it (Gallhofer & Jim Haslam, 1991; Gallhofer & Haslam, 2004; Moerman, 2006; Naipaul, 1999). Since Toussaint Louverture's achievements, the slave population had been educated to the understanding of accounting by the Black foremen in charge of supervising fieldwork. The abolition of slavery in 1848 made the education of indigenous peoples easier. Informally, generations of subalterns and weak people have shared and cumulated this accounting knowledge, until some were in a capacity of keeping their own records that would support a major protest (Alawattage & Wickramasinghe, 2009a, 2009b). Progressively, colonised peoples could keep their own books and manage their resources on their own. The presence of the White colonist as an administration and accounting authority was no longer an imperative (Marseille, 2001, 2005). Through accounting, colonised peoples could be self-standing and self-managed (Harney, 2006). As a result, the *raison d'être* of a colonial state could be called into question, thereby opening for decolonisation in the West Indies first, followed by Asia and Africa.

As with the Roman Catholic Church and Reformers in the sixteenth century (Joannidès de Lautour, 2016), colonisation and decolonisation took control over accounting to serve their own fate. Similarly, debates surrounding the way of keeping records and accounting for people and resources opposed conservatives (colonists) and reformers (slaves and then colonised peoples). As in the sixteenth century, issues raised by accounting related to information transparency and production. Notwithstanding these debates, colonists as well as slaves and colonised people managed to take advantage of accounting technologies: either to become wealthier or to free oneself. The dialectic movement engaged with religious discussions continued with the opposing of conservatives and progressists.

In line with the concerns expressed by colonial people after World War II, imperial powers found themselves forced to engage in a decolonisation process. After the war, political oppression began to be denounced in public discourses. The utmost expression of this denunciation and aspiration to a new world order was the Universal Declaration of Human Rights in 1949. Amongst human rights were the people's self-determination, thereby announcing the advent of decolonisation. As with motivations for colonising Asia, those for colonising empires differed between France and the United Kingdom. At this critical juncture, both countries were confronted with the same dilemma: decolonising or not. Discussions at the House of Parliament in both countries revolved around questioning whether independence should or should not be granted to a colony. The answer was not easy and proved to be contingent upon political matters peculiar to each country, that is, cost of independence, cost of the colony and probably the cost of war, if any (Alam et al., 2004; Alawattage & Wickramasinghe, 2009a; Bakre, 2008; Bush & Maltby, 2004; Davie, 2007; Gallhofer, Haslam, & Kamla, 2011; Hooper, Pratt, & Kearins, 1993; Kamla, 2007; Neu, 2000b).

If a colony was to be totally independent, this aspiration to self-determination may result in the new country fully detaching itself from the former colonial power. If this occurred, France or the United Kingdom would certainly incur a major cost of opportunity expressed as decline in GDP. Both countries reacted differently to this dilemma. The United Kingdom decided that it would be possible to maintain a special relationship to former colonies through trade, as has always been done, and a privileged access to each other's markets. New sovereign countries could decide to remain within the Commonwealth or leave. By remaining, they would maintain this privileged access to markets. Conversely, by leaving, they would be considered third-party countries without any special relationship to others. For its part, the French government saw in independence a major destabilisation of its own sovereignty and power. The political and economic élite living in the colonies would have to return to the metropole, thereby losing all their possessions. Back to the metropole, they would certainly not be welcome and would have to be looked after. Losing colonies would not just be a loss of GDP and resources but a real political risk. Therefore, unlike the UK, France first decided not to relinquish its colonies, which resulted in decolonisation wars. At the House of Parliament, opposition to wars could be found on the left wing and the right wing, but on different grounds. The leftist opposition to war was claiming the new right to self-determination. Rightist opponents were claiming the cost of war, as developed during World War I. Notwithstanding

Table 1.3 Management accounting in history

Historical era	*Management concern*	*Accounting response*
Pre-capitalism dualism	Reconcile world dualism (mankind and God)	Double-entry bookkeeping Valuation Verification
Second industrial capitalism	Profit maximisation	Total profit accounting Time management Supply chain management
Bureaucracies	Economies of scale	Division of labour and specialisation Standard cost and cost accounting Budgeting and budgetary control Open-book accounting
Scientific management	Process optimisation Profit maximisation	Cost classification Sophisticated costing systems Capital budgeting Mathematics-based management control
Financial capitalism	Optimise risk, return and liquidity	Job-order accounting Value chain accounting Financial ratios Reporting standards Integrated accounting (IR and XBRL) Inter-organisational controls
World War I	Align strategy, operations and control	Forecasts Operations management accounting Supply chain management Management accounting concepts
World War II	The Shoah	Management accounting selection criteria Operations management accounting Quality management accounting Supply chain management
Colonisation	Valuation Political justification or protest	Benchmark accounting Performance accounting Off-balance sheet accounting Accrual accounting Accounting figures' contingency Accounting manipulations

this twofold opposition, the French government engaged in a 17-year-long war to preserve its colonies (Roepstorff, 2012). Humanism on the leftist side and economics on the rightist side were uniting to oppose and denounced the war effort. In 1962, when Algeria gained independence, France had lost all its colonies and most of its influence over its former empire.

1.4 Conclusion

Notwithstanding its non-exhaustiveness, this chapter shows that management accounting and control are much broader than mere budgeting, costing and variance analysis. It can however not be denied that these are important, but it is crucial to put them in context. These have emerged as such in response to the spread of Capitalism and have characterised industrialisation. Prior to and irrespective of the industrial revolution, accounting and controls have developed to serve various purposes and to respond to specific needs. Not all of these needs were economic, with finance being peripheral to most of them. In fact, management accounting and control have developed as responses to strategic (military), ethical (religion) or political concerns (war and colonisation). Interestingly, contemporary management control systems appear as the colligation of technologies developed at different times and in different places to serve different purposes. This implies that some concerns we think are specific to present-day Capitalism have been expressed long before in a different situation. In other words, management accounting and control appear as highly contingent upon the situation, place and time where they are practised (Table 1.3).

Bibliography

Abrahamsson, P., Oza, N., & Bunce, P. G. (2010). How the beyond budgeting management model enables lean thinking and the agile organization. In W. Aalst, J. Mylopoulos, N. M. Sadeh, M. J. Shaw, & C. Szyperski (Eds.), *Lean enterprise software and systems* (Vol. 65, pp. 153–153). Berlin and Heidelberg: Springer.

Adams, C. A. (2015). The International Integrated Reporting Council: A call to action. *Critical Perspectives on Accounting, 27*(1), 23–28.

Ahmad, M. F., Zakuan, N., Jusoh, A., & Takala, J. (2012). Relationship of TQM and business performance with mediators of SPC, lean production and TPM. *Social and Behavioral Sciences, 65*, 186–191.

Alam, M., Lawrence, S., & Nandan, R. (2004). Accounting for economic development in the context of post-colonialism: The Fijian experience. *Critical Perspectives on Accounting, 15*(1), 135–157.

Alawattage, C., & Wickramasinghe, D. (2009a). Institutionalisation of control and accounting for bonded labour in colonial plantations: A historical analysis. *Critical Perspectives on Accounting, 20*(6), 701–715.

Alawattage, C., & Wickramasinghe, D. (2009b). Weapons of the weak: Subalterns' emancipatory accounting in Ceylon Tea. *Accounting, Auditing & Accountability Journal, 22*(3), 379–404.

Alcouffe, S., Berland, N., & Levant, Y. (2008). Actor-networks and the diffusion of management accounting innovations: A comparative study. *Management Accounting Research, 19*(1), 1–17.

Alles, M., & Debreceny, R. (2012). The evolution and future of XBRL research. *International Journal of Accounting Information Systems, 13*(2), 83–90. https://doi.org/10.1016/j.accinf.2012.03.006

Allsop, D., & Calveley, M. (2009). Miners' identity and the changing face of the labour process within the UK coal mining industry. *Qualitative Research in Accounting & Management, 6*(1/2), 57–69.

Annisette, M. (2003). The colour of accountancy: Examining the salience of race in a professionalisation project. *Accounting, Organizations and Society, 28*(7–8), 639–674.

Annisette, M., & Neu, D. (2004). Accounting and empire: An introduction. *Critical Perspectives on Accounting, 15*(1), 1–4.

Anthony, R. N. (1952). *Management controls in industrial research organizations.* Chicago, IL: Harvard University Press.

Anthony, R. N. (1965). *Planning and control systems: A framework for analysis.* Boston, MA: Harvard Business School Publishing.

Anthony, R. N. (1988). *The management control function.* Boston, MA: Harvard Business School Publishing.

Anthony, R. N., Dearden, J., & Bedford, N. M. (1984). *Management control systems.* Homewood, IL: Irwin.

Anvari, A., Ismail, Y., & Hojjati, S. M. (2011). A study on total quality management and lean manufacturing: Through lean thinking approach. *World Applied Sciences Journal, 12*(9), 1585–1596.

Anvari, A., Sorooshian, S., & Moghimi, R. (2011). The strategic approach to exploration review on TQM and lean production. *International Journal of Lean Thinking, 3*(2), 13–26.

Appadurai, A. (1996). *Modernity at large cultural dimensions of globalization.* Minneapolis: Minnesota University Press.

Arendt, H. (1961). *The human condition.* Chicago: The University of Chicago Press.

Arendt, H. (1963). *Eichmann in Jerusalem.* London: Penguin.

Arendt, H. (1968). *Totalitarianism: Part three of the origins of totalitarianism.* Boston: Harvest Books.

Badiou, A. (2006). The factory as event site: Why should the worker be a reference in our vision of politics?, in PRELOM. *Journal of Images and Politics, 8*, 171–176.

Bakre, O. M. (2008). Financial reporting as technology that supports and sustains imperial expansion, maintenance and control in the colonial and post-colonial globalisation: The case of the Jamaican economy. *Critical Perspectives on Accounting, 19*(4), 487–522.

Baraldi, E., & Waluszewski, A. (2005). Information technology at IKEA: An "open sesame" solution or just another type of facility? *Journal of Business Research, 58*(9), 1251–1260.

Barney, D., & Flesher, D. (1994). Early nineteenth-century productivity accounting: The Locust Grove Plantation slave ledger. *Accounting, Business & Financial History, 4*(2), 275–294.

Bauer, B. (2019). *Disraelis Romantischer Und Bismarcks Sozialistischer Imperialismus*. London: Wentworth Press.

Bebbington, J., & Gray, R. (2001). An account of sustainability: Failure, success and a reconceptualization. *Critical Perspectives on Accounting, 12*(5), 557–588.

Bébel-Ghisler, L., & Hurbon, L. (1997). *Culture et pouvoir dans la Caraïbe: Haïti et la Guadeloupe*. Paris: L'Harmattan.

Belden, F. A., & Haven, C. T. (2011). *A history of the Colt revolver and other arms made by Colt's patent fire arms manufacturing company from 1836–1940*. Whitefish, MT: Literary Licensing.

Berland, N. (1998). The availability of information and the accumulation of experiences as motors for the diffusion of budgetary control: The French experience from the 1920's to the 1960's. *Accounting, Business & Financial History, 8*(3), 303–329.

Berland, N. (1999). *L'histoire du contrôle budgétaire en France. Les fonctions du contrôle budgétaire, influences de l'idéologie, de l'environnement et du management stratégique*. Dauphine: Université Paris.

Berland, N., & Boyns, T. (2002). The development of budgetary control in France and Britain from the 1920s to the 1960s: A comparison. *European Accounting Review, 11*(2), 329–356.

Berland, N., & Chiapello, E. (2009). Criticisms of capitalism, budgeting and the double enrolment: Budgetary control rhetoric and social reform in France in the 1930s and 1950s. *Accounting, Organizations and Society, 34*(1), 28–57.

Berland, N., Levant, Y., & Joannidès, V. (2010). *Rhetorics and the fate of budgeting*. Paper presented at the Asia-Pacific Interdisciplinary Research in Accounting Conference, Sydney.

Black, F., & Scholes, M. S. (1973). The pricing of options and corporate liabilities. *Journal of Political Economy, 81*(3), 637–654.

Boyns, T., Edwards, J. R., & Emmanuel, C. (1999). A longitudinal study of the determinants of transfer pricing change. *Management Accounting Research, 10*(2), 85–108. https://doi.org/10.1006/mare.1998.0093

Broehl, W. G., Jr. (1992). *Cargill: Trading the world's grain*. London: Dartmouth Publishing.

Broehl, W. G., Jr. (2008). *Cargill: From commodities to customers.* London: Dartmouth Publishing.

Browning, C. R. (2007). *The origins of the Final Solution: The evolution of Nazi Jewish policy, September 1939–March 1942.* Lincoln: Bison Books.

Bryer, R. (1993). Double-entry bookkeeping and the birth of capitalism: Accounting for the commercial revolution in medieval Northern Italy. *Critical Perspectives on Accounting, 4*(2), 113–140.

Bryer, R. (2000a). The history of accounting and the transition to capitalism in England. Part one: Theory. *Accounting, Organizations and Society, 25*(2), 131–162.

Bryer, R. (2000b). The history of accounting and the transition to capitalism in England. Part two: Evidence. *Accounting, Organizations and Society, 25*(4–5), 327–381.

Bryer, R. (2006a). Accounting and control of the labour process. *Critical Perspectives on Accounting, 17*(5), 551–598.

Bryer, R. (2006b). Capitalist accountability and the British Industrial Revolution: The Carron Company, 1759–circa. 1850. *Accounting, Organizations and Society, 31*(8), 687–734.

Bryer, R. (2006c). The genesis of the capitalist farmer: Towards a Marxist accounting history of the origins of the English agricultural revolution. *Critical Perspectives on Accounting, 17*(4), 367–397.

Bryer, R. (2013). Americanism and financial accounting theory—Part 2: The 'modern business enterprise', America's transition to capitalism, and the genesis of management accounting. *Critical Perspectives on Accounting, 24*(4–5), 273–318. https://doi.org/10.1016/j.cpa.2012.09.002

Burns, T., & Stalker, G. (1961). *The management of innovation.* Oxford: Oxford University Press.

Busco, C., & Quattrone, P. (2014). Exploring how the Balanced Scorecard engages and unfolds: Articulating the visual power of accounting inscriptions. *Contemporary Accounting Research, 32*(3), 1236–1262.

Busco, C., & Quattrone, P. (2018). Performing business and social innovation through accounting inscriptions: An introduction. *Accounting, Organizations and Society.* https://doi.org/10.1016/j.aos.2018.03.002

Bush, B., & Maltby, J. (2004). Taxation in West Africa: Transforming the colonial subject into the "governable person". *Critical Perspectives on Accounting, 15*(1), 5–34.

Carlsson-Wall, M., Kraus, K., & Lind, J. (2011). The interdependencies of intra- and inter-organisational controls and work practices' The case of domestic care of the elderly. *Management Accounting Research, 22*(4), 313–329. https://doi.org/10.1016/j.mar.2010.11.002

Carnegie, G. D., & Napier, C. (2002). Exploring comparative international accounting history. *Accounting, Auditing & Accountability Journal, 15*(5), 689–718.

Carruthers, B. G., & Espeland, W. N. (1991). Accounting for rationality: Double-entry bookkeeping and the rhetoric of economic rationality. *The American Journal of Sociology, 97*(1), 31–69.

Carter, C., & Mueller, F. (2006). The colonisation of strategy: Financialisation in a post-privatisation context. *Critical Perspectives on Accounting, 17*(8), 967–985.

Carter, C., & Tinker, A. M. (2006). Critical accounting and the labour process. *Critical Perspectives on Accounting, 17*(5), 525–528.

Catchpowle, L., Cooper, C., & Wright, A. (2004). Capitalism, states and accounting. *Critical Perspectives on Accounting, 15*(8), 1037–1058.

Chandler, A. J. (1977). *The visible hand: The managerial revolution in American business.* Boston: Belknap Press.

Chandler, A. J., & Deams, H. (1979). Administrative coordination, allocation, and monitoring: A comparative analysis of the emergence of accounting and organization in the USA and Europe. *Accounting, Organizations & Society, 2*(2), 189–205.

Chew, A., & Greer, S. (1997). Contrasting world views on accounting: Accountability and Aboriginal culture. *Accounting, Auditing & Accountability Journal, 10*(3), 276–298.

Chiapello, E. (2007). Accounting and the birth of the notion of capitalism. *Critical Perspectives on Accounting, 18*(3), 263–296.

Cho, C. H., Guidry, R. P., Hageman, A. M., & Patten, D. M. (2012). Do actions speak louder than words? An empirical investigation of corporate environmental reputation. *Accounting, Organizations and Society, 37*(1), 14–25. https://doi.org/10.1016/j.aos.2011.12.001

Cho, C. H., & Patten, D. M. (2013). Green accounting: Reflections from a CSR and environmental disclosure perspective. *Critical Perspectives on Accounting, 24*(6), 443–447. https://doi.org/10.1016/j.cpa.2013.04.003

Chwastiak, M., & Lehman, G. (2008). Accounting for war. *Accounting Forum, 32*(4), 313–326. https://doi.org/10.1016/j.accfor.2008.09.001

Clausewitz (von), C. (1832). *On war.* Princeton, NJ: Princeton University Press.

Cordery, C. (2015). Accounting history and religion: A review of studies and a research agenda. *Accounting History, 20*(4), 430–463.

Davie, S. S. K. (2005). The politics of accounting, race and ethnicity: A story of a Chiefly-based preferencing. *Critical Perspectives on Accounting, 16*(5), 551–577.

Davie, S. S. K. (2007). A colonial "social experiment": Accounting and a communal system in British-ruled Fiji. *Accounting Forum, 31*(3), 255–276.

Davison, J. (2004). Sacred vestiges in financial reporting: Mythical readings guided by Mircea Eliade. *Accounting, Auditing & Accountability Journal, 17*(3), 476–497.

Davison, J. (2010). [In]visible [in]tangibles: Visual portraits of the business Élite. *Accounting, Organizations and Society, 35*(2), 165–183.

Davison, J. (2011). Barthesian perspectives on accounting communication and visual images of professional accountancy. *Accounting, Auditing & Accountability Journal, 24*(2), 250–283.

Derks, H. (2008). Religion, capitalism and the rise of double-entry bookkeeping. *Accounting, Business & Financial History, 18*(2), 187–213.

Dikolli, S. S., & Vaysman, I. (2006). Information technology, organizational design, and transfer pricing. *Journal of Accounting and Economics, 41*(1–2), 201–234. https://doi.org/10.1016/j.jacceco.2005.06.001

Doray, B. (1990). *From Taylorism to Fordism: A rational madness.* New York: Free Association Books.

Dragu, I.-M., & Tiron-Tudor, A. (2013). The integrated reporting initiative from an institutional perspective: Emergent factors. *Procedia—Social and Behavioral Sciences, 92*(0), 275–279. https://doi.org/10.1016/j.sbspro.2013.08.672

Duan, C., Grover, V., & Balakrishnan, N. (2009). Business process outsourcing: An event study on the nature of processes and firm valuation. *European Journal of Information Systems, 18*(5), 442–457.

Dunne, T., Helliar, C., Lymer, A., & Mousa, R. (2013). Stakeholder engagement in internet financial reporting: The diffusion of XBRL in the UK. *The British Accounting Review, 45*(3), 167–182. https://doi.org/10.1016/j.bar.2013.06.012

Durkheim, E. (1902). *Division of labour in society* (K. A. Fields, Trans., 1984 ed.). London: Free Press.

Edwards, J. R., & Boyns, T. (2012). *A history of management accounting: The British experience.* London: Routledge.

Edwards, J. R., Coombs, H. M., & Greener, H. T. (2002). British central government and "the mercantile system of double entry" bookkeeping: A study of ideological conflict. *Accounting, Organizations and Society, 27*(7), 637–658.

Ezzamel, M. (1994). The emergence of the 'accountant' in the institutions of Ancient Egypt. *Management Accounting Research, 5*(3–4), 221–246.

Ezzamel, M. (1997). Accounting, control and accountability: Preliminary evidence from ancient Egypt. *Critical Perspectives on Accounting, 8*(6), 563–601.

Ezzamel, M. (2009). Order and accounting as a performative ritual: Evidence from ancient Egypt. *Accounting, Organizations and Society, 34*(3–4), 348–380.

Ezzamel, M., & Hoskin, K. (2002). Retheorizing accounting, writing and money with evidence from Mesopotamia and ancient Egypt. *Critical Perspectives on Accounting, 13*, 333–367.

Ezzamel, M., Willmott, H., & Worthington, F. (2004). Accounting and management-labour relations: The politics of production in the 'factory with a problem'. *Accounting, Organizations and Society, 29*(3–4), 269–302.

Fabozzi, F. J., & Markowitz, H. (2011). *The theory and practice of investment management: Asset allocation, valuation, portfolio construction, and strategies* (2nd ed.). Hoboken, NJ: Wiley.

Fabozzi, F. J., Markowitz, H., & Kostovetsky, L. (2004). *The theory and practice of investment management workbook: Step-by-step exercises and tests to help you master the Theory and practice of investment management.* Hoboken, NJ: John Wiley & Sons.

Fenton, S. (1999). *Ethnicity—Racism, class and culture*. London: Macmillan Press.
Fleischman, R. K. (2000). Completing the triangle: Taylorism and the paradigms. *Accounting, Auditing & Accountability Journal, 13*, 597–623.
Fleischman, R. K., & Boyns, T. (2008). The search for standard costing in the United States and Britain. *Abacus, 44*(4), 341–376.
Fleischman, R. K., Oldroyd, D., & Tyson, T. N. (2011). The efficacy/inefficacy of accounting in controlling labour during the transition from slavery in the United Stated and British West Indies. *Accounting, Auditing & Accountability Journal, 24*(6), 718–750.
Fleischman, R. K., & Tyson, T. N. (2004). Accounting in service to racism: Monetizing slave property in the antebellum South. *Critical Perspectives on Accounting, 15*(3), 376–399.
Fleischman, R. K., & Tyson, T. N. (2007). The history of management accounting in the US. In C. Chapman, A. Hopwood, & M. D. Shields (Eds.), *Handbook of management accounting research* (Vol. 2, pp. 1071–1089). London: Elsevier.
Flower, J. (2015). The International Integrated Reporting Council: A story of failure. *Critical Perspectives on Accounting, 27*(1), 1–17.
Free, W. W. (1977). *Short history of the metric system of weights and measures*. London: Vantage Press.
Frías-Aceituno, J. V., Rodríguez-Ariza, L., & García-Sánchez, I. M. (2013). Is integrated reporting determined by a country's legal system? An exploratory study. *Journal of Cleaner Production, 44*(0), 45–55. https://doi.org/10.1016/j.jclepro.2012.12.006
Funnell, W. (1998). Accounting in the service of the Holocaust. *Critical Perspectives on Accounting, 9*(4), 435–464.
Funnell, W. (2006). National efficiency, military accounting and the business of war. *Critical Perspectives on Accounting, 17*(6), 719–751. https://doi.org/10.1016/j.cpa.2004.11.008
Funnell, W., & Chwastiak, M. (2015). *Accounting at war: The politics of military finance*. London: Routledge.
Gallhofer, S., & Chew, A. (2000). Introduction: Accounting and indigenous peoples. *Accounting, Auditing & Accountability Journal, 13*(3), 256–267.
Gallhofer, S., & Haslam, J. (1991). The aura of accounting in the context of a crisis: Germany and the first world war. *Accounting, Organizations and Society, 16*(5–6), 487–520. https://doi.org/10.1016/0361-3682(91)90039-h
Gallhofer, S., & Haslam, J. (1996). Accounting/art and the emancipatory project: Some reflections. *Accounting, Auditing & Accountability Journal, 9*(5), 23–44.
Gallhofer, S., & Haslam, J. (2003). *Accounting and emancipation: Some critical interventions*. New York: Routledge.
Gallhofer, S., & Haslam, J. (2004). Accounting and liberation theology: Some insights for the project of emancipatory accounting. *Accounting, Auditing & Accountability Journal, 17*(3), 382–407.

Gallhofer, S., & Haslam, J. (2006). Mobilising accounting in the radical media during the First World War and its aftermath: The case of Forward in the context of Red Clydeside. *Critical Perspectives on Accounting, 17*(2–3), 224–252. https://doi.org/10.1016/j.cpa.2003.06.009

Gallhofer, S., Haslam, J., & Kamla, R. (2011). The accountancy profession and the ambiguities of globalisation in a post-colonial, Middle Eastern and Islamic context: Perceptions of accountants in Syria. *Critical Perspectives on Accounting, 22*(4), 376–395. https://doi.org/10.1016/j.cpa.2010.09.003

García-Sánchez, I.-M., Rodríguez-Ariza, L., & Frías-Aceituno, J.-V. (2013). The cultural system and integrated reporting. *International Business Review, 22*(5), 828–838. https://doi.org/10.1016/j.ibusrev.2013.01.007

Gibson, K. (2000). Accounting as a tool for Aboriginal dispossession: Then and now. *Accounting, Auditing & Accountability Journal, 13*(3), 289–306.

Gleadle, P., & Cornelius, N. (2008). A case study of financialization and EVAÆ. *Critical Perspectives on Accounting, 19*(8), 1219–1238.

Glissant, E. (1997). *Le discours antillais.* Paris: Folio.

Gordon, L. A., Loeb, M. P., & Stark, A. W. (1990). Capital budgeting and the value of information. *Management Accounting Research, 1*(1), 21–35. https://doi.org/10.1016/s1044-5005(90)70043-1

Gray, R. (1992). Accounting and environmentalism: An exploration of the challenge of gently accounting for accountability, transparency and sustainability. *Accounting, Organizations and Society, 17*(5), 399–425.

Gray, R. (2006). Social, environmental and sustainability reporting and organisational value creation?: Whose value? Whose creation? *Accounting, Auditing & Accountability Journal, 19*(6), 793–819.

Gray, R. (2010). Is accounting for sustainability actually accounting for sustainability…and how would we know? An exploration of narratives of organisations and the planet. *Accounting, Organizations and Society, 35*(1), 47–62.

Gray, R., & Collison, D. (2002). Can't see the wood for the trees, can't see the trees for the numbers? Accounting education, sustainability and the public interest. *Critical Perspectives on Accounting, 13*(5–6), 797–836.

Gray, R., Owen, D., & Maunders, K. (1988). Corporate social reporting: Emerging trends in accountability and the social contract. *Accounting, Auditing & Accountability Journal, 1*(1), 6–20.

Greer, S., & Patel, C. (2000). The issue of Australian indigenous world-views and accounting. *Accounting, Auditing & Accountability Journal, 13*(3), 307–329.

Grinyer, J. R., & Daing, N. I. (1993). The use of abandonment values in capital budgeting' Äîa research note. *Management Accounting Research, 4*(1), 49–62. https://doi.org/10.1006/mare.1993.1003

Gumbrell-McCormick, R., & Hyman, R. (2013). *Trade unions in Western Europe: Hard times, hard choices.* Oxford: Oxford University Press.

Hammond, T., Clayton, B. M., & Arnold, P. J. (2012). An "unofficial" history of race relations in the South African accounting industry, 1968–2000: Perspectives of South Africa's first black chartered accountants. *Critical Perspectives on Accounting, 23*(4/5), 332–350. https://doi.org/10.1016/j.cpa.2011.10.005

Harney, S. (2006). Management and self-activity: Accounting for the crisis in profit-taking. *Critical Perspectives on Accounting, 17*(7), 935–946.

Hooper, K., Pratt, M., & Kearins, K. (1993). Accounting, auditing and the business establishment in colonial Auckland 1880–1895. *Accounting, Auditing & Accountability Journal, 6*(1), 79–98.

Hope, J., & Fraser, R. (2001). *Questions and answers—Beyond Budgeting Cam-I—Beyond Budgeting Round Table*. London: Beyond Budgeting Round Table.

Horringan, J. O. (1968). A short story of financial ratio analysis. *The Accounting Review, 43*, 284–294.

Houze, H. (2004). *Winchester repeating arms company: Its history & development from 1865 to 1981*. Iola, WI: Krause Publications.

Icon_Group_International. (2009). *The metric system: Webster's timeline history, 1781–2006*. London: ICON Group International, Inc.

Isakov, E. (2014). *International system of units (SI): How the world measures almost everything, and the people who made it possible*. London: Industrial Press.

Jacobs, K. (2011). Enlightenment and emancipation: Reflections for critical accounting research. *Critical Perspectives on Accounting, 22*(5), 510–515. https://doi.org/10.1016/j.cpa.2010.11.005

Jacobs, K., & Walker, S. P. (2004). Accounting and accountability in the Iona Community. *Accounting, Auditing & Accountability Journal, 17*(3), 361–381.

James, K. L., & Hill, C. (2009). Race and the development of career interest in accounting. *Critical Perspectives on Accounting, 27*(4), 210–222.

James, K. L., & Otsuka, S. (2009). Racial biases in recruitment by accounting firms: The case of international Chinese applicants in Australia. *Critical Perspectives on Accounting, 20*(4), 469–491.

James, L. (1997). *The rise and fall of the British Empire*. London: Martin's Press.

Jensen, M. (1986). Agency costs of free cash flow, corporate finance, and takeovers. *American Economic Review, 76*(2), 329–326.

Jensen, M. (2001). Corporate budgeting is broken, let's fix it. *Harvard Business Review*, November, 94–101.

Jensen, M. (2003). Paying people to lie: The truth about the budgeting process. *European Financial Management, 9*(3), 379–406.

Joannidès, V. (2012). Accounterability and the problematics of accountability. *Critical Perspectives on Accounting, 23*(3), 244–257.

Joannidès de Lautour, V. (2016). *Capitalism, accounting and the revealed religions—A study of Judaism, Christianity and Islam*. London: Palgrave Macmillan.

Joannidès de Lautour, V. (2018a). *Strategic management accounting—Volume I: Aligning strategy, operations and finance*. London: Palgrave Macmillan.

Joannidès de Lautour, V. (2018b). *Strategic management accounting—Volume II: Beyond the numbers*. London: Palgrave Macmillan.

Jones, C. T., & Dugdale, D. (2002). The ABC bandwagon and the juggernaut of modernity. *Accounting, Organizations and Society, 27*(1–2), 121–163.

Jørgensen, B., & Messner, M. (2010). Accounting and strategising: A case study from new product development. *Accounting, Organizations & Society, 35*(2), 184–204.

Kabinga, L. (2016). *Warehouse and supply chain management: Concept, history and trends*. Detroit: Amazon Digital Services.

Kamla, R. (2007). Critically appreciating social accounting and reporting in the Arab MiddleEast: A postcolonial perspective. *Advances in International Accounting, 20*, 105–177. https://doi.org/10.1016/S0897-3660(07)20005-4

Kaplan, R. (1984). The evolution of management accounting. *The Accounting Review, 59*(3), 390–418.

Kaplan, R., & Johnson, T. (1987). *Relevance lost: Rise and fall of management accounting*. Boston, MA: Harvard University Press.

Kershaw, I. (2013). *Fateful choices: Ten decisions that changed the world, 1940–1941*. London: Penguin.

Kershaw, I. (2016). *To hell and back: Europe 1914–1949*. London: Penguin Books.

Kershaw, I., & Sandys, N. (2019). *Hitler, the Germans, and the final solution*. London: Brilliance Publishing.

Keynes, J. M. (1919). *The economic consequences of the peace*. London: Macmillan & Co..

Kim, S. N. (2004a). Imperialism without empire: Silence in contemporary accounting research on race/ethnicity. *Critical Perspectives on Accounting, 15*(1), 95–133.

Kim, S. N. (2004b). Racialized gendering of the accountancy profession: Toward an understanding of Chinese women's experiences in accountancy in New Zealand. *Critical Perspectives on Accounting, 15*(3), 400–427.

Kim, S. N. (2008). Whose voice is it anyway? Rethinking the oral history method in accounting research on race, ethnicity and gender. *Critical Perspectives on Accounting, 19*(8), 1346–1369.

Kline, C. A., & Hessler, H. L. (1955). The du Pont chart system for appraising operating performance. In W. E. Thomas (Ed.), *Readings in cost accounting, budgeting, and control* (p. 752). South-Western Publishing.

Kraus, K. (2012). Heterogeneous accountingisation: Accounting and inter-organisational cooperation in home care services. *Accounting, Auditing & Accountability Journal, 25*(7), 1080–1112.

Lamminmaki, D. (2008). Accounting and the management of outsourcing: An empirical study in the hotel industry. *Management Accounting Research, 19*(2), 163–181.

Langfield-Smith, K., & Smith, D. (2003). Management control systems and trust in outsourcing relationships. *Management Accounting Research, 14*(3), 281–307. https://doi.org/10.1016/s1044-5005(03)00046-5

Laswad, F., & Baskerville, R. F. (2007). An analysis of the value of cash flow statements of New Zealand pension schemes. *The British Accounting Review, 39*(4), 347–355. https://doi.org/10.1016/j.bar.2007.08.002

Laughlin, R. (1996). Principals and higher-principals: Accounting for accountability in the caring professions. In R. Munro & J. Mouritsen (Eds.), *Accountability: Power, ethos and the technologies of managing* (pp. 225–244). London: International Thomson Business Press.

Lawrence, J. W., & Lorsch, P. R. (1967). *Organization and environment: Managing differentiation and integration.* New York: Irwin Inc..

Leonhard, J., & Camiller, P. (2018). *Pandora's box: A history of the First World War.* Harvard: Belknap Press.

Levi, P. (1991). *If this is a man.* London: Abacus.

Levi, P. (1995). *Survival in Auschwitz.* London: Simon & Schuster.

Littell, J. (2007). *Les Bienveillantes.* Paris: Garnier-Fammarion.

Liu, C., Wang, T., & Yao, L. J. (2014). XBRL's impact on analyst forecast behavior: An empirical study. *Journal of Accounting and Public Policy, 33*(1), 69–82. https://doi.org/10.1016/j.jaccpubpol.2013.10.004

Machiavel, N. (1520). The art of war. In E. Farneworth & J. Adams (Eds.), *The complete works of Machiavelli.* London: Nabu Press.

MacIntosh, N., Shearer, T., & Riccaboni, A. (2009). A Lévinassian ethics critique of the role of management and control systems by large corporations: The General Electric/Nuovo Pignone example. *Critical Perspectives on Accounting, 20*, 751–761.

Magee, H. C. (1915). Department store account. *The Journal of Accountancy*, April, 268–291.

Manne, A. S., Markowitz, H., & Yale University. Cowles Foundation for Research in Economics. (1963). Studies in process analysis: Economy-wide production capabilities. In *Proceedings of a conference sponsored by the Cowles Foundation ...* April 24–26, 1961, Wiley, New York.

Markowitz, H., Sharpe, W. F., & Miller, M. H. (1991). *The founders of modern finance: Their prize-winning concepts and 1990 Nobel lectures.* Charlottesville, VA: Research Foundation of the Institute of Chartered Financial Analysts.

Marrus, M., Paxton, R., & Hoffmann, S. (1995). *Vichy France and the Jews.* Stanford, CA: Stanford University Press.

Marseille, J. (2001). *L'âge d'or de la France coloniale.* Paris: Albin Michel.

Marseille, J. (2005). *Empire colonial et capitalisme français: Histoire d'un divorce.* Paris: Albin Michel.

Martin, W. (2010). Accounting for varieties of capitalism: The case against a single set of global accounting standards. *The British Accounting Review, 42*(3), 137–152. https://doi.org/10.1016/j.bar.2010.04.003

Marx, K. (1894). *Das Kapital: Kritik der politischen Oekonomie—Band III.* Hamburg: Verlag von Otto Meissner.
McKernan, J. F. (2007). Objectivity in accounting. *Accounting, Organizations and Society, 32*(1–2), 155–180.
McKernan, J. F., & Kosmala, K. (2004). Accounting, love and justice. *Accounting, Auditing & Accountability Journal, 17*(3), 327–360.
McKernan, J. F., & Kosmala, K. (2007). Doing the truth: Religion—Deconstruction—Justice, and accounting. *Accounting, Auditing & Accountability Journal, 20*(5), 729–764.
McNicholas, P., & Barrett, M. (2005). Answering the emancipatory call: An emerging research approach [']on the margins' of accounting. *Critical Perspectives on Accounting, 16*(4), 391–414.
McNicholas, P., Humphries, M., & Gallhofer, S. (2004). Maintaining the empire: Maori women's experiences in the accountancy profession. *Critical Perspectives on Accounting, 15*(1), 57–93.
Mederos, L. A. (2018). *Backsourcing processes: A decision support tool.* DBA thesis, Grenoble École de Management.
Mederos, L. A. (2020). *Strategic management controls and the backsourcing decision.* London: Palgrave Macmillan.
Merino, B. D. (1998). Critical theory and accounting history: Challenges and opportunities. *Critical Perspectives on Accounting, 9*(6), 603–616.
Merton, R. C. (1973). Theory of rational option pricing. *The Bell Journal of Economics and Management Science, 4*(1), 141–183.
Miller, P. (1992). Accounting and objectivity: The invention of calculating selves and calculable space. *Annals of Scholarship, 9*(1/2), 61–86.
Miller, P. (2008). Governing by numbers: Why calculative practices matter. In A. Amin & N. J. Thrift (Eds.), *The Blackwell cultural economy reader* (pp. 179–190). Malden: Blackwell Publishing.
Miller, P., Hopper, T., & Laughlin, R. (1991). The new accounting history: An introduction. *Accounting, Organizations and Society, 16*(5–6), 395–403.
Miller, P., & Napier, C. (1993). Genealogies of calculation. *Accounting, Organizations and Society, 18*(7–8), 631–647.
Miller, P., & O'Leary, T. (1987). Accounting and the construction of the governable person. *Accounting, Organizations and Society, 12*(3), 235–265.
Miller, P., & O'Leary, T. (1997). Capital budgeting practices and complementarity relations in the transition to modern manufacture: A field-base analysis. *Journal of Accounting Research, 35*, 257–271.
Miller, P., & O'Leary, T. (2007). Mediating instruments and making markets: Capital budgeting, science and the economy. *Accounting, Organizations and Society, 32*(7–8), 701–734.
Modigliani, F., & Miller, M. H. (1958). The cost of capital, corporation finance and the theory of investment. *The American Economic Review, 48*(3), 261–297.

Moerman, L. (2006). People as prophets: Liberation theology as a radical perspective on accounting. *Accounting, Auditing & Accountability Journal, 19*(2), 169–185.

Molisa, P. (2011). A spiritual reflection on emancipation and accounting. *Critical Perspectives on Accounting, 22*(5), 453–484.

Mouritsen, J., & Thrane, S. (2006). Accounting, network complementarities and the development of inter-organisational relations. *Accounting, Organizations and Society, 31*(3), 241–275. https://doi.org/10.1016/j.aos.2005.04.002

Müller, J. (2014). An accounting revolution? The financialisation of standard setting. *Critical Perspectives on Accounting, 25*(7), 539–557.

Naipaul, V. S. (1961). *The middle passage: Impressions of five colonial societies.* London: Picador.

Naipaul, V. S. (1999). *La traversée du milieu.* Paris: Folio.

Napier, C. (2009). Defining Islamic accounting: Current issues, past root. *Accounting History, 14*(1/2), 121–144.

Neu, D. (2000a). Accounting and accountability relations: Colonization, genocide and Canada's first nations. *Accounting, Auditing & Accountability Journal, 13*(3), 268–288.

Neu, D. (2000b). "Presents" for the "Indians": Land, colonialism and accounting in Canada. *Accounting, Organizations & Society, 25*(2), 163–184.

Neu, D., & Graham, C. (2004). Accounting and the holocausts of modernity. *Accounting, Auditing & Accountability Journal, 17*(4), 578–603.

Neu, D., & Graham, C. (2006). The birth of a nation: Accounting and Canada's first nations, 1860–1900. *Accounting, Organizations and Society, 31*(1), 47–76.

Neu, D., & Heincke, M. (2004). The subaltern speaks: Financial relations and the limits of governmentality. *Critical Perspectives on Accounting, 15*(1), 179–206.

O'Riain, S., Curry, E., & Harth, A. (2012). XBRL and open data for global financial ecosystems: A linked data approach. *International Journal of Accounting Information Systems, 13*(2), 141–162. https://doi.org/10.1016/j.accinf.2012.02.002

Oldroyd, D., Fleischman, R. K., & Tyson, T. N. (2008). The culpability of accounting practice in promoting slavery in the British Empire and antebellum United States. *Critical Perspectives on Accounting, 19*(5), 764–784.

Østergren, K., & Stensaker, I. (2011). Management control without budgets: A field study of 'Beyond Budgeting' in practice. *European Accounting Review, 20*(1), 149–181.

Otley, D. (1990). Issues in accountability and control: Some observations from a study of colliery accountability in the British Coal Corporation. *Management Accounting Research, 1*(2), 101–123.

Owen, D. L., & Lloyd, A. J. (1985). The use of financial information by trade union negotiators in plant level collective bargaining. *Accounting, Organizations and Society, 10*(3), 329–350. https://doi.org/10.1016/0361-3682(85)90023-6

Parker, L. D. (2002a). Budgetary incrementalism in a Christian bureaucracy. *Management Accounting Research, 13*(1), 71–100.
Parker, L. D. (2002b). It's been a pleasure doing business with you: A strategic analysis and critique of university change management. *Critical Perspectives on Accounting, 13*(5–6), 603–619.
Parker, L. D. (2016). The global Fayol: Contemporary management and accounting traces. *Entreprises et Histoire, 83*(3), 51–63.
Pfeiffer, T., & Schneider, G. (2010). Capital budgeting, information timing, and the value of abandonment options. *Management Accounting Research, 21*(4), 238–250. https://doi.org/10.1016/j.mar.2010.07.001
Player, S. (2003). Why some organizations go "Beyond Budgeting". *The Journal of Corporate Accounting & Finance*, March/April, 3–9.
Power, M. (2003). Auditing and the production of legitimacy. *Accounting, Organizations & Society, 28*(3), 379–394.
Power, M. (2009). The risk management of nothing. *Accounting, Organizations and Society, 34*(6–7), 849–855. https://doi.org/10.1016/j.aos.2009.06.001
Pratt, M. G., Rockmann, K. W., & Kaufmann, J. B. (2006). Constructing professional identity: The role of work and identity learning cycles in the customization of identity among medical residents. *Academy of Management Journal, 49*(2), 235–262. https://doi.org/10.5465/amj.2006.20786060
Quattrone, P. (2004). Accounting for God: Accounting and accountability practices in the Society of Jesus (Italy, XVI-XVII centuries). *Accounting, Organizations and Society, 29*(7), 647–683.
Quattrone, P. (2009). Books to be practiced: Memory, the power of the visual, and the success of accounting. *Accounting, Organizations & Society, 34*(1), 85–118.
Ramirez, C. (2009). Constructing the governable small practitioner: The changing nature of professional bodies and the management of professional accountants' identities in the UK. *Accounting, Organizations and Society, 34*(3–4), 381–408. https://doi.org/10.1016/j.aos.2008.05.004
Reid, A. J. (2005). *United we stand: A history of Britain's trade unions.* London: Penguin.
Rickards, R. (2006). Beyond budgeting: Boon or Boondoggle? *Investment Management and Financial Innovations, 3*(2), 62–76.
Roach, M. (2003). *Dr. Martens: The story of an icon.* London: Anova Books.
Roepstorff, K. (2012). *The politics of self-determination: Beyond the decolonisation process* (Vol. 95). London: Routledge.
Rosa, J.-J. (2000). *Le second vingtième siècle.* Paris: Grasset.
Schain, M. A., & Kesselman, M. (1998). *A century of organized labor in France: A union movement for the twenty first century?* London: Palgrave Macmillan.
Schweiker, W. (1993). Accounting for ourselves: Accounting practices and the disclosure of ethics. *Accounting, Organizations & Society, 18*(2–3), 231–252.

Semelin, J. (2019). *The survival of the Jews in France, 1940–44*. Oxford: Oxford University Press.

Shearer, T. (2002). Ethics and accountability: From the for-itself to the for-the-other. *Accounting, Organizations and Society, 27*(6), 541–573.

Shirrer, W., & Rosenbaum, R. (2011). *The rise and fall of the Third Reich: A history of Nazi Germany*. London: Simon & Schuster.

Silving, H. (1961). In Re Eichmann: A dilemma of law and morality. *The American Journal of International Law, 55*(2), 307–358. https://doi.org/10.2307/2196122

Sombart, W. (1916). *The quintessence of capitalism*. London: T. Fisher Unwin, Ltd..

Srivastava, R. P., & Kogan, A. (2010). Assurance on XBRL instance document: A conceptual framework of assertions. *International Journal of Accounting Information Systems, 11*(3), 261–273. https://doi.org/10.1016/j.accinf.2010.07.019

Taylor, F. W. (1911). *The principles of scientific management*. Eastford, CT: Martino Fine Books.

Thomas, M. (2012). *The French colonial mind, Volume 1: Mental maps of empire and colonial encounters* (Vol. I). Lincoln: University of Nebraska Press.

Thrane, S. (2007). The complexity of management accounting change: Bifurcation and oscillation in schizophrenic inter-organisational systems. *Management Accounting Research, 18*(2), 248–272. https://doi.org/10.1016/j.mar.2007.03.004

Tregidga, H., Milne, M., & Kearins, K. (2014). (Re)presenting 'sustainable organizations'. *Accounting, Organizations and Society, 39*(6), 477–494. https://doi.org/10.1016/j.aos.2013.10.006

Triplett, A., & Scheuman, J. (2000). Managing shared services with ABM. *Strategic Finance, 81*(8), 40–45.

Tyson, T. N., & Davie, S. S. K. (2009). The Livret system: The interface of accounting and indentured labor in British Guiana. *Accounting History, 14*(1–2), 145–165.

Tyson, T. N., Fleischman, R. K., & Oldroyd, D. (2004). Theoretical perspectives on accounting for labor on slave plantations of the USA and British West Indies. *Accounting, Auditing & Accountability Journal, 17*(5), 758–778.

Tzu, S.. (1078). *The art of war* (First Thus ed.). London: Filiquarian.

Upton, D., & Arrington, C. E. (2012). Implicit racial prejudice against African-Americans in balanced scorecard performance evaluations. *Critical Perspectives on Accounting, 23*(4–5), 281–297.

Vaivio, J. (1999). Examining "The quantified customer". *Accounting, Organizations and Society, 24*(8), 689–715.

Weber, M. (1922). *Economy and society*. Berkeley: The University of California Press.

Wickramasinghe, D., Hopper, T., & Rathnasiri, C. (2004). Japanese cost management meets Sri Lankan politics: Disappearance and reappearance of bureaucratic management controls in a privatised utility. *Accounting, Auditing & Accountability Journal, 17*(1), 85–120.

Williamson, O. E. (1985). *The economic institutions of capitalism*. New York: Free Press.

Williamson, O. E. (1999). Public and private bureaucracies: A transaction cost economics perspectives. *Journal of Law, Economics, & Organization, 15*(1), 306–342.

Wonning, P. (2018). *A history of time: A chronicle of calendars, clocks and time zones (history of things)*. London: Independently Published.

CHAPTER 2

Trust in Management Accounting: From Transparency to Confidence

It is commonly agreed in the literature that management accounting produces information deemed relevant for decision-making (Anthony, 1965, 1988; Anthony, Dearden, & Bedford, 1984). This implies that decision-makers should be in a capacity of relying on and trusting management accountants and management control systems. What makes this trust and reliance is left unaddressed in the management accounting literature, as though these were assumed and taken for granted. Interestingly, the management and organisation literature has abundantly informed this notion of trust, following a functionalist paradigm. Most authors dealing with trust have endeavoured to provide a working definition thereof, devising its features or components.

The notion of trust has been mostly exploited and developed by economists—and subsequently by "daughter sciences" such as sociology—according to which trust is the result of a calculated decision rationally or emotionally made by individuals or a group of individuals. For some reason, trust has been of lesser interest to humanities and philosophy in general. Economists and sociologists began working on the topic of trust in the late 1950s (Deutsch, 1962). Even though each researcher gravitates towards his or her own version of trust, a consensus has arisen regarding a common basic definition of this notion (Rousseau, Sitkin, Burt, & Camerer, 1998). Trust is generally understood as a threefold phenomenon. Firstly, trust rests upon "the willingness to be vulnerable" towards an individual, a group of individuals or an organisation. Second, the existence

V. Joannidès de Lautour, *Strategic Management Accounting, Volume III*, https://doi.org/10.1007/978-3-030-20157-9_2

of risk that one accepts to incur by engaging in a relationship with a third party is at the core of trust. Thirdly, trust lies in the interdependency between the two parties (Mayer, Davis, & Schoorman, 1995).

In addition to shedding light on the positive aspects of trust within managerial contexts, the literature is also prolific by proposing explanations on how trust can be built, retained and broken. Since trust is a topic that has attracted researchers' interest for about 60 years, what is important at this juncture is to highlight the contradictions, paradoxes and limits of the theories that have been proposed for explaining the concept of trust. When applicable, ways of overcoming these limits or solving these contradictions are discussed. Notwithstanding the possible merits of having a working definition of trust with clear analytical categories and taxonomies or measures, the literature has neglected the ontology of trust. Therefore, this chapter seeks to reveal a possible ontology of *trust* and its implications for management accounting by trying to answer the question of how trust in management control systems and accountants can be built. The ontology of trust is likely not to be found in the management literature, but in philosophical writings. Convinced that ontology can be traced through a form of genealogy of this word trust, such writings originate from the sixteenth century when the French word *confiance* was translated into *trust* and *confidence* into English.

It is commonly accepted in the literature that management accounting is tasked with the production and diffusion of figures telling the truth about an organisation (Bayou, Reinstein, & Williams, 2011; Jensen, 2003; Lambert & Pezet, 2011; McKernan & Kosmala, 2007). It is therefore important to understand how this management accounting truth is formed and acknowledged as such. Under this purview, as in most management accounting research publications dealing with truth and knowledge, this idea is informed with Michel Foucault's philosophy. In particular, his ideas about power, knowledge and normalisation are important in the context of this study to understand why there is a low compliance with accounting standards, as supported by the force of law and stock exchange requirements.

The truth spoken by management accounting can be accepted as true because those at whom it is directed consider it is trustworthy or reliable. These two notions have often—mistakenly—been associated with the idea that transparency would be central to the acceptance of truth. Albeit, appraising truth's trustworthiness is more complex than it looks, raising multiple challenges. Amidst these is a transparency that is not inseparable from truth and trust. Rather, trust (worthiness) can be best reasonably viewed as a novel form of religious faith applied to mundane concerns, and this is an extension of Pascal's (1657, 1670) works.

2.1 Appraising Trustworthiness as a Dual Challenge

When deciding that someone is trustworthy, those granting their benevolence consider three items (Mayer et al., 1995), each being a challenge in itself. The first object that must be judged is the ability of the other part to conduct the expected job properly. Initially, this component is the only one that was tested in the first research on trust (Cummings & Bromiley, 1996). Management accountants supposedly produce reliable information. This is what makes them trustworthy. It is however unclear how management can decide that management accountants are trustworthy. Appraising trustworthiness is a dual challenge whereby trust's intrinsic contradictions are to be solved. The first contradiction lies in that trust requires a prior knowledge of the other party, deemed impossible before the relation is initiated. The second contradiction is that trust requires the trustor's willingness, a mindset that can be modelled or predicted. It is impossible to explain how trust is granted at times and is not in other situations. Trust would just appear as an abstraction impossible to grasp.

2.1.1 Impossible Ante-knowledge-Based Trust

The question that must be answered is the following: "Is the other professional enough for the job?" The second object of trustworthiness that remains to be judged is the benevolence of the other part: maybe the other is able to complete the task that is delegated but does he really want to work with the trustor? Does he really want to help him? Finally, the last object to be judged is honesty, the assurance that the other does not expect to take part of the vulnerability and serving his own purposes. Even though the three objects that have to be measured by individuals for evaluating the trustworthiness of the others are identified, the question of the way they all can be judged remains opened. The literature on trust pretends to present three answers but we notice that these answers are contradictory.

2.1.1.1 The Impossibility of Trustworthiness

The first answer to the question on how to assess the trustworthiness of the other is given by economists who recall that access to knowledge on the other is key. Any problem that occurs within a trust-based governance system for managing alliances comes from a lack of knowledge of the other part prior to contracting (Carson, Madhok, Varman, & John, 2003). Consequently, there is distrust in a sense that trust is given to the wrong partner. Notwithstanding such claims, finding the key to open the door to such knowledge looks like the Holy Grail quest: How can such knowledge be acquired? Based on this knowledge, how can the judgement be made?

Mayer et al. (1995) state that such access remains difficult, since that ability is firstly learnt by reputation whilst benevolence and honesty can only be taught and learnt by experience and direct interactions between the two parts. In that sense, can we still talk about trust when trust is the result of a judgement based on past experience? Trust seems to be relevant prior to the experience, but not afterwards. At least, one can notify that there is either distrust or a good choice. Such a contradiction on the moment of the judgement is abundantly discussed in the literature (Becerra & Gupta, 2003; Gulati & Nickerson, 2008): trust can be learnt once the translation has occurred.

In fact, one does not really judge the propensity of the other part to be either capable, benevolent or honest but also his or her propensity to act consistently with the trustor's expectations.

The processes of knowledge acquisition on the potential trustee differ from the complexity of the context and, therefore, rely on more or less sophisticated systems (Zucker, 1986). This theory of trust building was resting upon a deep analysis of the process by which immigrants have been accepted within the US nation, from the late eighteenth century to the 1940s. During the first immigration wave, mechanisms for judging the trustworthiness of immigrants are quite simple: "intuitu personae", that is, "I know who you are, you know who I am. Therefore, I trust you." As long as the number of applicants increases, mechanisms evolve. In particular, over time, job applicants were to declare their ethnicity, which has caused the rejection of people having certain backgrounds. Pursuantly, the judging mechanism would be "I do trust you because you are son of X. I do not know who you are, but I know the community you belong to and I know that such a community has no problem with us… by transitivity, I trust you because I trust the community you belong to."

After the Great Depression, immigration policy changes required applicants not only to declare their ethnicity but also to prove they are educated and healthy. The trust-creation process was then based on a judgement regarding immigrants' ability to serve the American community. This formed the first institutionally calculated process for assessing a third-party's trustworthiness. Whatever their form, the judgement on trustworthiness seems to be linked to the propensity of the other to confirm through a behaviour perceived as consistent with the trustor's expectations. This judgement does not rest upon the other party's trustworthiness, which could be objectively assessed and therefore perceived as actual. To some extent, social controls operate as wardens or trustworthiness, assessing a party's capability of behaving like others.

2.1.1.2 *The Impossibility of Knowledge Prior to Trusting*

Trust's first intrinsic contradiction is that it requires a previous experience and knowledge of the other party involved in the transaction. As this is precisely a prerequisite for current trust, it may appear as impossible to occur. There may be ways of overcoming this apparent impossibility by relying on third-party experiences of the one claiming to be trustworthy. Such experiences can consist of reference checks, whereby there are records of this party's past behaviour and achievements, *namely* performance assessed through effective control systems. This is where visuals produced by management accounting figures can help (Busco & Quattrone, 2014, 2018). These are especially popular through rating systems, such as a number of stars, a mark or likes and dislikes as on TripAdvisor or any other online platform (Jeacle & Carter, 2011). Where this impossibility of trust cannot be overcome is when the demanding party can claim no history and is totally new to the transaction. In this situation, this organisation or person, too young to have been proved trustworthy, may not be considered. This is typically what characterises the job market, where applicants for a position must have proven records of past successful experiences in a similar role. This operates as an impediment to young graduates or people deciding to change career (Bhattarai, 2016; Donayre & Panovska, 2018; Ortego-Marti, 2017).

Management accounting contributes to the aggravation of this contradiction by producing figures relating to known situations and the past but incapable of anticipating future prospects. That is, management accounting only succeeds in assessing the trustworthiness of what is known and visible but fails to address what is unknown and invisible (Davison, 2010;

Fearfull, Carter, Sy, & Tinker, 2008; Komori, 2012). This means that management accounting succeeds in extrapolating the past but fails to envision the future. However, it is one of management accountants' roles to articulate forecast for the future, irrespective of what occurred in the past (Chotiyanon & Joannidès de Lautour, 2018; Joannidès de Lautour, 2018; Molridge & Player, 2010). Management accounting ontologically finds itself confronted with the impossibility of completing the task which is its *raison d'être*.

2.1.2 *Trust as Intentionality and Being in the Mood for It*

The second challenge raised by trust is that it is granted by a party to another. It is entrusted, which requires willingness to do so from the giving side (Dodgson, 1993). Mainly three factors allow knowledge access on the potential trustee: a shared interest for pursuing a common purpose, a cultural propensity to be open to external knowledge and accept external outputs, and an intensified culture through regular communication between trustor and potential trustee. This is generally referenced as organisational trust, that is, trust that can occur between people who do belong to different organisations. This observation of the organisational level is consistent with the results on the individual propensity to trust (Mayer et al., 1995), contingent upon individual characteristics.

2.1.2.1 Trust as the Offshoot of a Process

Trust is the offshoot of a process but that is strongly linked to a "natural" individual willingness. One would trust simply because one does want to trust the other. In that respect, knowledge of the other party would bear no consequences. Judgement on trustworthiness is positive, just because the individual wants it to be the case. Most often, this willingness to trust someone is associated with confidence in one's capability to hedge or minimise the risks associated with this trusting. One is willing to trust because one believes there is little risk that the trustee will adopt deviant behaviour and ultimately would not honour his or her commitment. This notion of risk-based willingness bears its own as yet unresolved contradiction: reducing risk simply means controlling and, therefore, reducing trust. I agree to trust someone because I can control how this person is behaving. This mindset appears incompatible with the notion of trust. In fact, by trusting the other, I should willingly relinquish any possibility of controlling his or her deeds. Any attempt at minimising the risk associated with trust does not imply a better knowledge of the other but the quest of signs of conformity to what the expectations are.

This challenge raised by trust perfectly applies to management accounting, as evidenced in the limits of Agency Theory (Booth & Schulz, 2004; Bricker & Chandar, 2000; Dirsmith, Heian, & Covaleski, 1997; Englund & Gerdin, 2011; Kilfoyle & Richardson, 2011). Management accounting and control are organisational institutions tasked with producing information that can be trusted for efficient and effective managerial decision-making. To this end, management accountants collect, colligate and process figures produced by other departments. Management accountants assess the trustworthiness of the information produced by other departments in charge of day-to-day operations. This raises the question of why management would trust management accountants more than other organisational actors.

2.1.2.2 The Idiosyncrasy of Trust and Trustworthiness

The grounds for trusting management accountants and the figures they produce are unclear or idiosyncratic: they are trusted because they are trustworthy. What makes their trustworthiness is precisely the fact that management trusts them. This circularity is the same as an egg-and-hen problem: what comes first and what follows. Breaking this circularity would lead to consider that the people in charge of controlling the trustworthiness of others' behaviour requires that the controllers should be controlled themselves. This then raises another series of questions left unanswered: who should control the controllers? How far should the chain of controls go and when should controls stop? It is easily understandable that this would lead to infinite controls if there were no willingness to trust at some point in time. With management accounting, the limits of the willingness to trust may well be manifested in the growing role played by internal audit and controls exerted on the whole organisation, including management control figures (Christopher, Savrens, & Leung, 2009; Harrell, Taylor, & Chewning, 1989; Norman, Rose, & Rose, 2010; Schneider, 2010; Vinnari & Skærbæak, 2014). Assuming management trusts these super-controllers, it does seem that stakeholders, namely stockholders, do not trust as much, since external auditing is required (Dillard & Bricker, 1992; Mennicken, 2010; Pentland, 1993; Richardson, 2009; Schneider, 2010). This major issue is raised by the imperatives of internal audit and control systems associated with IFRS 9, as though management control systems were not trusted. At least, stockholders seem to trust these mechanisms imposed by IFRS 9, perceived as wealth enhancers (Onaldi & Ginesti, 2014).

All this means is that willingness to trust controllers occurs at some juncture, whatever the control order is (first-order management accounting, second-order internal audit or third-order external audit). As this willingness can be identified at some stage, the question of its grounds remains unanswered: why would management decide to trust at this particular juncture? It does seem that management on one hand (in the case of management accountants or internal auditors) or stockholders on the other hand (in the case of external auditors) trust a profession rather than its members *intuitu personae*. This implies that the profession should have developed procedures to select only those people deemed capable of sustaining its respectability and trustworthiness (Caplan, Janvrin, & Kurtenbach, 2007; Caramanis, 2005; Retief & Villiers (de), 2013; Ryan, 2001). This may have a series of implications for management accounting.

Firstly, the profession is already known for having established clear trustworthiness criteria and applies them to the selection of applicants or new joiners. In this case, the willingness to trust management accountants rests upon certificates and degrees granted by the profession. In fact, management accountants are trusted because they are trusted by a profession that is itself trusted. This first implication actually operates as a way of overcoming the initial difficulty by returning to the first challenge (Boyce, 2004; Gray & Collison, 2002; James, 2009; McPhail, 1999).

Secondly, the profession has established its own rules and control bodies and appears capable of self-regulation. Lateral and social controls exerted by peers and the profession appear as guarantees of professionalism and professional trustworthiness. People deemed undeserving of this trust would be rejected from the profession and be forbidden to practise anymore. Such could be the case if the management accounting profession were very structured and regulated, as the medical or legal professions (Backhof & Martin, 1991; Kurunmäki, 2004; Livingstone & Balachandran, 1977; Pratt, Rockmann, & Kaufmann, 2006). Whilst the auditors and chartered accountants can be professionally regulated through norms, standards and procedures, the management accounting profession can hardly mimic these. This difficulty in organising and structuring the management accounting profession certainly lies in the diversity of management accountants' background and the large variety of roles they can have (Chotiyanon & Joannidès de Lautour, 2018; Hopper, 1980; Lambert &

Pezet, 2011; Puyou, 2018). Maybe one could consider that management accountants coming from the organisation's core profession and thereby having a dual professional identity can be trusted as management accountants, because they are trusted as professionals. This is what may explain the fact that the management accounting profession hardly gains legitimacy as such institutes, for example the Chartered Institute of Management Accountants, have an unsystematic recognition and credits across organisations (Allen, 1991; Caramanis, 2005; Carnegie & Napier, 2010; Cooper & Robson, 2006; Covaleski, Dirsmith, & Rittenberg, 2003; Gambling, 1985; Greenwood, Suddaby, & Hinings, 2002; Kurunmäki, 1999; Lee, 1995; Mataira & Van Peursem, 2010; Mueller & Carter, 2007; Norris & Niebuhr, 1984; Pratt et al., 2006; Ramirez, 2009; Rueschemeyer, 1986; Suddaby, Gendron, & Lam, 2009; Vough, Cardador, Bednar, Dane, & Pratt, 2013; Walker, 2003, 2004; Willmott, 1986).

2.2 Trust Without Transparency

As trust is associated with a certain degree of knowledge of the other, it would be tempting to consider that the relationship is enabled through transparency. Assuming this would deem that trust can be granted because I can read in the Other as in an open book. In itself, this transparency imperative is incompatible with trust, which appears precisely as a consequence of insufficient or impossible transparency. It is therefore important to understand how trust and transparency are related in the literature. This takes a twofold path. On one hand, the relationship between trust and transparency is circular and thereby contradictory. On the other hand, the impossibility of transparency would imply an impossibility of trust, albeit trust is happening.

2.2.1 The Circularity of Trust and Transparency in the Management Literature

The accounting literature has not addressed the issues associated with trust per se but has discussed transparency. Most often, transparency is associated with a means of accountability, even if critical accounting scholars consider this poses a number of ontological and epistemological problems (Messner, 2009; Roberts, 2009). In quite a similar vein, management research has often amalgamated trust and transparency, as though the latter were the condition of possibility for the former. In so doing, the relationship between trust and transparency has appeared as circular, if not tautological, appearing as an egg-and-hen problem, unless trust is understood as a process rather than a state or a set of criteria.

2.2.1.1 Trust as a Tautological Concept in Microeconomics

The management literature generally relies on two definitions of trust: *confidence or predictability in one's expectations [...] and confidence in the other's goodwill* (Ring & van de Ven, 1992, p. 488). Both are derived from neoclassical microeconomics, as they imply that trust does not exist *per se*. Rather, most authors tend to consider that distrust is the natural state of mind of relationships between people and organisations (Ring & van de Ven, 1992). Influenced by agency theory and transaction cost economics, key authors on trust in the management literature seem to consider that humans in essence are motivated by self-interest pursuit and utility maximisation. In nature too, they seem to consider that A's interest necessarily diverges from B's. Therefore, A and B disregard each other and need to establish some institutions aimed at making the other in the relationship prove that he or she is pursuing his or her counterpart's interest. Therefore, these authors contend that it is necessary that contracts bind these two parties, so that each can know what to expect from the other (Fried, 1982; MacAulay, 1963). Even if it is not sufficient, *trust is more likely to be extended to an organization when that organization earns a reputation in the market place for following norms of equity* (Ring & van de Ven, 1992, p. 489). Accordingly, trust is deemed to emerge as a consequence of repeated market transactions between the same parties affirming the observance of the same norms.

Although the authors in this stream of thought arrive at factors explaining determinants or features of trust, they leave essential questions unanswered and even prove some as yet unresolved contradictions. The very first unanswered question raised by this school of thought is whether distrust means absence of trust or the opposite of trust. In other words, the proponents of this paradigm do not clarify to us whether *trust* is built *ex nihilo* or whether it is the antithesis of prior (natural) situations. As these authors stress that trusting is risky, they implicitly reason that the *trust* of which they are speaking probably does not exist. Thence, by leaving the first question unanswered, they discard an entire stream of research seeking to define trust. This argument proves to be circular when these authors contended that trust emerges through the development of a reliable reputation, which they call *trustworthiness*. Following their own arguments, we could wonder why someone would engage in a relationship with someone else he or she does not trust as yet. For this reputation to be gained, there should be trust at some stage enabling its initial development. This would mean that trust is established and determined by itself regardless of agency issues. Anew, the initial assumption finds itself contradicted.

2.2.1.2 Trust as a Process and Not a State

A way of overcoming this unresolved contradiction seems to be found in the expressed need for defining trust by its components and as a process. To do so, other concepts seem to be needed. Henceforth, the reputation on which trust is built stems from transparent conduct, transparency being summarised as doing what one says and saying what one does. Beyond this trivial functional summary, transparency has been conceived of as readability and predictability by the other (Foucault, 1972, 1975). Because A makes his or her deeds accessible to B, he or she is trustworthy. Although many authors have tried to measure and determine transparency (van de Ven & Walker, 1984), this is still a new question unanswered: how can an emerging business or a new person be transparent when they have no past records? We are facing a huge egg-and-hen dilemma. What comes first of trust and transparency? Apparently, we trust they will be transparent. With this reasoning, microeconomics-based management research turns the full circle: one determinant of trust is past trust. As most of these works are qualitative research, this contradiction has not yet been highlighted. In quantitative research, such reasoning would be rejected because it is multicollinear.

2.2.2 The Impossibility of Transparency as a Condition of Possibility for Trust

To solve the contradiction of trust and transparency, the possibility of transparency needs to be questioned. Starting from *Giving an account of oneself* (Butler, 2005), this chapter reasons that transparency is impossible and subsequently that *trust* cannot be conditioned by transparent conduct. Opening oneself in full to the other and letting him or her know what our deeds are is not always desirable or possible, Butler (2005) explains for three reasons.

Firstly, the self is *opaque*: it is not always capable of reflecting on its deeds and their rationale. It is not always capable of relating its actions to a purpose: sometimes no intelligible reason can be given. It then becomes very difficult for it to open itself to others and put its actions and the reasons for these actions into words and numbers.

Secondly, forcing the giving of an account *exposes* the self to violence exerted by others whose demands for good transparency imply suspicion. Transparency appears as a constraint over people and organisations whereby the subject is constituted as answerable, that is, as one compulsorily able to give evidence of the reasonableness of his or her actions to a community of others. Being effectively transparent becomes equally difficult because these others are also *opaque*, meaning I cannot exactly know what they want of me. If my understanding of the Other's expectations is inconsistent, an account of myself cannot be intelligible to him or her, even though it may be a fair representation of the perception I have of myself. Conversely, I may fully understand what the Other wants of me and be compelled to distort my account to make it intelligible. In this case, the account I give is not a fair representation of how I perceive the events I am reporting.

The third limit follows: when the norms by which I must open myself to the Other are not issued by this Other, my relationship to him or her is *mediated*. In this situation, I do not know to whom I am eventually transparent and whether this transparency meets this Other's requirements. Building on the Derridean notion of *resistance* (Derrida, 1993, 1998, 2002a, 2002b, 2002c, 2003; Kamuf, 2002) and the Levinassian concept of the *face* (Lévinas, 1969, 1972, 1987), Butler (2005) reasons that this notion of transparency stresses the impossibility of any absolute obligation to the Other. At best, obligation can only be relative. Defending the absoluteness of any obligation to the Other takes for granted that the summary offered by conduct objectively mirrors reality. Due to the three limits to giving an account of oneself, the truth told cannot be absolute: it is selective and therefore contingent upon the teller's subjectivity. Its confrontation with the listener's subjectivity reveals accountability as a nexus of inter-subjective transparency appropriations of observed conduct and forges a form of trust: an implicit agreement on what is acceptable in a bounded relationship.

2.3 *Con fide* as the Ontology of Trust

In the quest for the ontology of trust, we know what trust is not. The limits of transparency result in trust being ontologically no offspring of transparent conduct. Accordingly, the essence of trust is to be found in other forms of relationships. Such a relationship can be identified if etymology and its deformation over time were considered. The Latin expression meaning *trust* is *con fides*, that is, with faith. Over centuries, the Latin expression has resulted in two words in English: *confidence* and in the eighteenth century *trust* when the first corporations started emerging (Freytag, 1855; Maltby, 1997; Sombart, 1911, 1916; Weber, 1921, 1922).

2.3.1 Trust as Historical Faith in the Other

Freytag (1855) and Sombart (1911, 1916) describe how the notion of *trust* in management accounting inscriptions has stepwise emerged when modern companies started needing financing. Funding was supplied by Jewish families managing financial institutions, whilst demand was on the Christian business leaders' side. Anti-Semitism at that time prevented the latter from having faith in the former. Yet, relationships were necessary. On both sides, argues Freytag (1855), individuals gave evidence of their respective faithfulness to reassure their counterpart. As it was impossible for a Christian to have faith in a Jew and vice versa, it was agreed upon that the confidence relationship would have a mediator: a financial *trust* gathering and allocating funds. *Trust* seemed to be a locus for lesser confidence as actors did not share the same faith in God (Sombart, 1911, 1916).

This historical digression seems necessary to us in the understanding of the religious origins of *trust* and *confidence*. The notion was first developed by Roman Catholic thinkers in the seventeenth century to explain the relationship to God whom we cannot know in person (Pascal, 1656a, 1656b, 1670; Saint-Augustin, 1637). When individuals have faith in the Lord, they do not seek obvious manifestations of His existence or deeds. He is opaque to them, while they are by nature transparent to Him. The assumption that the Lord is omniscient results in accounts of oneself being useless: accounting books are instruments *mediating* relationships between humans *exposed* to impossible reflexivity on themselves. Agency Theory or Transaction Costs Theory, and more broadly neoclassical microeconomics, cannot compete with God's hyper-essentiality (Derrida, 1994; Derrida & Anidjar, 2002).

Considering God entering into an agency relationship would lead to an impossible contradiction: humans entrust their lives to an omniscient God, never knowing what He might do with them. They would find themselves in the position of the principals whilst the Lord would be the agent. In such a principal-agent relationship, mankind would be expected to develop institutions aimed at controlling God's actions. This is impossible, if God's hyper-essentiality is taken for granted, and is even blasphemy, as *men blaspheme what they do not know* (Pascal, 1670, *Pensée* 555, p. 152). And even, it is *dangerous for man to know God without knowing his own wretchedness, and to know his own wretchedness without knowing the Redeemer who can free him from it* (*op. cit.* p. 153). Moreover, making God transparent to people means that the Lord loses His hyper-essentiality. Doing *with faith* would make no more sense (Derrida, 1992a, 1992b, 1992c). *Confidence* and subsequently *trust* would be impossible: *confidence* is the ontological impossibility of knowing, seeing or showing/disclosing.

This impossibility can be solved easily if one considers first that the very issue is more on the knowledge we have of God than on information. Whilst information has some objective claims, knowledge is more subjective and is the offspring of a direct relationship to the Other (Arendt, 1961, 1989). The self cannot know God and can just imagine and represent Him through various pictures, whereof the Other can be part, as, *when I speak to a Christian, the relation to God is presented as a relation to another person. It is not a metaphor: in the other, there is a real presence of God* (Lévinas, 1991, p. 94).

All these temporal representations conflate faith (beliefs), imagination (approximations), values and norms in substitutive conduct *vis-à-vis* God throughout the *confidence* relationship whereby I operate as a *substitution for another, one in the place of another, expiation* (Lévinas, 1974, p. 15). The believer knows neither God nor His expectations and can at best approximate them by faith, which is his privacy. Self and God opacity operate here in the *guise* of ontological limitations. In this context, the relationship is mediated through faith, with the self being confident that God will provide (Lévinas, 1974, 1975).

Trust is a lesser form of confidence, that is, operations *with faith*, the latter term as yet being undefined. Given the religious roots of the linguistic issues of the discussion, it is now critical returning to the origin of all these debates to understand this key notion. Butler, Derrida and Lévinas have all built their works on the notion of faith developed by Pascal (Cohen, 1972). Pascal was a major thinker of the seventeenth century. A member of the *Jansenist* order, Pascal intended to reform the Roman Catholic Church without engaging in a religious schism, bitterly opposing Calvin and Pelage (Pascal, 1656a). Pascal's (1656a, 1656b, 1656c, 1670) as well as Pascal & Montaigne's (1654) writings were aimed at defining the essence of belief in God, assuming that the Lord exists. Pascal starts considering that *we should fight firmly and invincibly with heretics of our time who pretend to know the real meaning of the Scriptures* (1656c, p. 104).[1]

2.3.2 Trust as a Dual Wager

Pascal (1656a, 1656b, 1656c) states that we cannot know God but have an idea of His capabilities and promise when we entrust to Him our lives: *God fills the soul and heart of those whom He possesses, a God who makes them conscious of their inward wretchedness, and His infinite mercy, who unites Himself to their inmost soul, who fills it with humility and joy, with confidence and love, who renders them incapable of any other end than Himself* (Pascal, Pensée 555, p. 154). It stems from this contention in Pascal's philosophy that *faith*—and confidence, accordingly—is the reflection of a dual wager.

2.3.2.1 First Wager: I Entrust My Life to God Without Guarantee of Salvation

The first wager lies in that we entrust our lives to God without having a guarantee that we will be saved. Salvation is such a great promise transcending us and to which you all aspire that believing in its existence is not an issue. If I believe in God and His plan, I have a chance to get it. I have nothing to lose but everything to win. Accordingly, wagering on God in the uncertainty that He eventually exists has no risk. I can have eternal life if He exists and I have no idea of what I can get if He does not exist. Thence, *shall all men in the world believe, but faith should a mélange of credit and fear accompanied by no certainty* (Pascal, 1656a, p. 123). Emotionally or rationally, we should be confident in His existence and *have in ourselves principles of the true [...] in which we do believe and which we call axioms or common notions* (Pascal, 1656c, p. 105). In his Pensée 194, Pascal further develops this thought:

> *What do we gain by hearing it said of a man that he has now thrown off the yoke, that he does not believe there is a God who watches our actions, that he considers himself the sole master of his conduct, and that he thinks he is accountable for it only to himself? Does he think that he has thus brought us to have henceforth complete confidence in him, and to look to him for consolation,*

[1] *Combat avec une fermeté invincible les heretiques de son temps sur ce qu'ils s'assuraient de connaître seuls le veritable sens de l'Écriture.*

advice, and help in every need of life? Do they profess to have delighted us by telling us that they hold our soul to be only a little wind and smoke, especially by telling us this in a haughty and self-satisfied tone of voice? Is this a thing to say gaily? Is it not, on the contrary, a thing to say sadly, as the saddest thing in the world?

If they thought of it seriously, they would see that this is so bad a mistake, so contrary to good sense, so opposed to decency and so removed in every respect from that good breeding which they seek, that they would be more likely to correct than to pervert those who had an inclination to follow them. And indeed, make them give an account of their opinions, and of the reasons which they have for doubting religion, and they will say to you things so feeble and so petty, that they will persuade you of the contrary. The following is what a person one day said to such a one very appositely: "If you continue to talk in this manner, you will really make me religious." And he was right, for who would not have a horror of holding opinions in which he would have such contemptible persons as companions!

Thus those who only feign these opinions would be very unhappy, if they restrained their natural feelings in order to make themselves the most conceited of men. If, at the bottom of their heart, they are troubled at not having more light, let [Pg 58] them not disguise the fact; this avowal will not be shameful. The only shame is to have none. Nothing reveals more an extreme weakness of mind than not to know the misery of a godless man. Nothing is more indicative of a bad disposition of heart than not to desire the truth of eternal promises. Nothing is more dastardly than to act with bravado before God. Let them then leave these impieties to those who are sufficiently ill-bred to be really capable of them. Let them at least be honest men, if they cannot be Christians. Finally, let them recognise that there are two kinds of people one can call reasonable; those who serve God with all their heart because they know Him, and those who seek Him with all their heart because they do not know Him.

But as for those who live without knowing Him and without seeking Him, they judge themselves so little worthy of their own care, that they are not worthy of the care of others; and it needs all the charity of the religion which they despise, not to despise them even to the point of leaving them to their folly. But because this religion obliges us always to regard them, so long as they are in this life, as capable of the grace which can enlighten them, and to believe that they may, in a little time, be more replenished with faith than we are, and that, on the other hand, we may fall into the blindness wherein they are, we must do for them what we would they should do for us if we were in their place, and call upon them to have pity upon themselves, and to take at least some steps in the endeavour to find light. Let them give to reading this some of the hours which they otherwise employ so uselessly; whatever aversion they may bring to the task, they will perhaps gain something, and at least will not lose much. But as for those who bring

to the task perfect sincerity and a real desire to meet with truth, those I hope will be satisfied and convinced of the proofs of a religion so divine, which I have here collected, and in which I have followed somewhat after this order.
Pensées (n. 194, pp. 55–57)

2.3.2.2 Second Wager: Divine Grace Is Selective, Will I Be Chosen?

The second wager is on the eventuation of the promise God took before us. The promise of eternal salvation does not eventuate in all circumstances and is driven by divine grace only (Pascal, 1656b, 1657, 1670). Before Adam attempted to equal God by acquiring knowledge, the Lord wanted to grant grace to mankind unconditionally. After the Fall, *God, by punishing for current or Original sin, denies by His justice any graces without which thou cannot do the things to which thou art compelled, such as loving God and believing in the articles of faith* (Pascal, 1656a, pp. 132–133). It transpires from this that not everyone is granted divine grace and ultimately saved. Rather, men are predestined to salvation and are chosen for reasons unknown to men and angels and for the mere sake of mercy (Pascal, 1656a, pp. 136–137). It stems from this that nobody knows in advance if they are chosen or not. If chosen, holy conduct is expected from them as a condition for salvation. Through their good conduct, they must prove before God that they deserved to be chosen and saved. But, as reasons for being chosen are unknown, men cannot know if they are eventually until they decease. *Confidence* is what leads them to behave as though they were chosen so as to deserve predestination. Because they have chosen to believe in God (first wager), they choose to conduct themselves as they understand He expects them to do. And this in the view of being saved if they were chosen or making God change His plan if they proved to have led a particularly holy life.

In sum, *it is thence obvious that God's will and that of men concur to salvation and damnation for those who are either saved or damned* (Pascal, 1656a, p. 117). The second wager on which confidence is based consists of the ignorance of whether I am or not predestined to salvation. Again, if I am, I lose nothing by conducting myself in a holy manner. If I am not, I might encounter God's mercy on Judgement Day. Be I chosen or not, by faith I believe that holy life can only have an outcome good to me. Trust is a matter of faith more than evidence and subsequent transparency. Having faith means that the two parties involved in the relationship believe in what the other party will do; the relationship then implies belief in the other's ability to conduct as per expectations or an explicit agreement

(Latour, 2002, 2010). Obviously, having faith in the Other is no guarantee. In some cases (*e.g.* religion, family), faith needs no proof, while in others (*e.g.* organisational contexts) at least some evidence is expected (Kamuf, 2007).

Given the historical and etymological roots of *trust* as a concept, two types of contemporary issues for trust arise. *Confidence*, as faith in the other and belief in his or her capability of keeping a promise taken, is an absolute relationship to the Other. In contexts in which organisational actors are reluctant to make any decision without knowing its outcome or at least effect, the relationship to the Other can be relative and imply agreements and evidence giving. In other words, what the management literature calls *trust* is a lesser commitment to the Other than the ontology of the concept as found in *confidence.*

2.4 Conclusion

This chapter drew on the ontology of *trust.* Microeconomics-based approaches to the notion reveal what *trust* is not transparency. This argument is informed with Butler's (2005) on the impossibility of giving an account of oneself. Drawing a genealogy of Butler's work in parallel of the notion of *trust*, this chapter shows that *trust* is historically and etymologically a religious notion. *Confidence* and *entrusting* both have religious roots as discussed with Pascal's writings on the question who was the earliest modern addressing this issue of confidence. The discussion offered in this chapter shows that the ontology of *trust* is not to be found in transparency but in faith and belief in the Other. The contribution of this chapter lies in that its conclusion totally rejects those drawn by prior management literature attempting to define *trust*, its features and its determinants.

Given its religious roots, *trust* rests, not on distrust, as neoclassical microeconomics-based management literature contend, but on the belief that something might happen. Contrary to that literature purporting that trust is granted to someone with already a good reputation, we reason that in a contemporary trust relationship, no prior good reason is expected to believe in the counterpart's capabilities. Belief lies in my subjective appreciation of whether the Other is likely to keep the promise he or she takes before me. I am wagering on this Other and believe there might be an outcome. Whilst prior management literature on *trust* calls this risk, we must call it *uncertainty* or *ignorance*, because there is no known probability of eventuation. In sum, trusting someone consists of believing in the capabilities of a person unbeknown to me.

In this *trust* relationship in which I engage, I can essentially not expect the Other to be transparent. Rather, I am the person opening oneself to him or her. If trust were to require transparency, this would come from the person who gives and not the one who receives, because trust is granted by the one who is in the position of being confident but cannot be claimed by the person who wants to be trusted. I cannot declare myself trustworthy. I must be acknowledged as such by those who will hopefully trust me.

These two ontological dimensions of *trust* seem to collide with what the management literature has found to date. The straightest reason for this is known: economics is not the ontology of this phenomenon. Beyond this easy critique, it is likely that economic reasons now dominate because we have lost faith. Nowadays we are living in the *knowledge society* in which Capitalism is based on the knowledge we can acquire and trade (Boltanski & Chiapello, 1999, 2006). Claims for knowledge seem to result in us being incapable of tolerating ignorance and consequently belief, as belief is a substitute to knowledge. We nowadays tend to believe in our capability of and right for knowing. This right of knowing is aggravated by the decline of religious thought characterising our postmodern societies. Unsurprisingly, in a trust relationship we expect good reasons for believing coming from the Other, as though we were scared of gratuitously believing (Derrida & Wieviorka, 2001; Latour, 2002, 2010).

Bibliography

Allen, K. (1991). In pursuit of professional dominance: Australian accounting 1953–1985. *Accounting, Auditing & Accountability Journal, 4*(1), 51–67.

Anthony, R. N. (1965). *Planning and control systems: A framework for analysis.* Boston, MA: Harvard Business School Publishing.

Anthony, R. N. (1988). *The management control function.* Boston, MA: Harvard Business School Publishing.

Anthony, R. N., Dearden, J., & Bedford, N. M. (1984). *Management control systems.* Homewood, IL: Irwin.

Arendt, H. (1961). *The human condition.* Chicago: The University of Chicago Press.

Arendt, H. (1989). *La crise de la culture.* Paris: Folio.

Backhof, J. F., & Martin, C. L. J. (1991). Historical perspectives: Development of the codes of ethics in legal, medical and accounting professions. *Journal of Business Ethics, 10*, 99–110.

Bayou, M. E., Reinstein, A., & Williams, P. F. (2011). To tell the truth: A discussion of issues concerning truth and ethics in accounting. *Accounting, Organizations and Society, 36*(2), 109–124.

Becerra, M., & Gupta, A. K. (2003). Perceived trustworthiness within the organization: The moderating impact of communication frequency on trustor and trustee effects. *Organization Science, 14*(1), 32–44.

Bhattarai, K. (2016). Unemployment–inflation trade-offs in OECD countries. *Economic Modelling, 58*, 93–103.

Boltanski, L., & Chiapello, E. (1999). *Le nouvel esprit du Capitalisme*. Paris: La Découverte.

Boltanski, L., & Chiapello, E. (2006). *The new spirit of capitalism*. London: Verso.

Booth, P., & Schulz, A. K. D. (2004). The impact of an ethical environment on managers' project evaluation judgments under agency problem conditions. *Accounting, Organizations and Society, 29*(5–6), 473–488.

Boyce, G. (2004). Critical accounting education: Teaching and learning outside the circle. *Critical Perspectives on Accounting, 15*(4–5), 565–586.

Bricker, R., & Chandar, N. (2000). Where Berle and Means went wrong: A reassessment of capital market agency and financial reporting. *Accounting, Organizations and Society, 25*(6), 529–554.

Busco, C., & Quattrone, P. (2014). Exploring how the Balanced Scorecard engages and unfolds: Articulating the visual power of accounting inscriptions. *Contemporary Accounting Research, 32*(3), 1236–1262.

Busco, C., & Quattrone, P. (2018). Performing business and social innovation through accounting inscriptions: An introduction. *Accounting, Organizations and Society*. https://doi.org/10.1016/j.aos.2018.03.002

Butler, J. (2005). *Giving an account of oneself*. Fordham: Fordham University Press.

Caplan, D., Janvrin, D., & Kurtenbach, J. (2007). Internal audit outsourcing: An analysis of self-regulation by the accounting profession. *Research in Accounting Regulation, 19*(0), 3–34. https://doi.org/10.1016/s1052-0457(06)19001-3

Caramanis, C. (2005). Rationalisation, charisma and accounting professionalisation: Perspectives on the intra-professional conflict in Greece, 1993–2001. *Accounting, Organizations & Society, 30*(3), 195–221.

Carnegie, G. D., & Napier, C. J. (2010). Traditional accountants and business professionals: Portraying the accounting profession after Enron. *Accounting, Organizations and Society, 35*(3), 360–376.

Carson, S. J., Madhok, A., Varman, R., & John, G. (2003). Information processing moderators of the effectiveness of trust-based governance in interfirm R&D collaboration. *Organization Science, 14*(1), 45–56.

Chotiyanon, P., & Joannidès de Lautour, V. (2018). *The changing role of the management accountants—Becoming a business partner*. London: Palgrave Macmillan.

Christopher, J., Savrens, G., & Leung, P. (2009). A critical analysis of the independence of the internal audit function: Evidence from Australia. *Accounting, Auditing & Accountability Journal, 22*(2), 200–220.

Cohen, R. A. (1972). Introduction. In E. Lévinas (Ed.), *Humanism of the other* (pp. vii–xliv). Chicago: University of Illinois Press.

Cooper, D. J., & Robson, K. (2006). Accounting, professions and regulation: Locating the sites of professionalization. *Accounting, Organizations and Society, 31*(4–5), 415–444. https://doi.org/10.1016/j.aos.2006.03.003

Covaleski, M. A., Dirsmith, M. W., & Rittenberg, L. (2003). Jurisdictional disputes over professional work: The institutionalization of the global knowledge expert. *Accounting, Organizations and Society, 28*(4), 323–355. https://doi.org/10.1016/s0361-3682(02)00029-6

Cummings, L. L., & Bromiley, P. (1996). The Organizational Trust Inventory (OTI): Development and validation. In R. Kramer & T. Tykler (Eds.), *Trust in organizations: Frontiers of theory and research* (pp. 302–330). New York: Sage Publishing.

Davison, J. (2010). [In]visible [in]tangibles: Visual portraits of the business Élite. *Accounting, Organizations and Society, 35*(2), 165–183.

Derrida, J. (1992a). How to avoid speaking: Denials. In H. Coward & T. Foshay (Eds.), *Derrida and negative theology* (pp. 73–142). Albany: State University of New York Press.

Derrida, J. (1992b). Of an apocalyptic tone newly adopted in philosophy. In H. Coward & T. Foshay (Eds.), *Derrida and negative theology* (pp. 25–72). Albany: State University of New York Press.

Derrida, J. (1992c). Post-scriptum: Aporias, ways and voices. In H. Coward & T. Foshay (Eds.), *Derrida and negative theology* (pp. 283–323). New York: State University of New York Press.

Derrida, J. (1993). *Aporias: Dying—Awaiting (one another at) the "limits of truth" (mourir—s'attendre aux "limites de la vérité")*. Stanford, CA: Stanford University Press.

Derrida, J. (1994). *Specters of Marx: The state of the debt, the work of mourning, and the New International.* New York: Routledge.

Derrida, J. (1998). Resistance. In J. Derrida (Ed.), *Resistances of psychoanlysis* (pp. 1–38). Stanford, CA: Stanford University Press.

Derrida, J. (2002a). History of the Lie. In P. Kamuf (Ed.), *Without alibi* (pp. 28–70). Stanford, CA: Stanford University Press.

Derrida, J. (2002b). "Le parjure", *Perhaps*: storytelling and lying. In P. Kamuf (Ed.), *Without alibi* (pp. 161–201). Stanford, CA: Stanford University Press.

Derrida, J. (2002c). Typewriter Ribbon: Limited Ink (2). In P. Kamuf (Ed.), *Without alibi* (pp. 71–160). Stanford, CA: Stanford University Press.

Derrida, J. (2003). Letter to a Japanese friend. In J. Derrida (Ed.), *Psyche—Invention of the other* (Vol. II, pp. 1–6). Stanford, CA: Stanford University Press.

Derrida, J., & Anidjar, G. (2002). *Acts of religion.* New York: Routledge.

Derrida, J., & Wieviorka, M. (2001). *Foi et savoir.* Paris: Seuil.

Deutsch, M. (1962). Cooperation and trust: Some theoretical notes. In M. R. Jones (Ed.), *Nebraska symposium on motivation* (pp. 275–319). Lincoln: Nebraska University Press.

Dillard, J. F., & Bricker, R. (1992). A critique of knowledge-based systems in auditing: The systemic encroachment of technical consciousness. *Critical Perspectives on Accounting, 3*(3), 205–224.

Dirsmith, M. W., Heian, J. B., & Covaleski, M. A. (1997). Structure and agency in an institutionalized setting: The application and social transformation of control in the Big Six. *Accounting, Organizations and Society, 22*(1), 1–27.

Dodgson, M. (1993). Learning, trust, and technological collaboration. *Human Relations, 46*(1), 77–95.

Donayre, L., & Panovska, I. (2018). U.S. wage growth and nonlinearities: The roles of inflation and unemployment. *Economic Modelling, 68*, 273–292.

Englund, H., & Gerdin, J. (2011). Agency and structure in management accounting research: Reflections and extensions of Kilfoyle and Richardson. *Critical Perspectives on Accounting, 22*(6), 581–592. https://doi.org/10.1016/j.cpa.2011.03.002

Fearfull, A., Carter, C., Sy, A., & Tinker, A. M. (2008). Invisible influence, tangible trap: The clerical conundrum. *Critical Perspectives on Accounting, 19*(8), 1177–1196.

Foucault, M. (1972). *Histoire de la folie à l'âge classique*. Paris: Gallimard.

Foucault, M. (1975). *Surveiller et punir*. Paris: Gallimard.

Freytag, G. (1855). *Soll und Haben*. Berlin: Weichert.

Fried, C. (1982). *Contract as promise*. Cambridge, MA: Harvard University Press.

Gambling, T. (1985). The accountant's guide to the galaxy, including the profession at the end of the universe. *Accounting, Organizations & Society, 10*(4), 415–425.

Gray, R., & Collison, D. (2002). Can't see the wood for the trees, can't see the trees for the numbers? Accounting education, sustainability and the public interest. *Critical Perspectives on Accounting, 13*(5–6), 797–836.

Greenwood, R., Suddaby, R., & Hinings, C. (2002). Theorizing change: The role or professional associations in the transformation of institutionalized fields. *Academy of Management Journal, 45*(1), 58–80.

Gulati, R., & Nickerson, J. (2008). Interorganizational trust, governance choice, and exchange performance. *Organization Science, 19*(5), 688–708.

Harrell, A., Taylor, M., & Chewning, E. (1989). An examination of management's ability to bias the professional objectivity of internal auditors. *Accounting, Organizations and Society, 14*(3), 259–269. https://doi.org/10.1016/0361-3682(89)90027-5

Hopper, T. M. (1980). Role conflicts of management accountants and their position within organisation structures. *Accounting, Organizations and Society, 5*(4), 401–411. https://doi.org/10.1016/0361-3682(80)90039-2

James, K. (2009). "This is England": Punk rock's realist/idealist dialectic and its implications for critical accounting education. *Accounting Forum, 33*(2), 127–145.

Jeacle, I., & Carter, C. (2011). In TripAdvisor we trust: Rankings, calculative regimes and abstract systems. *Accounting, Organizations and Society, 36*(4–5), 293–309. https://doi.org/10.1016/j.aos.2011.04.002

Jensen, M. (2003). Paying people to lie: The truth about the budgeting process. *European Financial Management, 9*(3), 379–406.

Joannidès de Lautour, V. (2018). *Strategic management accounting—Volume I: Aligning strategy, operations and finance*. London: Palgrave Macmillan.

Kamuf, P. (2002). Introduction: Event of resistance. In P. Kamuf (Ed.), *Without alibi* (pp. 1–27). Stanford, CA: Stanford University Press.

Kamuf, P. (2007). Accounterability. *Textual Practice, 21*(2), 251–266.

Kilfoyle, E., & Richardson, A. J. (2011). Agency and structure in budgeting: Thesis, antithesis and synthesis. *Critical Perspectives on Accounting, 22*(2), 183–199. https://doi.org/10.1016/j.cpa.2010.06.013

Komori, N. (2012). Visualizing the negative space: Making feminine accounting practices visible by reference to Japanese women's household accounting practices. *Critical Perspectives on Accounting, 23*(6), 451–467. https://doi.org/10.1016/j.cpa.2012.04.006

Kurunmäki, L. (1999). Professional vs financial capital in the field of health care—Struggles for the redistribution of power and control. *Accounting, Organizations and Society, 24*(2), 95–124.

Kurunmäki, L. (2004). A hybrid profession—The acquisition of management accounting expertise by medical professionals. *Accounting, Organizations & Society, 29*, 327–347.

Lambert, C., & Pezet, E. (2011). The making of the management accountant, Becoming the producer of truthful knowledge. *Accounting, Organizations and Society, 36*(1), 10–30. https://doi.org/10.1016/j.aos.2010.07.005

Latour, B. (2002). *Jubiler ou les tourments de la parole religieuse*. Paris: Seuil.

Latour, B. (2010). *On the modern cult of factish Gods*. Durham: Duke University Press.

Lee, T. A. (1995). The professionalization of accountancy: A history of protecting the public interest in a self-interested way. *Accounting, Auditing & Accountability Journal, 8*, 48–59.

Lévinas, E. (1969). *Totality and infinity*. Pittsburgh: Duquesne University Press.

Lévinas, E. (1972). *Humanism of the other* (N. Poller, Trans.). Chicago: University of Illinois Press.

Lévinas, E. (1974). *Otherwise than being or beyond essence* (A. Lingis, Trans.). Pittsburgh: Duquesne University Press.

Lévinas, E. (1975). *God, death and time* (B. Bergo, Trans.). Stanford, CA: Stanford University Press.

Lévinas, E. (1987). *Time and the other* (R. A. Cohen, Trans.). Pittsburg: Duquesne University Press.

Lévinas, E. (1991). *Entre nous: Thinking-of-the-other*. New York: Continuum.

Livingstone, J. L., & Balachandran, K. R. (1977). Cost and effectiveness of physician peer review in reducing medicare overutilization. *Accounting, Organizations and Society, 2*(2), 153–164.

MacAulay, S. (1963). Non-contractual relationships in business. *American Sociological Review, 28*, 55–70.

Maltby, J. (1997). Accounting and the soul of the middle-class: Gustav Freytag's *Soll und Haben*. *Accounting, Organizations & Society, 22*(1), 69–87.

Mataira, K., & Van Peursem, K. A. (2010). An examination of disciplinary culture: Two professional accounting associations in New Zealand. *Accounting Forum, 34*(2), 109–122. https://doi.org/10.1016/j.accfor.2010.02.001

Mayer, R. C., Davis, J. H., & Schoorman, F. D. (1995). An integrative model of organizational trust. *Academy of Management Review, 20*, 709–734.

McKernan, J. F., & Kosmala, K. (2007). Doing the truth: Religion—Deconstruction—Justice, and accounting. *Accounting, Auditing & Accountability Journal, 20*(5), 729–764.

McPhail, K. (1999). The threat of ethical accountants: An application of Foucault's concept of ethics to accounting education and some thoughts on ethically educating for the other. *Critical Perspectives on Accounting, 10*(6), 833–866.

Mennicken, A. (2010). From inspection to auditing: Audit and markets as linked ecologies. *Accounting, Organizations and Society, 35*(3), 334–359.

Messner, M. (2009). The limits of accountability. *Accounting, Organizations and Society, 34*(8), 918–938.

Molridge, S., & Player, S. (2010). *Future ready—How to master business forecasting*. London: Wiley.

Mueller, F., & Carter, C. (2007). 'We are all managers now': Managerialism and professional engineering in UK electricity utilities. *Accounting, Organizations and Society, 32*(1–2), 181–195.

Norman, C. S., Rose, A. M., & Rose, J. M. (2010). Internal audit reporting lines, fraud risk decomposition, and assessments of fraud risk. *Accounting, Organizations and Society, 35*(5), 546–557. https://doi.org/10.1016/j.aos.2009.12.003

Norris, D. R., & Niebuhr, R. E. (1984). Professionalism, organizational commitment and job satisfaction in an accounting organization. *Accounting, Organizations and Society, 9*(1), 49–59.

Onaldi, E., & Ginesti, G. (2014). Pre-adoption market reaction to IFRS 9: A cross-country event-study. *Journal of Accounting and Public Policy, 33*(6), 628–637.

Ortego-Marti, V. (2017). Loss of skill during unemployment and TFP differences across countries. *European Economic Review, 100*, 215–235.

Pascal, B. (1656a). Ecrits sur la grâce. In B. Pascal (Ed.), *De l'esprit géométrique* (pp. 120–140). Paris: Garnier-Flammarion.

Pascal, B. (1656b). Entretien de M. Pascal et de M. de Sacy sur la lecture d'Épictète et de Montaigne. In B. Pascal (Ed.), *De l'esprit géométrique* (pp. 97–114). Paris: Garnier-Flammarion.

Pascal, B. (1657). *Provincial letters*. London: Mobi Classics.

Pascal, B. (1670). *Pensées*. Paris: Garnier-Flammarion.

Pascal, B., & Montaigne (de), M. (1654). *De l'art de persuader*. Paris: Garnier-Flammarion.

Pentland, B. T. (1993). Getting comfortable with the numbers: Auditing and the micro-production of macro-order. *Accounting, Organizations and Society, 18*(7–8), 605–620. https://doi.org/10.1016/0361-3682(93)90045-8

Pratt, M. G., Rockmann, K. W., & Kaufmann, J. B. (2006). Constructing professional identity: The role of work and identity learning cycles in the customization of identity among medical residents. *Academy of Management Journal, 49*(2), 235–262. https://doi.org/10.5465/amj.2006.20786060

Puyou, F.-R. (2018). Systems of secrecy: Confidences and gossip in management accountants' handling of dual role expectations and MCS limitations. *Management Accounting Research, 40*(Sep.), 15–26.

Ramirez, C. (2009). Constructing the small local practitioner: The changing nature of professional bodies and the management of professional accountants' identities in the UK. *Accounting, Organizations & Society, 24*, 381–408.

Retief, V. E., & Villiers (de), C. (2013). The accounting profession's influence on academe: South African evidence. *Accounting, Auditing & Accountability Journal, 26*(8), 1246–1278.

Richardson, A. J. (2009). Regulatory networks for accounting and auditing standards: A social network analysis of Canadian and international standard-setting. *Accounting, Organizations & Society, 34*, 571–588.

Ring, P. S., & van de Ven, A. H. (1992). Structuring cooperative relationships between organizations. *Strategic Management Journal, 13*(7), 483–498.

Roberts, J. (2009). No one is perfect: The limits of transparency and an ethic for 'intelligent' accountability. *Accounting, Organizations and Society, 34*(8), 957–970.

Rousseau, D. M., Sitkin, S. B., Burt, R. S., & Camerer, C. (1998). Not so different after all: A cross-discipline view of trust. *Academy of Management Review, 23*, 393–404.

Rueschemeyer, D. (1986). Comparing legal professions cross-nationally: From a professions-centered to a state-centered approach. *American Bar Foundation Research Journal, 11*(3), 415–446. https://doi.org/10.2307/828140

Ryan, J. (2001). Moral reasoning as a determinant of organizational citizenship behaviors: A study in the public accounting profession. *Journal of Business Ethics, 33*, 233–244.

Saint-Augustin. (1637). *Les confessions.* Paris: Garnier-Flammarion.
Schneider, A. (2010). Analysis of professional standards and research findings to develop decision aids for reliance on internal auditing. *Research in Accounting Regulation, 22*(2), 96–106. https://doi.org/10.1016/j.racreg.2010.07.004
Sombart, W. (1911). *The Jews and modern capitalism* (2001 ed.). Kitchener, ON: Batoche Books Limited.
Sombart, W. (1916). *The quintessence of capitalism.* London: T. Fisher Unwin, Ltd..
Suddaby, R., Gendron, Y., & Lam, H. (2009). The organizational context of professionalism in accounting. *Accounting, Organizations and Society, 34*(3–4), 409–427.
van de Ven, A. H., & Walker, G. (1984). The dynamics of interorganizational coordination. *Administrative Science Quarterly, 29*, 598–621.
Vinnari, E., & Skærbæak, P. (2014). The uncertainties of risk management: A field study on risk management internal audit practices in a Finnish municipality. *Accounting, Auditing & Accountability Journal, 27*(3), 489–526.
Vough, H. C., Cardador, M. T., Bednar, J. S., Dane, E., & Pratt, M. G. (2013). What clients don't get about my profession: A model of perceived role-based image discrepancies. *Academy of Management Journal, 56*(4), 1050–1080. https://doi.org/10.5465/amj.2011.0490
Walker, S. P. (2003). Professionalisation or incarceration? Household engineering, accounting and the domestic ideal. *Accounting, Organizations and Society, 28*(7–8), 743–772.
Walker, S. P. (2004). The genesis of professional organisation in English accountancy. *Accounting, Organizations and Society, 29*(2), 127–156.
Weber, M. (1921). *The Protestant ethic and the spirit of capitalism.* New York: Routledge.
Weber, M. (1922). *Economy and society.* Berkeley: The University of California Press.
Willmott, H. (1986). Organising the profession: A theoretical and historical examination of the development of the major accountancy bodies in the U.K. *Accounting, Organizations and Society, 11*(6), 555–580.
Zucker, L. G. (1986). Production of trust: Institutional sources of economic structure. *Research in Organizational Behavior, 8*, 53–111.

CHAPTER 3

Corporate Social Responsibility and Accounting for Externalities

Since the early 2000s, corporate social responsibility (CSR) has been a growing concern in society and business. In the twenty-first century, issues associated with global warming and breaches of human rights in a number of countries have made social and environment matters appear as central to business accountability. This is how the notion of the triple bottom line has emerged and become increasingly central to management accounting and accountability. Organisations' accountability evolved as to make its whole philosophy change. Until 2002, it was strongly believed that organisations would be accountable to capital only and for value creation (M. Jensen, 2001). It was believed that private companies' *raison d'être* was profit maximisation for stockholders, owing to their residual claims. This was neglecting other stakeholders and other purposes associated with the conduct of business.

After the 1973 oil crisis, business economics has been strongly influenced by neoclassical microeconomic theory. Economic theory has been resting upon profit maximisation as unique objective companies should pursue (R. E. Jensen, 1990). As social and environmental matters have arisen, the economic paradigm at play has slightly changed: welfare economics (Pigou, 1946) has eventually started to be echoed in business. The idea that economics is aimed at utilising resources in a way maximising the largest population's wellbeing started to spread after World War II but has gained practical interest with the advent of corporate social responsibility concerns. Once stakeholders other than mere capital providers have been

V. Joannidès de Lautour, *Strategic Management Accounting, Volume III*, https://doi.org/10.1007/978-3-030-20157-9_3

taken into consideration, economic concerns have embraced more than just financial value creation (Bebbington & Gray, 2001; Cho, 2009; Cho, Guidry, Hageman, & Patten, 2012; Cho & Patten, 2007, 2013; Cho, Roberts, & Patten, 2010; Gray, 1992, 2002a, 2002b, 2006, 2010, 2013a; Gray & Collison, 2002; Gray, Dey, Owen, Evans, & Zadek, 1997; Gray, Kouhy, & lavers, 1995; Gray & Laughlin, 2012; Gray, Owen, & Maunders, 1988). CSR matters, associated with social and environmental management accounting, relate to a form of accounting for externalities requiring that these externalities be identified and measured as convincingly as possible.

Social and environmental management accounting has developed since the 1990s alongside concerns regarding the ozone hole (Zehr, 1994). In the 1990s, this was the environmental problem confronting society *par excellence*; for the first time, society became conscious of the impact human activities would have on the planet and people's health. In particular, the ozone hole has been presented as responsible for the fast development of skin cancer in the Southern hemisphere (Abarca & Casiccia, 2002; Henriksen, Dahlback, Larsen, & Moan, 1990). This problem was announcing the beginning of global warming and associated concerns (Ungar, 1998, 2000). Accordingly, it seems important to first discuss the measuring of and accounting for environmental externalities.

This chapter is organised around three areas of discussion. The philosophy of welfare economics is discussed, since corporate social responsibility rests upon the awareness an organisation has of the good and evil it does to the rest of the world, outside of competition. This philosophy is subsumed into two themes organised around the two sections: accounting for environmental externalities on the one hand and accounting for social externalities on the other. Then, assuming this awareness has arisen, the third section addresses issues in reporting and disclosing environmental and social matters, thereby presenting major initiatives and the politics associated therewith: the impossibility of issuing and enforcing standards.

3.1 Accounting for Environmental Externalities

Issues in green accounting first arose in the United States in 1992, as come West-Coast companies would report the good they were doing for the environment, such as planting trees or saving water and electricity (Gray & Laughlin, 2012). Since then, individual initiatives have further developed until social and environmental reporting has become mandatory in a series of countries, such as France (Déjean & Martinez, 2009). Although such practices are not compulsory in every country, increasingly companies are disclosing their social and environmental performance. Many do so on a voluntary basis, generally perceived as a way of enhancing their own legitimacy before stakeholders (Aerts & Cormier, 2009; Castelló & Lozano, 2011; Cho & Patten, 2007; Du & Viera Jr., 2012; Laine, 2009; Mäkelä, 2011; Rahaman, Lawrence, & Roper, 2004; Wilmshurst & Frost, 2000). Irrespective of the motivations driving disclosure, it is important to understand what is being accounted for and eventually disclosed to organisational stakeholders: environmental externalities on one hand and social externalities on the other.

3.1.1 Measuring Externalities

According to welfare economics, externalities are the good or the harm economic activities do to others. Whichever they are, externalities are part of an organisation's performance. Therefore, they need to be measured and accounted for, first physically and if applicable financially (Hansen, 2010).

3.1.1.1 Physical Measures

Externalities are generally associated with physical measures, that is, measures that can be expressed through tangible units other than money. A general phenomenon cannot be considered an externality *per se*, if it is not accompanied with metrics (Callon, 2009). These physical measures can borrow from the metric or the Imperial system to express externalities as weight, volume or surface. For intelligibility purposes, the metric system is more widely used than that of the Imperial system even though it is however utilised.

Measures can be, for instance, kilograms or tons of CO_2 or NO_2 emissions to express pollution. Such is often the case with transport. When an airline passenger purchases a ticket, the weight of CO_2 emissions associated with this journey is often specified on the reservation (Jane Andrew & Cortese, 2011; Engels, 2009; Lohmann, 2009; MacKenzie, 2009). This particular measure is appropriate, as gas can be weighed, even though this metric remains relatively abstract. At least, one can figure out more or less clearly what this represents. This particular measure has become emblematic of environmental pollution as the main externality generated by human activity (Callon, 2009; Lohmann, 2009; Villiers (de), Chen, Jin, & Zhu, 2013).

Even if greenhouse gas emissions expressed in weight are the most common measure of environmental externalities, numerous other measures exist. For instance, climate change and global warming are expressed in Celsius degrees in international discussions, such as the Kyoto Accords or the annual Conference of Parties a.k.a. COP (Careira, Aguiar, Onça, & Monzoni, 2017; Chan, 2018). Other forms of metrics exist but are not widely used, partly because they are not as intelligible to the public. These are metrics relating to abstract measures non-scientists can hardly represent themselves, and yet express various forms of environmental externalities. For instance, luminous pollution at night when a city's neon lights are turned on can be expressed in lumens measuring luminosity (Fan, Yung, & Pecht, 2015). Noise externalities, such as those of an airport in a neighbourhood or night life in a city centre, can be expressed in decibels (Newell, 2012), which are not intelligible to most people. Similarly, air pollution can be measured through bars or Pascals expressing (ab)normal pressure; but, again, such a metric is not easily intelligible to the public. Lastly, any tangible externality could be measured as matter quantity, expressed with moles. This measure is however much more abstract than any others and is probably the least intelligible for non-chemists (Wolff, in press).

Seemingly, physical metrics respond to an imperative not of being perfectly accurate at measuring environmental externalities but of being intelligible and imprinting in people's mind. As intelligibility seems to be predominant in the use of performance management systems and related metrics, accuracy seems to be a secondary concern when raising collective awareness and interest in a problem (Alcouffe, Berland, & Levant, 2008; Callon, 2009). Pursuant to this intelligibility imperative, a number of metrics employed are just approximations of the phenomenon, inconsistent with what scientists or specialists would recommend. At least, people can visualise these in their day-to-day lives and make decision on those grounds. Such approximate metrics, notwithstanding their ontological limitation, reveal the power of the visual and intelligible in management accounting metrics (Busco & Quattrone, 2014, 2018; Quattrone, 2009).

This power of the visual is especially vivid in a series of metrics that involve representation. Dry and objective metrics often do not suffice to give a clear view of a phenomenon. Therefore, they are often replaced with equivalents that are more accessible to the public. For instance, electricity savings are expressed in megawatts or megawatts per hour, which poses two problems. Firstly, it is never perfectly clear what electric consumption a watt or kilowatt represents. Hence, the unit is not very insightful per se. Secondly, kilowatts or megawatts are such big units that they are beyond understanding. Therefore, this unintelligible unit often associated with a comparison against something that can be represented, such as "equivalent to the electric consumption of Paris for *x* days"(Gémes, 2015; Mueller & Carter, 2007). Surfaces or volumes can also make much more sense when presented in a comparative format rather than in a dry way. The issues raised by deforestation cannot be easily understood when these are expressed in square kilometres or hectares. Therefore, an intelligible way of presenting these metrics can consist in "*x* times the surface of country *y*" (Cukston, 2013; Mäkelä, 2011). The same can apply to volumes or capacities, where a mining company discloses the dust it generates. Tons, or hectolitres may not be easily understandable whilst a comparison in terms of "equivalent to *x* containers" would make much more sense (Alawattage, 2011; Coetzee & van Staden, 2011; De Waal & Orcotoma-Escarente, 2011).

3.1.1.2 Financial Measures

Even though physical measures have the virtue of clarity, they have two major limitations. Firstly, they cannot be integrated into conventional reporting, since they are not expressed in monetary terms. Therefore, they can only appear as additional insights into an organisation's environmental performance. In fact, the externalities generated through economic activity cannot be formally accounted for and presented in annual reports as part of total performance. Secondly, as externalities are manifold, the same is said of metrics: tons, litres, square metres and so on. They are so different in nature that they cannot be summed and put together in the same report. This is one of the main challenges confronting anyone involved in the Integrated Reporting initiative: finding a way of making all these metrics intelligibly coexist in one single report (Adams, 2015; de Villiers, Rinaldi, & Unerman, 2014; Flower, 2014; Higgins, Stubbs, & Love, 2014). Unsurprisingly, most organisations set out to express most of their activities' externalities in monetary terms (Hansen, 2010). Environmental externalities tend to be financialised in three different ways.

The first way of converting externalities into money consists in assigning them a direct trading or replacement value. In the case of deforestation for instance, the value of fallen trees can be expressed through direct economic benefits for the local population (*e.g.* employment). The environmental cost of a fallen tree could be expressed as the direct cost of a new seed and the gardening activities enabling this replacement tree to grow.

The second way of ascribing a financial value to externalities consists in estimating the direct cash flows associated with the externality. Inflows are the cost of opportunity associated with this externality when it results in reduced cash. Still with the case of a fallen tree, inflows can be estimated as this tree's absence of activity, such as the non-absorption of CO_2 emissions as expressed through the cost of emission trading (Villiers (de) et al., 2013). Similarly, the outflows associated with this externality are assessed: the cash benefits for the environment or local population. These cover direct cash benefits plus indirect ones, lingering in the future.

The third way of financialising externalities appears as theoretical as of 2019, owing to its very abstract nature, and consists of environmental discounted cash flows. As with the second option, the inflows and outflows are associated with an externality. The difference lies in that the third option models all future inflows and outflows discounted at the cost of environmental capital. This implies that the discount rate should not just be the well-known Weighted Average Cost of Capital but should include an environmental dimension. To date, such a discount rate does not exist, because such a metric requires profoundly renewed financial models (Chava, 2014).

3.1.2 Costing Externalities

When it comes to environmental matters, externalities are generally negative, probably because these are the most visible and especially easy to identify. Very often, the identification of such costs relates to incantations, reflecting what should be done, as on a political agenda (Cho et al., 2012; Helfaya & Moussa, 2017; Mathews, 1997; Russell, Milne, & Dey, 2017). Accordingly, these costs must be understood as expenses incurred to prevent, monitor or report environmental impact, *for example*, cost of waste management systems, environmental training, legal activities and legal fines, record keeping and reporting, cost of remediation of environmental impact and so on. To some extent, accounting for all these costs is equivalent to computing this company's environmental period cost, using an absorption costing system (Schaltegger & Burritt, 2017a; Schaltegger & Csutora, 2012).

3.1.2.1 Environmental Product Costing

Environmental product costing relates to the environmental footprint of business activities and can be delineated into the environmental product cost for each activity taken in isolation from others (Schaltegger & Burritt, 2017a). Accordingly, environmental product cost sets out to answer to the question of how much of the total environmental cost a manufacturing company should allocate to a given product. To some extent, answering this question is similar to answering that of how indirect and overhead costs can be assigned to a specific product or activity. In the twenty-first century, the environmental cost of any product purchased has become a concern. Such has been the case, mainly for two reasons. Firstly, environmental awareness has been growing. Secondly, some very popular products (*e.g.* high-tech or luxury products) as well as some very useful products (*e.g.* agro-food products or drugs) may rest upon a polluting business model. Nowadays, with the development of cloud computing and the dematerialisation of most human activities, the question of the damage that servers cause to the environment is arising. As with the allocation of overhead, product costing can rest upon either absorption costing or variable costing. As compared to overhead allocation, the choice of a method is driven, not by strategic concerns but by environmental exposure (Schaltegger & Burritt, 2017a; Schaltegger & Csutora, 2012; Schaltegger & Wagner, 2017).

If the company is known to be highly environment-friendly, variable costing could be sufficient, just accounting for the direct environmental cost of business activities. Conversely, if the company is known for having a strong environmental footprint, absorption costing may be more adequate. Such is the case because public demand for accountability highlights a need for disclosure revealing the actual impact of business activities on the environment. Company environmental accountability would thereby consist in proving commitment to environmental value and safety. Therefore, the cost of the damages caused must be comprehensive and accurate; hence, corrective actions can be clearly stated and undertaken. In other words, the more accurate and comprehensive environmental disclosure is, greater is the company credibility and legitimacy. Incurring high environmental costs is an acknowledgement of the environmental footprint. If costs are to be cut, not only product and period costs should be considered, but also environmental costs. The public can expect the company to reduce some of its environmental costs, so that product total cost can be less (Du & Viera Jr., 2012; Laine, 2009; Mäkelä, 2011).

Environmental product costing shifts the traditional management accounting reflection from strategic concerns to environmental positioning. Unlike strategy, which is imposed by competitors and can be managed, environmental positioning consists in the way the organisation is perceived by the public. Accordingly, on environmental matters, the public is a company's main stakeholder (Darnall, Seol, & Sarkis, 2009; Freeman, 2010; Kevin Gibson, 2000b; Orij, 2010; Passetti, Bianchi, Battaglia, & Frey, 2017). All told, an environmental costing system is imposed by society and the environment with whose expectations accounting must remain consistent.

3.1.2.2 Environmental Period Cost

The need for environmental period costing, a.k.a. environmental full-cost accounting (Schaltegger & Burritt, 2017a) is especially vivid in the case of environmental disasters, such as oil spills along a coastline (Cho, 2009; Hefln & Wallace, 2017) or the explosion of a factory producing chemicals (Chabbal, 2005). The most recent and most traumatic environmental disaster was the BP oil spill caused by the Deepwater Horizon in the Gulf of Mexico on 20 April 2010 (Williams et al., 2011) or the Fukushima (Betzer, Doumet, & Rinne, 2013). As the Fukushima case is still having lingering effects, the BP accident now belongs to the past and can be discussed more freely. Subsequent to the sinking of BP's Deepwater Horizon, the cost of the accident could be estimated: USD 15 billion in repairing the direct damage caused (removing the oil, conserving endangered species, renewing marine flora and fauna etc.). As this total cost was made public, competitors, like Royal Dutch Shell, could anticipate these in case something similar happened to them.

Foremost, other oil and gas companies found themselves encouraged to take account of the BP case to prevent future events from happening. Preventative measures were taken, whose cost was accounted for as product cost (Hefln & Wallace, 2017; Hoogevorst, 2013). Accordingly, competitors, such as Royal Dutch Shell, Total SA, Exxon Mobil or Aramco, would hire people for research and development, for safety, security, whose salaries and equipment are accounted for as product cost. Also, growing environmental awareness has resulted in numerous companies hiring environmental specialists or officers and departments. Similarly, consultants are often called on to articulate environmental recommendations aimed at preventing catastrophes and disasters.

3.1.2.3 Environmental Capital Expenditures and Revenues

As with any product or business activity, environmental matters include capital expenditures and revenues. These relate to investments made to protect or preserve the environment by reducing one's environmental footprint. In order to achieve this, environmental investments necessarily lead to revising internal business processes, the corporate business as well as the value chain. In the twenty-first century, these environmental capital expenditures are undertaken in the context of ecological transition (Schaltegger & Burritt, 2017a, 2017b; Schaltegger & Wagner, 2017; Schaltegger & Zvedzov, 2016). This can be understood through practical examples.

In a factory, managers can choose between numerous sources of energy, amongst which are coal or windmill energy. The latter is non-polluting, so that environmental impact using windmill energy will be zero. Conversely, using coal is highly polluting, thereby having a high environmental cost. In order to reduce this cost, shifting from one source of energy to another cannot be done without massive capital investment in new machines: the whole way of doing things needs to be revisited. This capital expenditure is taken into account in these accounts of environmental footprint. As the negative externalities generated by a polluting source of energy should be accounted for as savings, some future outflows shall be averted. Similarly, the positive externalities generated by the new source of energy should be accounted for as future inflows. For instance, if the new source of energy generates more than necessary, the excess can be sold to third parties or donated to other organisations. In the case of a sale, the new source of energy generates profit. In the case of a donation, corporate legitimacy can be enhanced through a behaviour deemed socially responsible (Harjoto & Jo, 2011; Iivonen & Moisander, 2014; Sheehy, 2014).

It can proceed from environmental investments an increase of corporate profitability visible in two ways. Firstly, by reducing its environmental cost, a company finds itself eventually reducing the total cost it incurs. Mechanically, if sales remain unchanged, profit margin can increase (Khojastehpour & Johns, 2014; Malik, 2015). Secondly, it can occur that a revised environmental strategy results in the company positioning its products differently and sell it as a better-quality product at a higher price. Thence, product cost decreases, just as selling prices increase; profit margin can mechanically increase. In fact, acknowledged environment-friendliness, by enhancing corporate legitimacy to its stakeholders, can result in higher sales and thereby contribute to greater profitability (Aerts & Cormier, 2009; Bessire & Onnée, 2010; Castelló & Lozano, 2011; Cho & Patten, 2007; Kuruppu & Milne, 2010).

3.1.3 Four-Tiers-Based Environmental Accounting

Even though environmental management accounting is not subjected to reporting standards, commonly observed practices reveal some recurrent patterns: four-tiers environmental costs and benefits (Schaltegger & Burritt, 2017a). Traditionally, environmental costs are emphasised, although environmental benefits are what makes corporate social responsibility profitable and therefore attractive (Schaltegger & Burritt, 2017b; Schaltegger & Wagner, 2017). These can be grouped in four tiers.

3.1.3.1 Conventional Costs and Benefits

Conventional costs are direct costs associated with capital expenditure, raw materials and other operating and maintenance costs relating to an organisation's environmental footprint or change in business model. When management is environment conscious, investments are undertaken to keep the environmental footprint in control. All these costs that are known as part of this policy are conventional costs. Symmetrically, conventional benefits are direct revenues generated from these investments and conventional expenses. Very often, these conventional benefits result from savings associated with these environmental expenses, *namely* expenses that are not incurred. These can also be direct revenues generated through the revised business model to which environmental expenses may have led.

3.1.3.2 Hidden Costs and Benefits

Hidden costs are unexpected and indirect cost eventually incurred when an organisation becomes environment conscious. These hidden costs can comprehend regulatory costs from activities such as those relating to managing and reporting environmental activities, cost of searching for environmentally responsible suppliers or the ongoing cost of cleaning up contaminated premises. In other words, hidden costs are all these costs induced by an organisation's ecological footprint at two levels. Firstly, these hidden costs cover regulatory obligations to repair or disclose. Secondly, these are comprised of costs incurred through corrective behaviours and practices.

Symmetrically, hidden benefits can be regulatory benefits from environmentally friendly activities. These can be manifested in three ways. Firstly, these can be exemption from the paying of fines for environmental damages. Because business processes have been revised, the damages caused to the environment are lesser and no longer subject to fines or repairs. In other words, these fine exemptions equal savings enabled by environmental expenses. Secondly, increasingly more governments support environmental initiatives through public subsidies or tax exemptions. These are not necessarily expected at the outset, since they may only be devised, as environmental awareness grows. These can be comprised of any exemptions or subsidies granted to enhance buildings' environmental performance (*e.g.* solar panel, insulation, dry toilets). Thirdly, environment-friendly practices may result in unexpected higher activity level, owing to enhanced corporate legitimacy to the public.

3.1.3.3 Contingent Costs and Benefits

Contingent costs and benefits explicitly relate to organisational activity and environmental footprint. These occur precisely because the organisation has had a certain behaviour or practices with an impact on the environment (Schaltegger & Wagner, 2017).

Contingent costs are liabilities arising from failure to actually comply with environmental regulations. These are generally comprised of fines and penalties organisations have to pay for such failure. Such is the case, as increasingly more countries associate breaches of environmental laws and regulations with penal law. For instance, the illegal use of pesticides known for polluting soils can be subject to major fines. These are contingent upon laws' trespassing. Other than fines and penalties, contingent costs also relate to fees organisations have to pay to the casualties of environmental damages they have caused.

Conversely, contingent benefits reflect direct and explicit gains generated by complying with environmental laws and regulations. Unlike hidden benefits that are not predictable, contingent benefits are, since they directly proceed from existing laws and regulations promoting virtuous environmental practices. These contingent benefits include anticipated tax exemptions, grants or awards received in relation to commendable behaviours and practices. As these are generally expressed in monetary terms, they can be easily and directly accounted for as benefits.

3.1.3.4 Relationship and Image Costs and Benefits

Relationship and image costs and benefits relate to the way the company is perceived by its main stakeholders and how this perception affects the conduct of business operations (Schaltegger & Burritt, 2017b). Depending on the way the organisation is perceived by the public, public authorities, its customers and employees, operations can be facilitated or made difficult. In case operations are made difficult, relationship and image costs proceed from a loss in confidence from these stakeholders (Freeman, 2010; Orij, 2010; Passetti et al., 2017). If employees distrust their company, they can lose motivation on the workplace and be less efficient or productive than previously. They can also resign, thereby resulting in the company losing its organisational memory and know-how. In this case, the relationship and image cost can be increased by the costs associated with new recruitment campaigns and new employees' training. If customers are lost, because they decide to boycott the company's product, the loss in sales can be accounted for as a relationship and image cost. As with employees, any costs incurred to restore this lost confidence shall be accounted for as relationship and image costs—marketing and communication on new processes, materials or technologies and so on—as with Volkswagen subsequent to the Dieselgate (Cleeren, Dekimpe, & Van Heerde, 2017; Frigessi di Rattalma, 2019).

Conversely, relationship and image benefits are revenues directly generated from virtuous behaviours and practices. These appear as commendable and result in stakeholders committing themselves to the organisation. On the employment front, an organisation known for commendable environmental practices can attract talent and highly devoted people (Jamali, El Dirani, & Harwood, 2015). Highly skilled and committed to their jobs, talents can be expected to be especially efficient and productive. Such is the case of Unilever known for its environmental consciousness and virtuous practices attracting and retaining talented applicants (Farndale, Scullion, & Sparrow, 2010). Similarly, as environmental awareness has been growing in society, customers are increasingly bound to purchase products from companies known for virtuous environmental behaviour and practices (Pérez, 2013). In this case relationship and image benefits can be just accounted for as the extra revenues from (popular) sales. This can explain the success of certain brands advertising organic produce or ways of growing (Hughner, McDonagh, Prothero, Schultz, & Stanton, 2007).

In conclusion, in order to avert environmental disasters, when these can be anticipated and modelled, organisations have been encouraged to raise their employees' environmental awareness through various forms of training. As with product cost, these are accounted for as expenses at the organisations' end. For instance, these companies offer their employees university degrees, environmental certificates or other trainings given by external consultants. These expenses are paid for by the company. The cost incurred is twofold. Firstly, companies pay for the service itself. Secondly, during their training period, employees are not working. The training itself is thereby a cost of opportunity for the company, from a mere financial perspective. From a CSR perspective, such an operation is an investment in environmental friendliness or awareness.

The company has to pay for this in order to have people knowing how to cope with the environment or how to protect it. For instance, in Australia, Victoria in particular regularly undergoes water restrictions. In order for people to know how to cope with these water restrictions, the State government subsidises a form of training (Chiew, Zhou, & McMahon, 2003; Hurliman, 2011). In order to cope with water restrictions, people are trained to have a three-minute shower. Likewise, they are trained to use dry toilets and so on.

3.2 Accounting for Social Externalities

Even if social externalities are often presented as an extension or part of environmental externalities, they are specific and therefore need special treatment. In welfare economics, social externalities have been identified before environmental ones, as ecological concerns were not as vivid as interest in other stakeholders (Freeman, 2010; Pigou, 1946).

3.2.1 Measuring Social Performance

Social performance is broader than environmental performance, since this notion covers every other type of externalities that is not directly relating to environmental matters. This implies all those positive and negative externalities affecting stakeholders in different ways. In order to assess an organisation's social performance, it is important to first identify its stakeholders and their expectations. Once these stakeholders are identified, social performance consists of organisation capability of creating the value these stakeholders expect (Bessire & Onnée, 2010; Mahoney & Roberts, 2007).

3.2.1.1 Measuring Internal Social Performance

Traditionally, value creation has been understood for stockholders, other stakeholders being neglected because they are not concerned by the corporate value maximisation function (M. Jensen, 2001). As Agency Theory has historically dealt with listed companies, the principal was simply considered stockholders expecting value maximisation expressed through the Capital Asset Pricing Model (Fama & Jensen, 1983a, 1983b; M. Jensen & Meckling, 1976). Corporate social performance can broadly be understood as commitment to value creation for society, value being unnecessarily financial (Gray, 2002a, 2002b).

Within the organisation, value takes differentiated forms relating to what counts as strategic (Ahrens & Chapman, 2002, 2007; Ahrens & Mollona, 2007; Jørgensen & Messner, 2009; Messner, 2009). Once such value has been commonly understood, subordinates are expected to provide managers with management accounting figures, which can also comprise of non-financial data. As part of the organisational management control system, these data are produced and circulated following the organisational standards and procedures. In a private sector organisation, such figures can address costs and income, number of units produced or sold, per unit value, inventory or delivery velocity. In public sector organisations and non-profits, management accounting figures can inform on the same issues as well as value for society as a multiple Higher-Stakeholder, that is, welfare produced (Bebbington & Gray, 2001; Gray, 2002a, 2002b, 2010; Gray et al., 1997; O'Dwyer & Unerman, 2007).

A major type of internal stakeholders is found in employees, so that a company's social performance is often amalgamated with the way workers are treated. This performance borrows from the Human Relations movement subsequent to the Hawthorne study (Jamali et al., 2015; L. Parker, 2014; Schaltegger & Wagner, 2017). Whilst approaches borrowing from Agency Theory rest upon the mere assumption that treating employees well shall result in higher economic performance, contemporary approaches consider that employee wellbeing is an end per se. This approach explicitly assumes the fact that it is a company's role to treat its employee as well as possible. This appears as a fair counterpart for making profit through their labour. Accordingly, social performance can first be visible in HR management (Jamali et al., 2015) through workplace organisation, work arrangements, Compensations & Benefits policy and other perks associated with employment (Day, 1994; Jansen, Merchant, & Van der Stede, 2009; Tornikoski, 2011). The organisation of the workplace can be more or less comfortable for employees and suitable for their health. Some companies, such as Google, offer a free cafeteria operating like a health food shop with only organic produce (Dann & Haddow, 2008; Jarvis, 2011; Vise, 2008). Work arrangements can consist in allowing employees to have flexible hours or work remotely, especially when they are caring for children and have similar outside responsibilities.

Internal social performance can also be assessed outside HR and therefore appears as an extension of general management practices. These could be practices whereby trans-generational relationships are encouraged or facilitated. This would not be just for the sake of transmitting know-how and experience but integrating the younger and the elder ones (Scholes-Fogg, 2011). Likewise, how diversity under all its possible forms is managed appears as an expression of social performance, that is, integration of minorities (Baldwin, Lightbody, Brown, & Trinkle, 2012; del Carmen Triana, Wagstaff, & Kim, 2012; Fearfull & Kamenou, 2006; Rupert, Jehn, Engen, & Reuver, 2010).

3.2.1.2 Measuring External Social Performance

Externally, the various stakeholders are periodically provided with financial reporting revealing how the organisational project was conducted operationally and financially (Ahrens, 1996). Traditional financial reporting is complemented with an annual social report that is increasingly integrated in the annual report, thereby operationalising the Integrated Reporting initiative (de Villiers et al., 2014; Higgins et al., 2014). Social value creation is disclosed to any party interested through generally accepted accounting principles. As in Agency Theory approaches, figures are audited and disclosed to the public (Gray, 2013b; Gray, Dey, et al., 1997; Gray, Owen, et al., 1988). Based on those premises, not only are private companies concerned by social performance, public sector organisations as well as non-profits also are. In the case of non-profits, these statements are directed at donors and public authorities interested in accounts for the righteous use of donations, that is, the completion of announced programmes, such as training, social work or otherwise (Goddard & Assad, 2006; Gray, Bebbington, & Collison, 2006; Lehman, 2007; Unerman & O'Dwyer, 2006a, 2006b, 2008). Lastly, public sector organisations disclose accounts revealing to citizens how taxes collected and returns on public investments were used to construct infrastructures or enable social transfers (Black, Briggs, & Keogh, 2001; Broadbent, Dietrich, & Laughlin, 1996; Collier, 2005; Ezzamel & Willmott, 1993; Humphrey, Miller, & Scapens, 1993).

These multiple external stakeholders have different and specific expectations, depending on their relation to the organisation. A company's neighbourhood may not expect exactly the same value as public authorities, suppliers or customers. The surrounding neighbourhood may expect employment and maybe facilities associated therewith, such as infrastructures that could benefit society (*e.g.* schools, hospitals, roads) Very often, when multinational companies settle into a developing country they build such infrastructures for their employees and at times make them accessible to the local population (Bonache, Sanchez, & Zárraga-Oberty, 2009). Public authorities may expect the organisation to keep their social and economic promises, by eventually recruiting people, training their staff and paying tax where they generate value (Col & Patel, 2016; Sikka, 2010; West, 2017). Public authorities may also consider that an organisation is socially performing well when it contributes to the wealth of the territory on which it is operating through namely job creation, participation in various local activities and so on. Suppliers may simply expect their client to honour the contract and pay for the sold merchandises. Depending on corporate strategic generic strategy, value for customers shall differ. If the company is cost-dominant, customers may expect a cheap price and ease at finding the product. Conversely, if the company seeks differentiation, customers may well expect the product or service to be different from that of competitors and to be of sufficient quality (no defect etc.)

All told, social performance is not unique but multifaceted. This particular type of performance is highly contingent upon the stakeholders under consideration but also upon the organisation itself. What is assessed, accounted for and disclosed, as with management accounting figures, appears as an extension of strategic concerns intertwined with specific stakeholders' social value expectations. Thence, there cannot be one single measure of social performance and standards can hardly be applicable.

3.2.2 Accounting for Social Issues

Accounting for social performance consists in associating the right measure to the right Key Performance Indicator (KPI) proceeding from the value stakeholders expect. To some extent, the logic underlying social accounting can be considered similar to that underpinning the Balanced Scorecard: a strategic critical success factor needs to be identified, a measure articulated, a target defined and an objective set. Based upon actual achievements, management shall seek for cause-effect explanations and take corrective actions, when necessary.

3.2.2.1 Internal Social Accounts

Unlike environmental issues that are mainly external with some internal actions, social matters may directly and explicitly relate to corporate practices and processes (Chetty, 2011; Cooper, Taylor, Smith, & Catchpowle, 2005; Gray, 2002b). Generally speaking, these cover themes relating to the HRM and the management or interactions between human beings within the organisation. Pursuantly, organisations are held accountable both to society at large and to their internal stakeholders for their extended HR policy (Boyce, 2018; Jamali et al., 2015). These matters of concern mainly relate to issues such as attitude towards discrimination and anti-discrimination policies and practices (del Carmen Triana et al., 2012; Tinker & Fearfull, 2007). In the twenty-first century, discrimination can take on multiple forms, such as ethnic background, class, age or gender. Organisations are more or less explicitly required to disclose figures and actions proving that they are not discriminating or that they endeavour at averting any forms of discrimination.

Racial and ethnic discrimination has long been a major problem in organisations, where ethnic minorities have barely found their way. For instance, ethnic minorities have long been more or less explicitly excluded from the accountancy profession (Baskerville, Jacobs, Joannidès de Lautour, & Sissons, 2016; Efferin, 2002; Fearfull & Kamenou, 2006; Kim, 2004a, 2004b, 2008). This observation is not just valid in countries known for forms of segregation between Whites and non-Whites, such as the United States or South Africa (Hammond, Clayton, & Arnold, 2009; Hammond, Clayton, & Arnold, 2012; Retief & Villiers (de), 2013), but any other countries with immigration, such as the UK or historic ethnic minorities, as in Trinidad and Tobago (Annisette, 2000, 2003). In order to account for non-discrimination based upon race or ethnicity, organisation's social disclosure can reveal figures of employees and management by ethnic background. This is possible for companies operating in countries where ethnic statistics are allowed or practised, generally Anglo-Saxon countries, as opposed to France where this is not permitted. What ethnic backgrounds are represented in the organisation and how many of them are on senior positions, management positions or even on the board could easily be disclosed. When it comes to board composition, it is not unusual that companies disclose photographs of their members, in order to prove the figures they announce (Bernardi, Bean, & Weippert, 2005).

Gender discrimination relates to the idea that women and men are not treated equally in organisations, generally owing to stereotypes regarding females' capabilities. Discrimination based upon gender can be evidenced through unequal pay for the same job and responsibilities (Grosser & Moon, 2008; Subramanian, 2008). Another form gender-based discrimination can take relates to the scope of responsibilities and promotion to senior positions, as it has been noticed women are often confronted with a glass ceiling (Broadbent & Kirkham, 2008; Dambrin & Lambert, 2008, 2012). In order to prove their concern for gender equality and actual policies aimed at fostering it, organisations tend to disclose more and more figures on gender-based pay gaps, expressed in percentages: how much on average women earn for the same responsibilities as men do (Fearfull & Kamenou, 2006). Also, organisations are increasingly expected to disclose figures relating to the number of women having an executive or senior role (Jeacle, 2011), such as board member or CEO (Tremblay, Gendron, & Malsch, 2016). In general, companies are increasingly demanded accounts of gender parity on most corporate roles (Ahmad, 2012).

Age discrimination has also appeared as an emerging concern within organisations, whereby senior employees would not be treated as well as younger ones. In particular, according to some myths, elder employees are either more expensive or less efficient than younger ones, thereby leading companies to privilege the hiring or promoting of junior staff at the detriment of senior people (Posthuma & Campion, 2009; A. Walker, 1999). This myth is especially popular in countries characterised with high unemployment rates amongst senior executives, such as France or Italy (Lippman, 2008). Whilst racial and gender-based discrimination can be made visible and have active opponents in society such is not necessarily the case with age discrimination. The problem of discriminating elder employees is less visible and thereby does not appear as an equally important concern. Therefore, organisations are not urged to disclose on this particular social account. Some do, whilst others do not. What can be disclosed are figures relating to the number of employees by age group and intertwine this information with responsibility levels. Apparently, research has not expressed a particular interest in this issue thus far.

3.2.2.2 Accounts of Corporate Social Impact

Organisations' social impact embraces HR-related issues, but also some broader themes concerning society at large. Apart from these discriminatory behaviours, it was noticed on occasions that some companies were more or less severely attending to human rights and people's dignity (Gray

& Gray, 2011; Li & McKernan, 2016; McPhail & Adams, 2016; McPhail & McKernan, 2011; O'Brien & Dhanarajan, 2016). It has therefore become a growing concern that organisations do protect human rights on the workplace and more broadly in their supply chain and should disclose what they do in their favour (Cooper, Coulson, & Taylor, 2011; Frankental, 2011; Islam & McPhail, 2011; McPhail & Ferguson, 2016). This can take on numerous forms. One of them could be disclosure of child labour either on corporate premises or at their suppliers. Another form could be inhumane work conditions, such as excessively heavy workload, long hours, without sufficient rest, and unsafe work premises that are dirty, dangerous and without sufficient ventilation (Cragg, 2000; Harcourt & Harcourt, 2002; Mena et al., 2010).

From a mere CSR perspective, it is arguable that organisations are expected not to abuse human rights at all. From an ethical viewpoint, apart from what they do in favour of human rights, organisations are expected to disclose figures directly relating to the way their business model exposes them to these issues. Obviously, not two companies would be expected to disclose the same things. For instance, C&A, caught in a scandal regarding work conditions in Bangladesh, is expected to disclose figures on health and safety. These could be expressed through actual measures taken to improve health and safety as well as amounts spent on these. In order to give an account of the extent of the phenomenon, the company is also expected to disclose figures relating to accidents on the workplace and professional diseases (Graafland, 2008). Likewise, a company like Nike, often accused of living off child labour in developing countries is expected to disclose figures regarding the age of its suppliers' workforce age. The number of people working under age is expected to be disclosed with the assumption this number should so decline over years as to reach zero (Locke, Kochan, Romis, & Qin, 2007). Lastly, a company like France Telecom—now known as Orange—has been confronted with a massive suicide wage amongst its employees. Scrutinised by the public, it is now expected to disclose accounts of suicides as well as actions taken and money spent to avert suicide (Chabrak, Craig, & Daidji, 2016).

All told, social accounts and disclosure also cover areas that are specific to one particular organisation, owing to its business model and supply chain. These items that are emphasised by society as important and deserving accountability vary from one organisation to another and must be accounted for contingently upon organisational exposure thither. Whilst it is possible to issue standards for non-discrimination reporting, it is impossible when it comes to social issues directly related to the way a particular organisation conducts its operations.

Organisations can have a social impact just by being present and active in a certain geographic area. Thence, their impact on this area needs to be measured, accounted for and disclosed. The main impact an organisation can have on its neighbourhood consists in employment. By conducting operations somewhere, an organisation is expected to hire locals and not just to bring expats from overseas or experts from the headquarters. When an organisation decides to locate some of its activities somewhere, it is implicitly expected that it will provide the local workforce with occupations. Held accountable to their local environment and local authorities, such organisations are expected to disclose figures revealing the number of jobs they have created for locals (Lee Parker, 2011). This is especially vivid when the organisation is large and becomes a major local employer or when the territory on which this organisation settles is characterised by high unemployment rates. In these two cases, disclosure of the number of local jobs created as well as the nature of jobs filled by locals appear as critical concerns.

When the organisation is perceived as the main employer in a particular area, it is implicitly assumed that it has a certain contribution to its social and economic development. Therefore, the organisation is held accountable before local authorities for this contribution. This can take on numerous forms, such as the building of infrastructures that can benefit employees and other locals, such as roads, schools or hospitals (Reimann, Ehrgott, Kaufmann, & Carter, 2012). Even though these companies are not explicitly and formally demanded to contribute and disclose, it becomes part of their implicit accountability to do so. Thence, they tend to disclose facts and figures highlighting the good they have locally done, expressed through accomplishments and amounts spent on these actions. For instance, Michelin is the main employer in the Auvergne region in central France and has contributed to local development through various infrastructures whereof it gives an account in its annual disclosure: hospitals, schools, accommodation, roads, university training and many others (Gueslin, 1999).

Not just is social impact positive. It also happens that an organisation would have a negative social impact, in which case it needs to be clarified and detailed in its disclosure. Some negative features of an organisation's social impact could be locals' expropriating or dispossessing to acquire land or buildings. Such has long been the case with first nations when settlers launched businesses, as in Australia, Canada or the United States, where the issue of native land is still prevailing in the twenty-first century (Fleischman, Oldroyd, & Tyson, 2011; Kathy Gibson, 2000a; Neu & Graham, 2004; Oldroyd, Fleischman, & Tyson, 2008; Tyson, Fleischman, & Oldroyd, 2004; S. P. Walker, 2003). In this case, concerned organisations are expected to disclose on the evil they may have done to the local population, expressed in quantified figures and detailed explanations. As such disclosure is voluntary, precisely because it cannot be subjected to reporting standard, organisations are less than bound to eventually disclose such information. And yet, it is important that they should, as part of their advanced CSR policy, at least by acknowledging the areas where they are failing to be socially responsible. Similarly, organisations whose business activities may affect people's health are expected to disclose figures of both their impact and the measures taken to prevent this from happening. For instance, McDonald's has long been known for delivering junk food contributing to obesity and other health issues. As a result, the company nowadays discloses in its restaurants the contents of its meals and expresses the sugar and fat absorbed as well as disclaimers addressed to the most vulnerable of its clients. Its annual social report discloses figures relating to its foundation's activity aimed at averting obesity and caring for ill people. These are expressed in terms of both actions taken and amounts of money spent on actions (Kroc, 2012).

3.2.2.3 Finding the Right Measure

As with performance management, once what counts has been identified, the next challenge is to identify an appropriate measure: an appropriate working unit. This difficulty is twofold. On one hand, what is a matter of concern for stakeholders needs to be identified and precisely named. This can pose a problem, as social matters are often diverse and loosely formulated (Banks et al., 2016; S. M. Cooper & Owen, 2007). Once these have been expressed, finding a measure may be difficult in itself, because metrics addressed to stakeholders must have two characteristics: accuracy and intelligibility. Any measures for social impact must be accurate, directly related to the matter of concern and appear as the fairest possible proxy for it. But also, these units must be understandable to stakeholders and relate to actual concerns of theirs. It proceeds from this that some measures that would be technically or scientifically accurate may be inappropriate because they do not make sense to stakeholders (Callon, 2009; Callon &

Rabeharisoa, 2008). For instance, in industries where employee health is at risk, as in mining, the quantity of toxic substances cannot be expressed in moles (*mol*), a purely abstract measure used by physicists only and yet appropriate to measure the quantity of a substance (Coetzee & van Staden, 2011; De Waal & Orcotoma-Escarente, 2011).

With corporate social responsibility issues at stake, organisations are confronted with a form of suspicion that they are doing wrong and must prove that they are doing the least evil rather than doing the good. This implies that social as well as environmental accounting tends to focus on problematic areas more than laudable initiatives. As with ethics, governance and accountability, corporate social responsibility seems to be operated as in response to scandals or cases of notorious misconduct (Badiou, 2006, 2012; Badiou & Gauchet, 2016). Social and environmental accounting unsurprisingly tends to focus on negative externalities, *namely* costs for stakeholders and the environment.

In so doing, as CSR reporting appears as a response to the evil the organisation can do, mainly costs accepted by society as a matter of concern tend to be reported. For instance, transport companies, including airlines, do report CO_2 emissions but not necessarily decibels for the noise generated through their activity. This has major implications for social and environmental accounting: even the identification of negative externalities is selective.

3.2.3 Difficulties in Identifying and Measuring Externalities

Accounting for social externalities is difficult, and this chiefly for two reasons. The identification itself of these externalities is not a simple task, since this requires a very good command of corporate value chain and knowledge of stakeholders. As these externalities are strictly contingent upon organisational activities, it is crucial to first know these activities very well.

3.2.3.1 Externalities We Can Measure

The main social and environmental costs that organisations disclose are those that can relatively easily be identified and measured. With the triple bottom-line logic, it would be expected that all these costs should at some point be expressed in a similar unit; hence, they can be summed or compared. By definition, social and environmental costs can hardly be converted into monetary value, namely because they relate to intangibles. In order to solve this problem, two positions exist to integrate within the same type of report these incommensurate matters of concern. The first approach consists in considering these externalities intangible assets and applying the same valuation models as for these assets. Thereby, these negative externalities are assigned a monetary value (Daum, 2002; Kaplan & Norton, 2004; Power, 2001), always with the same reservations that can be raised regarding the valuation of intangibles. The second approach is known as Integrated Reporting and consists in considering reporting as addressed to society as a whole and therefore every single stakeholder. Under this purview, reporting appears as a collection of numerous individual reports whereof all have the same status and value in general (de Villiers et al., 2014; Frías-Aceituno, Rodríguez-Ariza, & García-Sánchez, 2013; Higgins et al., 2014).

The first approach sets out to financialise and standardise stakeholder accounting whilst the second approach assumes measurements vary and are contingent. Considering externalities intangibles enables to account for them, using conventional reporting standards. Conversely, considering externalities are contingent liabilities assumes standardisation cannot occur, management accounting being central. To some extent, the first approach has a utilitarian view of externalities and reporting, enabling, for instance, to measure costs of collecting and disposing of waste, cost of control systems used to minimise gas spread into rivers or air, packaging costs, compensation paid to the wife of an employee killed at the plant or costs of a new waste water treatment plant and so on. In contradistinction, the second approach would rather focus on those physical measures that are accurate and as intelligible as possible, such as the number of suicides on the workplace, the total number of sick leave days with a distinction between short-term (the flu, a cold) and long-term (cancer, burnout etc.)

Positive externalities seem more difficult to measure or at least disclose, as though they were less legitimate or could be subject to self-marketing (Chava, 2014; Hansen, 2010). Disclosing positive externalities would appear as a means of legitimising an activity which is not (Elsbach & Sutton, 1992; Hampel & Tracey, 2016; Suchman, 1995). Interestingly, it does seem that measuring an impact is also easier when it is negative than when it is positive: measuring a negative impact would appear as clairvoyance and honesty whilst measuring a positive impact could appear as science fiction (impossible to prove) or arrogance (overestimation of the good done).

As a result, social accounting does not emphasise positive externalities as much as negative ones. At best, what is disclosed is what organisations do to minimise their negative externalities or raise their social and environmental awareness. These actions are not aimed at doing the good per se as a social project but at averting evil or minimising its effect. In other words, social and environmental accounting tends to highlight mainly these actions directed at negative externalities. These can be of two orders: corrective or preventative. In either case, they tend to be disclosed in two ways: concrete actions on one hand and amounts of money placed in these on the other. But the good the organisation does to its stakeholders just through its existence is rarely disclosed as such (Bessire & Onnée, 2010; Cho, 2009; Cho & Patten, 2007; Rayman-Bacchus, 2006; Suddaby & Greenwood, 2005). The good organisations do could be local direct and indirect employment caused by their existence. Local suppliers may have work because of the organisation. Indirectly, as employees may have children, these may populate local schools and lead to a need for more classes and teachers and so on.

3.2.3.2 Externalities We Cannot Measure

In contradistinction to externalities we can measure but do not always actually assess, some others can just not be. These mainly relate to three types of externalities.

The first type of externalities that cannot be measured are undoubtedly those externalities that can be named. An organisation's activity can have some social or environmental impact whereof management is certain. But these are loosely understood and relate to a mere intuition. As long as this intuition is not formalised and proved as correct, the externality under consideration cannot be measured. For instance, lean management can be stressful on employees who do not have much visibility and predictability for their work shifts: depending on demand, their timetable can unexpectedly change, causing some inconvenience and stress (Dankbaar, 1997; McCann, Hassard, Granter, & Hyde, 2015; Niepcel & Molleman, 1998). These can be intuited but not named, since the occasioned inconvenience may well have a differentiated meaning for each employee, whereas stress can take on different forms and extent. Conversely, there are some positive externalities that can hardly be named and therefore not measured: wishing an employee a happy birthday could do good to him or her (or unexpectedly bad in some cases), but this feeling shall differ from one person to another. A friendly work environment is hardly nameable and measurable.

The second type of externalities that cannot be measured are those long-term externalities whose effects may occur long after the event or last longer afterwards. The difficulty here relates to the fact that the time horizon is so large that estimating anything could be perceived as science fiction. In the future, technologies may change so radically that what we perceive today as an externality can be absorbed and fixed tomorrow. Conversely, some externalities may be largely underestimated today because we do not have the necessary technology and knowledge to anticipate its effects. Such has been the case with global warming: there is an international consensus on the phenomenon and on its global causes. However, it is very difficult, if not impossible to estimate every company's actual contribution thither or the lag effect organisation's today's behaviour shall have on climate tomorrow. Such externalities, positive or negative, can only be named and identified as a matter of concern but cannot be measured as such (Jones, 2016; Ungar, 1998). This often results in arbitrary measures, expressed as an upper-limit allowance. Corporate examples could be Cathay Pacific or Qantas. The two airlines are allowed to produce *X* grams of carbon per passenger. The reason for this metric remains unknown, as we have no idea of a measure showing the actual impact on the environment. As these companies' concern is not on the legitimacy of these metrics, they at best know about improving their practices so as to comply with standards. Nobody does really know how these metrics were defined; companies just abide by these without being certain this measure be actually pertinent or helpful.

The third type of externalities that pose a measurement problem is that relating to living beings: humans, fauna and flora. A ground principle of human ethics has always been that life is priceless and therefore cannot be assigned any value. Accordingly, social externalities whose impact is directly on people's lives can hardly be measured as such. When McDonald's was accused of causing morbid obesity, it was impossible to value the effect of junk food on people's lives. Some people would die, and some others would be so obese that they could be considered disabled. The estimated cost would necessarily be underestimated and would ethically pose a problem: if one can assign a value to a human life, the next step is their commodification and tradability (Abeysekera, 2008; Lawrence & Sharma, 2002). Doing so would deny the absolute and inviolable character of human nature, thereby almost breaching human rights: all humans are equal and have an equal right to live with dignity. By assigning a value to human nature, those with resources could purchase someone else's life by paying a fee or a fine if they attend to it (Chetty, 2011; Frankental, 2011; Islam & McPhail, 2011). For this simple reason, externalities attending to human life and health cannot be fully measured and should not be at all.

Even though human life should not be priced, there have been attempts at measuring and compensating for breaches of human dignity through fines, fees or other expenses companies would agree to incur to fix problems their activity caused. Contrary to human life per se, such social costs can be easily measured through all those expenses incurred to cure the person. This poses an ethical problem, since this is equivalent to considering that human nature and dignity can be managed. Even if it is not possible to purchase a life, it would be possible to purchase a right to attend to it, provided corrective actions are taken and financed. In fact, so doing would in itself be a breach of human rights: equal dignity and integrity would no longer be absolute but just relative, since one can just rebalance by paying in case of abuses (Blechman, Chari, & Hasan, 2012). This means there are externalities we can ethically not measure and whose measurement we prohibit.

There are other externalities we cannot measure because we are not equipped with technologies, knowledge or expertise to do so. At times, such is the case of those externalities that are indirect and proceed from the original externality associated with our activity. It is not always possible to assess the actual reach of an externality and therefore to measure it in full. This situation could be evidenced with the story of *Erin Brockovich*: an advocate who sued Pacific Gas and Electric Company on the ground that people died of drinking water with hexavalent chromium. The issue was twofold. Firstly, it was to identify a cause-effect relationship from the fact of people drinking tap water and die. Secondly, pursuant to the US legal system, the barrister was to assess this in dollar value; hence, the company would pay for the damages caused. This was an externality we could not measure at all, because assessing its actual reach was almost impossible. Pacific Gas and Electric Company's solicitors claimed no systematic cause-effect relationship, arguing claiming one is pure speculation. They substantiated their claims with the fact that nobody could measure the impact of neighbours' health on non-drinkers' health. Accordingly, Pacific Gas and Electric Company dealers would not pay for this damage. What this story revealed was the difficulty finding experts who would feed the argument that we can measure the impact on neighbours' health. The case eventually came to an end in 1996 with a USD 333 million settlement for Pacific Gas and Electric Company's victims (Cole, 2018).

3.2.3.3 Externalities We Forget

Whilst direct externalities can be identified some indirect ones can, but certainly not all of them. It proceeds from this observation that a number of externalities are unknown to organisations. Accordingly, they cannot even mention them and less account for those. Externalities we forget can be chiefly of three orders.

Firstly, externalities we forget are externalities to customers and society forced to dispose of the leftovers or waste generated by our activity but transferred on to them. Such can be the case with unwanted packaging and the imperative to recycle it, which implies the purchase of different rubbish bags and bins. Outside of this externality on the family, society is concerned: councils have to organise recycling, hiring people for this, which leads to raise tax from residents and so on. Typically, all these indirect externalities are just ignored. It is obvious that these costs are related to organisational activity. As this link is merely indirect, it is almost impossible to envisage all these externalities. If actually accounted for, these would dramatically increase the social and environmental cost associated with corporate activity (Degli Antoni & Marzetti, 2019).

Secondly, lagged externalities are externalities that cannot be anticipated *par excellence*. These relate to the reach of current externalities. In contradistinction to externalities that form a long chain, externalities having a lagged effect in time are bound to be those whose effects only occur at a much later stage and may find themselves ignored. Such can happen when these externalities occur further than corporate time horizon, even if the effect can be known. This trend to forget these externalities rests upon three implicitly assumptions. On one hand, it is considered that it is not realistic to claim visibility over a long time, circumstances can change. On the other hand, there is always hope that future technologies, unknown today, shall find solutions to the current problem and fix the negative externalities we generate. Lastly, our activity can do in the future good we ignore. In 2000, experts revealed that Monsanto's Roundup would cause dramatic social and environmental damages over the next 20 years: soil pollution and respiratory problems for farmers using it (Giesy, Dobson, & Solomon, 2000). Although these potential effects were confirmed in 2005 (Richard, Moslemi, Sipahutar, Benachour, & Seralini, 2005), the company considered they were not proved to actually occur, the future being known for its uncertainty and unpredictability. According to Monsanto's counsels, results from scientific research would not be evidence of certainty but just hypotheses. For this reason, the company did not plead guilty before a US court when former users sued it for severe health condition caused by an intensive Roundup usage. To Monsanto, these effects could not be anticipated at all at the time of first use (Cohen, 2019).

This second type of externalities we forget can to some extent relate to cynicism or a breach of the precautionary principle. According to this principle, every known or potential effect must be taken into consideration and measured. Unknown effects must be researched and taken into consideration when they become potential, that is, when science provides with some intuitions these may occur. Beyond cynicism and the precautionary principle, these externalities we forget from an ethical viewpoint may be acceptable if we have no knowledge and no intuition at all that these might someday eventuate. In other words, from a merely ethical viewpoint, these externalities we forget should only remain temporary. In the Monsanto case, the ethical problem lies in that there had long been warnings that Roundup could have dramatic effects on people's health. The company has been dismissive of these studies and warnings until people actually developed disease directly proceeding from using Roundup. Prosecutors considered Monsanto had long known and should have issued warnings and provisioned for possible effects, making the information clearer as intuitions were clearer, which has never been done.

Thirdly, any externality deemed subjective or contingent upon the person it affects can hardly be envisaged and are ignored. Such can be the case of any form of inconvenience activities can cause. For instance, when housing commission puts a large family with young children in a building with elderly people who need quiet and silent place, the inconvenience for residents is considered purely subjective and is therefore ignored (Collier, 2005; Courtney, Marnoch, & Williamson, 2009; Stewart, 2012). With subjective externalities, the difficulty is that there cannot be any collective agreement or external estimate of what they exactly mean to the concerned people. As a result, it would just be impossible to perfectly name them and measure them. Most often, organisations do not even imagine the existence of these externalities their activity can cause. This problem is manifest with externalities confronting internal stakeholders too: impact of an action on employee morale cannot systematically be anticipated and even less apprehended, since morale is a personal and individual feeling (Abdel-Maksoud, Cerbioni, Ricceri, & Velayutham, 2010).

In total, these externalities we forget are not just pure conjecture, they are small anecdotes. They can in fact be substantial in three respects: financially, socially or environmentally.

Financially speaking, these externalities may result in massive amounts of money paid for curing after the externality manifested itself, taking corrective actions and preparing the aftermath. In this respect, the 2010 Fukushima example can instance this problem: initially, externalities were estimated around USD 30–40 billion. After two years, because some had been initially forgotten, they amounted up to USD 300 billion, including site depollution, decontamination, power plant neutralisation, research into nuclear safety and renewable energies, as well as people's relocating (buying land and estate back above market value otherwise close to zero, offering similar accommodation on a safe site), and many others (Krooth, Edelson, & Fukurai, 2015).

Socially, thousands, if not millions, of people's lives can be affected by corporate activity, especially when health or security is at play. Additives or preservatives utilised in the food industry, known as these *E* products, may act as endocrine disrupters and thereby alter the functioning of human metabolism or body activity. Potentially, millions of people in the world eating processed food could be affected. If these disruptions result in malformation, malfunctioning or diseases, this may be a dramatic social cost: people whose lives may be shortened or damaged. Of course, this would also have a cost for society in countries where the welfare state looks after vulnerable people (Khetan, 2014; Patisaul & Belcher, 2017).

Environmentally, a report released on 6 May 2019 revealed that one million species are threatened to be extinguished, which would represent the sixth mass annihilation in human history (Brondizio, Settele, Díaz, & Ngo, 2019). According to the experts, the annihilation of species is problematic, since each of them has a contribution to the functioning of the world. If one is missing, the course of the world may be affected. The threat on bees is the most preoccupying because of their pollination activity without which fruits and vegetables would slowly disappear. Less known is the case of wasps who contribute to the functioning of the world by eating the corpses of animal mass graves, averting that these pollute soils.

3.3 Environmental and Social Disclosure

As social and environmental matters have become increasingly important over the past 20 years, methods of accounting for these and reporting them have become central to practitioners' concerns and research advances (Gray, 2010, 2013b; Gray & Laughlin, 2012). Unlike financial reporting, which is driven by compelling norms, social and environmental reporting has not been. There has therefore been room for disputes and competition to gain authority over this area, occurring at two levels. Firstly, some companies have endeavoured to so appear as authorities in CSR reporting practices as to diffusing them to other organisations. Secondly, global initiatives have arisen to articulate standards for social and environmental reporting, whereof Integrated Reporting seems to have emerged as the most popular and applicable.

3.3.1 Corporate Issuance of Best Practices and Associated Standards

This section seeks to demonstrate how the issuance and enforcement of norms regarding socially responsible practices reveals power relationships dominated by large companies considered legitimate authors. Given externalities' contingent nature, reporting is not uniform from one organisation to the other. In the past decade or so a series of initiatives has endeavoured at setting standards for social and environmental reporting: the Global Reporting Initiative (GRI) and the Integrated Reporting project. In the social and environmental reporting field, truth regarding tolerable or commendable practices can reveal such concerns that companies, public authorities and various unions pretending to be legitimate for uttering the truth through norm issuance (Adams, 2015; Dragu & Tiron-Tudor, 2013; Flower, 2014; Frías-Aceituno et al., 2013; Wilmshurst & Frost, 2000).

3.3.1.1 Knowledge and Authorship Authority

When seeking to precede public authorities in defining which socially responsible practices are tolerable or commendable, pioneer organisations position themselves *qua* authors of a truth, be it organisational or political. It is organisational, as it is first addressed to organisation actors and internal stakeholders (employees, stockholders). Such a truth can then be considered social, corporate social responsibility committing also external stakeholders to the organisational project (suppliers, clients, the public, environment). Lastly, this view is political, as it is also addressed to public authorities, which are a major stakeholder, whose role comprises orienting choices and subsequent decisions regarding life together (Bessire & Onnée, 2010; Castelló & Lozano, 2011; Cho & Patten, 2007; Du & Viera Jr., 2012; Laine, 2009; Rayman-Bacchus, 2006; Reimann et al., 2012; Suchman, 1995; Wilmshurst & Frost, 2000).

Companies would consider that they are the most legitimate to produce norms framing professional practices (Elsbach & Sutton, 1992; Jacobs & Jones, 2009; Power, 2003), as auditors (Pasewark, Shockley, & Wilkerson, 1995; Ramirez, 2009a, 2009b) or management accountants do (Chotiyanon, 2018; Chotiyanon & Joannidès de Lautour, 2018). *Qua* major actors of industrial production, they are obviously confronted with eventual everyday needs, possibilities and boundaries. Thence, they would be the sole actors capable of articulating what can or should be done.

French companies have been especially exposed to this legitimacy and authority issue, since standard-setting in France is traditionally the monopoly of the Parliament. Pursuant to this, any time a best practice is identified and presented as a role model, this mostly requires parliamentary work, French authorities being very sceptical *vis-à-vis* what they could perceive as the privatisation of standard-setting (Chiapello & Medjad, 2009). In August 2007, in a conference organised by the French Parliament entitled *Do not shoot the planet*, Veolia's spokesman uttered that "company, economic community, can enrol others to find rational and technical solutions to problems apparently difficult to solve." His declaration was immediately followed by an utterance from Air Liquide's CEO, recalling that business organisations must play an increasingly significant and active role, for their decisions and actions can have worldwide impacts, while laws and national regulations are geographically bounded. Vinci's CEO confirms this statement and emphasises the inevitable association of responsibility and authority: a responsible organisation must be legitimate to issue bylaws enforced at least within its premises, and at best outside. Therefore, the Minister for Ecology and Sustainable Development Affairs admitted that government is only one actor amongst others in charge of managing apparent contradictions in the normal conduct of business operations.

These utterances, produced by listed companies' spokespersons, stress the core issue in truth production: it is accepted as such to the extent that its author is considered having knowledge on the field in which he operates (Foucault, 1975, p. 75). Accordingly, the French government has decided to implement a sustainable development policy through 15 programmes based on companies' expertise. Thereby, ministers acknowledged that only these organisations are legitimate to speak about business operations and devise best practices. Through this shift in governmental attitude towards professional standard-setting, French public authorities granted these business leaders the necessary legitimacy *qua* truth authors in their field. Practical knowledge would give an individual or an institution sufficient authority to define an appropriate conceptual framework. Obviously, practical knowledge can result in conceptual knowledge, *namely* teachable, transferable and examinable knowledge (Bourdieu, 1977, 1990, 1992; Foucault, 1969, 1975).

Knowledge becomes truth only if its author is acknowledged as the sole legitimate to produce it (Foucault, 1975, p. 317), utterance by someone who is not accepted as the author appearing as illegitimate and therefore nil. Legitimacy is obtained through due references to the author, either in the business world—legitimacy *vis-à-vis* peer organisation—or in public discourses—social or political legitimacy—(Suddaby & Greenwood, 2005). The more these harbingers are in number, the greater legitimacy can be: a high number of references to the author's name operate as legitimacy. Conversely, if the uttered truth is not transferred, transformed into actions and enforced, its author cannot be considered legitimate. Hence, the Peugeot-Citroën CEO claimed supreme legitimacy and authorship for his company regarding environmental standards in the conduct of business operations. Henceforth, he has intensified communication on the subject through numerous interventions on TV, in newspapers and practitioner literature. This endeavour was apparently aimed at positioning himself and the company he was directing as authors of best practices and in some sense standards for social and environmental matters.

Once legitimacy is admitted, the author is the sole capable of producing, enriching and altering the truth told. Subsequently, only authorship acknowledgement by his audience enables him to be the truth teller (Ricœur, 1991). In other words, once legitimacy is granted, it is self-perpetuated (Foucault, 1966, 1969). Unsurprisingly, in the French business world and in governmental circles, the Veolia, Air Liquide, Vinci and Peugeot-Citroën CEOs are systematically presented as role models for other companies.

3.3.1.2 Struggles About Authorship Acknowledgement and Authority

Whereas internal legitimacy is not to be doubted, authorship *vis-à-vis* external actors is not guaranteed. Two struggles can be manifested, one against other business organisations (social struggle) and one against pubic authorities (political struggle). Ultimately, CSR standards will apply to other organisations. Governments will also be able to adopt them, which inevitably incurs disputes through competing standards and public realm occupation (Giddens, 1985) in the three realms.

In the social realm, society as a whole is interested in relationships between company and government, as these can ultimately influence work regulations, contract enforcement, environmental norms and so on. Accordingly, all stakeholders could be associated to norm issuance and conceptualisation processes (S. M. Cooper & Owen, 2007; Darnall et al., 2009; Freeman, 2010; Kevin Gibson, 2000b; Humber, 2002; Naszalyi & Slama, 2016; Orij, 2010). For instance, regarding employment and work conditions, government and trade unions could be participating in policy definition. Arguably, company knows its employment capacity as well as most of its constraints, whereas trade unions represent employees, who are first concerned by employment policies. Lastly, public authorities can consider that they are legitimate, as they are *in fine* solicited for social transfers and policies (Esping-Andersen, 1999).

In such a situation, although three contestants are involved, the relationship is only dual. Foucault (1975) recalls that authority acknowledgement is not made by peers, but by those whom it can be opposed (p. 300). If the company is considered legitimate, it will be able to impose its truth both to public authorities and to trade unions. Hence, one can easily imagine that their practices would be driven by capital accumulation and profit seeking (Chiapello, 2009). Conversely, if unions were considered legitimate, their perceptions would be likely to orient organisational policy towards employee welfare (Gumbrell-McCormick & Hyman, 2013; Ogden & Bougen, 1985; Owen & Lloyd, 1985). Lastly, admitting that public authorities are legitimate will probably result in policies securing the capital base of public investments through employment protection, as workers would pay more for social welfare than they would receive (Hood & Scott, 1996).

Political issues in the relationship can also incur struggles about legitimacy involving company and public authorities. For instance, Vinci calls for a simplification of public contracting justified by their numerous initiatives to protect employment and environment. The argument upholding legitimacy is that regulations compelling and regulations framing practices directly impact on its operations. Symmetrically, public authorities, through the administration of life together, can count on knowledge legitimating their intervention *qua* authors. Unsurprisingly, struggles about legitimacy would arise, public authorities claiming political and social knowledge, whereas companies stress practical knowledge. Tension stems from scattering of conceptual and practical knowledge (Bourdieu, 1977).

Struggles about legitimacy and subsequent authorship and authority acknowledgement can result in a twofold issue. Either, one of both actors can be acknowledged as author at the expense of the other, or none of them will be legitimate enough to dominate the other and subsequently conceive of CSR practices. In the latter case, the relationship could result in a dual legitimacy, *namely* acknowledgement of co-authorship and co-authority through partnerships and mutual influences.

3.3.2 *Standard-Setting as Political Struggle: Integrated Reporting Wins*

Arguably, disclosing organisations have a role to play in the determining of best social and environmental reporting, especially because such matters are contingent upon their activity. Best practices pose no particular problems when disclosure is entirely voluntary: home-made standards can apply to reveal what is critical to the organisation. When it comes to standard-setting, defining what matters and how to account for it and report reveals political struggles and actors' lobbying activism (Reuter & Messner, 2015).

3.3.2.1 Authorship as Predication

Authorship acknowledgement leads the actor to produce knowledge applicable as one worth truth (Foucault, 1972, pp. 502–503). Accordingly, power-knowledge relationships should in no way be analysed from the viewpoint of a free actor *vis-à-vis* the power relationship; rather, knowledgeable actor, topics and knowledge practicalities are fundamental implications of the relationship, authorship resulting in imposing ways of transmitting, teaching and applying them. Accordingly, a form of power is delivered and enabled norm issuance and standardisation. Thus far, numerous initiatives have endeavoured at being recognised as truth authors on social environmental reporting, such as the Global Reporting Initiative, although forgotten nowadays. The initiative that seems to have been accepted as a possible standard-setting authority is the International Integrated Reporting Council—the IIRC—(Adams, 2015; de Villiers et al., 2014; Dragu & Tiron-Tudor, 2013; Flower, 2014; Reuter & Messner, 2015).

The authors utter a (contingent) truth accepted as knowledge: "*we have all the truth, but under predictive and prophetic forms characterising both the oracle and the fortune-teller*" (Foucault, 1975, p. 430). Because, the author was granted legitimacy for truth production, this latter becomes normative. The author is the sole capable of issuing a practice theory imposing itself to all other actors involved in the practice. If the enterprise was considered legitimate, it is then likely to be granted authority to produce norms regarding socially responsible practices, these latter imposing themselves to all organisations claiming to practice social responsibility, which includes public authorities. The IIRC seems to have been accepted as such, namely for two reasons. The first reason lies in its consultative nature, whereby preparers and users of disclosure have been involved in designing the Integrated Reporting framework. The second reason is that the Integrated Reporting Framework is by no means constraining but appears as a philosophy consisting of managing in a holistic way (de Villiers et al., 2014; Reuter & Messner, 2015). Integrated Reporting is associated with the idea that the business model and processes are aimed at creating value for all stakeholders. Accordingly, these stakeholders and this value need to be acknowledged as contingent upon organisational activity (de Villiers et al., 2014; Higgins et al., 2014). What is especially interesting with the case of Integrated Reporting, as opposed to other initiatives, which failed, is precisely its non-constraining essence. It is by no means a formal reporting standard applying as norm to be enforced. Parliaments could be therefore bypassed and the development of this new management and reporting philosophy be transferred to mere private actors.

Integrated Reporting's predictive nature makes it drive conduct, while authorship identification protects it from contests. Most potential preparers and users can recognise themselves in the best practices and philosophy Integrated Reporting encourages. Its foundational truth and authority lies in its constitution: the 2011 discussion paper through which the bases were set (IIRC, 2011). Once produced, a standard or reference guide can be transmitted through due *quotations* (see Foucault, 1975, p. 430) and applied. In the Integrated Reporting case, the 2011 report is explicitly quoted and referenced by those companies engaged in pertinent social and environmental disclosure (Adams, 2015; Dragu & Tiron-Tudor, 2013; Higgins et al., 2014). These due quotations thereby enhance the aura of the framework or norm author (see Weber, 1922, p. 1142). The author defines, not only norm content, but also allowed interpretations and implied tolerated practices. With Integrated Reporting, what is remarkable is that interpretation is very broad and open. What may make it successful is the fact that it is compatible with most contingent interpretation, since it is a management and reporting philosophy rather than a rigid standard (Frías-Aceituno et al., 2013; García-Sánchez, Rodríguez-Ariza, & Frías-Aceituno, 2013). Thereby, the IIRC sets open boundaries for the CSR field, opening room for appropriation reversely what is not.

3.3.2.2 Integrated Reporting: From a Promise to a Translation Process

Integrated Reporting's core philosophy is simple and rests upon the idea that corporate reporting should be viewed as a holistic practice aimed at showing the value created for all stakeholders with whom the organisation interacts. It is preparers' duty to identify these pertinent stakeholders and the value they expect. Integrated management and Integrated Reporting rest upon seven principles with infinite declensions (IIRC, 2011):

- Strategic priorities and future orientations
- Information connectedness and complementarity across stakeholders
- Relationships with stakeholders
- Selectivity of relevant information only
- Concision and intelligibility of information
- Reliability and comprehensiveness of reporting
- Consistency and comparability of data

Within this framework, disclosing organisations can choose what they view as pertinent and can report it in a way they deem relevant for their stakeholders. Integrated Reporting can therefore be accommodated within any legal or cultural system (Frías-Aceituno et al., 2013; García-Sánchez et al., 2013). Contents per se are expected to follow some common-sense non-compelling principles:

- Presentation of the organisation and its ecosystem
- Presentation of organisational governance structures
- Presentation of corporate business model
- Risks and opportunities
- Strategic goal and resources allocation
- Corporate performance
- Perspectives and future prospects
- Presentation methodology

Even though some argue that Integrated Reporting has failed to enrol organisations within its philosophy (Flower, 2014), it seems that it remains very promising and has real potential to attract preparers and users of disclosed information (Adams, 2015; de Villiers et al., 2014). Like any other innovation, Integrated Reporting takes a promise: disclose holistic and pertinent information useful to all stakeholders. As such, it addresses a dual accounting problem: the reconciliation of management accounting (including social and environmental accounting) and financial reporting on one hand, and pertinence for all readers on the other. This promise is that the whole value created by the organisation can be disclosed, detailed and discussed in simple terms and with simple figures in one single document (Adams, 2015; de Villiers et al., 2014).

What makes Integrated Reporting especially powerful and promising is that its logic can be easily understood and appropriated. Preparers on one hand can identify for what they need to account, what they need to disclose and how they can do this. For their part, users can see what makes sense to them and better understand the organisation's whence and whither. What is especially interesting in the case of Integrated Reporting is the fact that it does not have any underlying technology and is not presented as a technical solution. In some sense, Integrated Reporting can be perceived as a management innovation similar to the Balanced Scorecard or Beyond Budgeting, in contrast to the GP method of fixed cost allocation. Having no technical promise but presenting itself as a philosophy, this approach can only be open and adaptive, thereby subject to appropriation (Alcouffe et al., 2008).

As a management accounting innovation, Integrated Reporting can be successful if it is eventually promoted by those who believe in it can keep its promise: users and preparers. To some extent, the spread of Integrated Reporting could follow the same path as Activity-Based Costing if professionals, organisation representatives and stakeholder representatives speak for it (Alcouffe et al., 2008). These will act as spokespersons for Integrated Reporting. To some extent, the development and spread of Integrated Reporting will follow a translation process, as Activity-Based Costing has done (Alcouffe et al., 2008).

In order to be widely adopted, Integrated Reporting needs to form a network of actors and allies, that is, a locus where debates are organised and conducted (Latour, 1987, 2005). In this respect, debates started in 2011 with the IIRC launched its international consultation aimed at issuing a framework (Reuter & Messner, 2015). These preliminary discussions revealed the interests and matters of concern for the community at a given point in time: improve reporting in such a way that all stakeholders and expected value be taken into consideration. The framework itself, acting as an open-ended approach, raises new concerns and questions (Frías-Aceituno et al., 2013; García-Sánchez et al., 2013; Higgins et al., 2014; Rensburg & Botha, 2014). On an ongoing basis, new matters of concern and of interest arise, altering the initial problem (Latour, 2004).

Gradually, a *translation* process is started whereby actors rephrase the terms of the discussion; they rename objects and model new artefacts that will be involved in further controversies. This process results in matters of interest becoming matters of concern (Latour, 2005). After the Integrated Reporting framework was issued, new questions related to its compatibility with different legal and cultural systems arose (Frías-Aceituno et al., 2013; García-Sánchez et al., 2013). Over time, it is more than plausible that new questions arise as to possible ways of making it systematic and issue an enforceable standard in order to compare similar organisations, as with any form of reporting (Jana Andrew & Cortese, 2013).

Translation usually comprises four *moments* (Callon, 1985). Firstly, *problematisation* is where a gap in the knowledge is identified and presented as a matter of concern for a community (Latour, 2004). Secondly comes *interessement*, where community members understand why this issue is worthy of investigation (Callon & Rabeharisoa, 2008). Thirdly, *mobilisation* occurs with the engagement of other community actors (Latour, 2008). Once community members appropriate the problem, disseminate it and enlist new allies, the fourth and last moment of *enrolment* is at work (Callon & Rabeharisoa, 2008). Now, the community can be considered relatively stable, with the issues and matters of concern broadly accepted and forming a "black box". Thereby the network that has commenced can have provisory boundaries (Latour, 1994). At this juncture, in 2019, Integrated Reporting seems to attract more and more scholars, consultants and organisations increasingly engaging in more practical discussions regarding materiality, contents and modes of reporting (Green & Cheng, 2019; Pavlopoulos, Magnis, & Iatridiis, 2019; Skouloudis, Malesios, & Dimitrakopoulos, 2019).

3.3.2.3 Rise of a Need for a Reporting Solution

A problematic situation has confronted the business world: reporting for holistic performance, including externalities (IIRC, 2011). Seemingly, according to research, this need has not been subject for much discussion, rather being unanimously acknowledged (Adams, 2015; de Villiers et al., 2014; Reuter & Messner, 2015). A collective strategy for responding to the *posed* and *qualified* problem is adopted on the spot through the organisation of a large consultation in 2011. As the problem posed related neither to economy nor to efficiency, it is no surprise that the expected solution be outside the remit of mere financial reporting. Thereby, mechanisms of a strict convergence of goals towards the common good are brought to light: a collective strategy can be followed; hence, all stakeholders find themselves involved and see their matters of concern taken into consideration (value creation for them). As a result, all these actors unambiguously could recognise themselves (de Haas & Algera, 2002). The problem could be posed and qualified, precisely because conventional reporting failed to fulfil all these stakeholders' needs. The problem *posed* was that issuing standards compelling organisations to one form of reporting would be rejected, precisely because they would not enable to take organisation specificities into consideration. Rather than standards, what seemed to be acceptable was a framework (as contrary to the Global Reporting Initiative, interrupted as soon as members pretended to issue reporting standards).

It was not just the problem itself that triggered the need for an integrated reporting system as its surface is just a technicality. Rather, discussions about the shape of this framework and lobbying from various actors revealed the need for so *qualifying* the problem as to identify the nature of the solution to be found (Reuter & Messner, 2015). As with any other apparently technical problem, although the problem *posed* seemed to be financial, the nature of the solution thither may address operations, organisation, HR, logistics or anything else at the core of organisational identity (Latour, 2009). Interestingly, early discussions did not reveal a particular need for an immediate technical solution but for an agreement on a framework and a philosophy (Reuter & Messner, 2015). Seemingly, it seems that Integrated Reporting has interested organisations, because discussions did not address its technical merits but focused on its organisational and managerial effects. If consequences remain relatively predictable and controllable, this reporting philosophy technology was deemed acceptable.

However, it is probable that discussions around Integrated Reporting be far from terminated, since this technology is still in its infancy and will certainly raise further questions regarding the measurement of externalities and possible standards for some recurring items, as with fixed costs in Activity-Based Costing (Alcouffe et al., 2008). This intuition can be confirmed by the fact that an accounting technology and a management philosophy are never a final product. Because they are open, they are more than likely to evolve over time and be fine-tuned, as new actors appropriate them (Joannidès, Jaumier, & Hoque, 2015). Once its foundations are stabilised, it can be enriched with new technologies responding to new needs (How & Alawattage, 2012). It therefore seems that the diffusion of Integrated Reporting will be an incremental and non-linear process made of trials and errors (de Villiers et al., 2014).

3.4 Conclusion

Growing concerns relating to human rights, gender equality and environmental issues such as climate change and global warming have shed light on organisations' responsibility outside their mere economic role. Concerns regarding corporate social responsibility and sustainable development have resulted in the public demanding accounts of good social and environment conduct. This is how companies have first voluntarily disclosed on these issues since the early 2000s, until social and environmental reporting has become compulsory in numerous countries. As these new concerns arose, neoclassical microeconomics has seemingly reached its limits. A company's objective is not just to generate surpluses for its stockholders. Welfare economics has enriched this traditional view, considering that any externalities generated from corporate activity must be accounted for and disclosed. It has been assumed an organisation does not function in isolation from the rest of the world but interacts with it and affects its course.

Social and environmental disclosure undoubtedly raises questions regarding the identifying and measuring of these externalities. Whilst it is often assumed that all organisations are confronted with the same issues it does seem that the associated ethical dilemmas differ from one to the other. Seemingly, as with conventional management accounting, what matters is to account for these externalities that count in a way that counts. Therefore, it is impossible to realistically consider setting standards for such measurements and reports. If any company supra-organisational institution pretends to issue standards, the politics behind these is bound to annihilate social and environmental reporting's purpose.

In 2019, as the Integrated Reporting initiative is gaining wider popularity around the world, new research challenges shall be on the identification of realistic, comprehensive and intelligible measures for most of these externalities. Whilst it is not realistic that all organisations would report on social and environmental matters in a uniform way, it would be a challenge that the same externality be measured in similar terms across organisations. How such standards are issued and enforced is certainly social and environmental accounting research's next challenge.

Bibliography

Abarca, J. F., & Casiccia, C. C. (2002). Skin cancer and ultraviolet-B radiation under the Antarctic ozone hole: Southern Chile, 1987–2000. *Photodermatology, Photoimmunology & Photomedicine, 18*(6), 294–302.

Abdel-Maksoud, A., Cerbioni, F., Ricceri, F., & Velayutham, S. (2010). Employee morale, non-financial performance measures, deployment of innovative managerial practices and shop-floor involvement in Italian manufacturing firms. *The British Accounting Review, 42*(1), 36–55. https://doi.org/10.1016/j.bar.2010.01.002

Abeysekera, I. (2008). Intellectual capital practices of firms and the commodification of labour. *Accounting, Auditing & Accountability Journal, 21*(1), 36–48.

Adams, C. A. (2015). The International Integrated Reporting Council: A call to action. *Critical Perspectives on Accounting, 27*(1), 23–28.

Aerts, W., & Cormier, D. (2009). Media legitimacy and corporate environmental communication. *Accounting, Organizations and Society, 34*(1), 1–27.

Ahmad, Z. Z. (2012). Women, business and the law: Measuring legal gender parity for entrepreneurs and workers. *Equality, Diversity and Inclusion: An International Journal, 31*(7), 681–689.

Ahrens, T. (1996). Styles of accountability. *Accounting, Organizations and Society, 21*(2–3), 139–173.

Ahrens, T., & Chapman, C. S. (2002). The structuration of legitimate performance measures and management: Day-to-day contests of accountability in a U.K. restaurant chain. *Management Accounting Research, 13*(2), 151–171.

Ahrens, T., & Chapman, C. S. (2007). Management accounting as practice. *Accounting, Organizations and Society, 32*(1–2), 1–27.

Ahrens, T., & Mollona, M. (2007). Organisational control as cultural practice—A shop floor ethnography of a Sheffield steel mill. *Accounting, Organizations and Society, 32*(4–5), 305–331.

Alawattage, C. (2011). The calculative reproduction of social structures—The field of gem mining in Sri Lanka. *Critical Perspectives on Accounting, 22*(1), 1–19. https://doi.org/10.1016/j.cpa.2010.10.001

Alcouffe, S., Berland, N., & Levant, Y. (2008). Actor-networks and the diffusion of management accounting innovations: A comparative study. *Management Accounting Research, 19*(1), 1–17.

Andrew, J., & Cortese, C. (2011). Accounting for climate change and the self-regulation of carbon disclosures. *Accounting Forum, 35*(3), 130–138. https://doi.org/10.1016/j.accfor.2011.06.006

Andrew, J., & Cortese, C. (2013). Free market environmentalism and the neoliberal project: The case of the Climate Disclosure Standards Board. *Critical Perspectives on Accounting, 24*(6), 397–409.

Annisette, M. (2000). Imperialism and the professions: The education and certification of accountants in Trinidad and Tobago. *Accounting, Organizations and Society, 25*(7), 631–659.

Annisette, M. (2003). The colour of accountancy: Examining the salience of race in a professionalisation project. *Accounting, Organizations and Society, 28*(7–8), 639–674.

Badiou, A. (2006). The factory as event site: Why should the worker be a reference in our vision of politics?, in PRELOM. *Journal of Images and Politics, 8*, 171–176.

Badiou, A. (2012). *Philosophy for militants (Pocket communism)*. London: Verso.

Badiou, A., & Gauchet, M. (2016). *What is to be done? A dialogue on communism, capitalism, and the future of democracy*. London: Polity Press.

Baldwin, A. A., Lightbody, M., Brown, C. E., & Trinkle, B. S. (2012). Twenty years of minority PhDs in accounting: Signs of successes and segregation. *Critical Perspectives on Accounting, 23*(4–5), 298–311.

Banks, G., Pollack, J., Bochantin, J., Kirkman, B., Whelpley, C., & O'Boyle, E. (2016). Management's science-practice gap a grand challenge for all stakeholders. *Academy of Management Journal*. https://doi.org/10.5465/amj.2015.0728

Baskerville, R. F., Jacobs, K., Joannidès de Lautour, V., & Sissons, J. (2016). Ethnicity as inclusion and exclusion: Drawing on concept and practice in accounting research. *Accounting, Auditing & Accountability Journal, 29*(8), 1262–1269. https://doi.org/10.1108/AAAJ-07-2016-2643

Bebbington, J., & Gray, R. (2001). An account of sustainability: Failure, success and a reconceptualization. *Critical Perspectives on Accounting, 12*(5), 557–588.

Bernardi, R. A., Bean, D. F., & Weippert, K. M. (2005). Minority membership on boards of directors: The case for requiring pictures of boards in annual reports. *Critical Perspectives on Accounting, 16*(8), 1019–1033.

Bessire, D., & Onnée, S. (2010). Assessing corporate social performance: Strategies of legitimation and conflicting ideologies. *Critical Perspectives on Accounting, 21*(6), 445–467.

Betzer, A., Doumet, M., & Rinne, U. (2013). How policy changes affect shareholder wealth: The case of the Fukushima Daiichi nuclear disaster. *Applied Economics Letters, 20*(8), 799–803.

Black, S., Briggs, S., & Keogh, W. (2001). Service quality performance measurement in public/private sectors. *Managerial Auditing Journal, 16*(7), 400–405.

Blechman, M., Chari, A., & Hasan, R. (2012). Human rights are the rights of the infinite: An interview with Alain Badiou. *Historical Materialism, 20*(4), 162–186.

Bonache, J., Sanchez, J., & Zárraga-Oberty, C. (2009). The interaction of expatriate pay differential and expatriate inputs on host country nationals' pay unfairness. *The International Journal of Human Resource Management, 20*(10), 2135–2149.

Bourdieu, P. (1977). *Outline of a theory of practice*. Cambridge: Cambridge University Press.

Bourdieu, P. (1990). *La logique de la pratique*. Paris: Seuil.

Bourdieu, P. (1992). *Les règles de l'art*. Paris: Seuil.

Boyce, G. (2018). Accounting, ethics and human existence: Lightly unbearable, heavily kitsch. *Critical Perspectives on Accounting, 25*(3), 97–109.

Broadbent, J., Dietrich, M., & Laughlin, R. (1996). The development of principal-agent, contracting and accountability relationships in the public sector: Conceptual and cultural problems. *Critical Perspectives on Accounting, 7*(3), 259–284.

Broadbent, J., & Kirkham, L. (2008). Glass ceilings, glass cliffs or new worlds?: Revisiting gender and accounting. *Accounting, Auditing & Accountability Journal, 21*(4), 465–473.

Brondizio, E. S., Settele, J., Díaz, S., & Ngo, H. T. (2019). Global assessment report on biodiversity and ecosystem services. In IPBES (Ed.), *Global assessment report*. New York: United Nations Organisation.

Busco, C., & Quattrone, P. (2014). Exploring how the balanced scorecard engages and unfolds: Articulating the visual power of accounting inscriptions. *Contemporary Accounting Research, 32*(3), 1236–1262.

Busco, C., & Quattrone, P. (2018). Performing business and social innovation through accounting inscriptions: An introduction. *Accounting, Organizations and Society*. https://doi.org/10.1016/j.aos.2018.03.002

Callon, M. (1985). Éléments pour une sociologie de la traduction: la domestication des coquilles St-Jacques et des marins pêcheurs dans la baie de St. Brieuc. *L'Année Sociologique, 36*, 169–208.

Callon, M. (2009). Civilizing markets: Carbon trading between in vitro and in vivo experiments. *Accounting, Organizations and Society, 34*(3–4), 535–548.

Callon, M., & Rabeharisoa, V. (2008). The growing engagement of emergent concerned groups in political and economic life: Lessons from the French Association of neuromuscular disease patients. *Science Technology Human Values, 33*, 230–261.

Careira, F., Aguiar, C., Onça, F., & Monzoni, M. (2017). The celsius game: An experiential activity on management education simulating the complex challenges for the two-degree climate change target. *The International Journal of Management Education, 15*(2), 350–361.

Castelló, I., & Lozano, J. M. (2011). Searching for new forms of legitimacy through corporate responsibility rhetoric. *Journal of Business Ethics, 100*, 11–29.

Chabbal, J. (2005). Le risque invisible—la non-émergence d'un problème public. *Politix, 70*(2), 169–195.

Chabrak, N., Craig, R., & Daidji, N. (2016). Financialization and the employee suicide crisis at France telecom. *Journal of Business Ethics, 139*(3), 501–515.

Chan, E. Y. (2018). Climate change is the world's greatest threat—In Celsius or Fahrenheit? *Journal of Environmental Psychology, 60*(Dec.), 21–26.

Chava, S. (2014). Environmental externalities and cost of capital. *Management Science, 60*(9), iv–vi.

Chetty, K. R. (2011). From responsibility to accountability—Social accounting, human rights and Scotland. *Critical Perspectives on Accounting, 22*(8), 759–761.

Chiapello, E. (2009). *La critique écologique et la nouvelle nébuleuse réformatrice du Capitalisme*. Paper presented at the IIIè congrès de l'Association Française de Sociologie, Paris.

Chiapello, E., & Medjad, K. (2009). An unprecedented privatisation of mandatory standard-setting: The case of European accounting policy. *Critical Perspectives on Accounting, 20*(4), 448–468. https://doi.org/10.1016/j.cpa.2008.09.002

Chiew, F. H. S., Zhou, S. L., & McMahon, S. L. (2003). Use of seasonal streamflow forecasts in water resources management. *Journal of Hydrology, 270*(1–2), 135–144.

Cho, C. H. (2009). Legitimation strategies used in response to environmental disaster: A French case study of Total SA's Erika and AZF incidents. *European Accounting Review, 18*(1), 33–62.

Cho, C. H., Guidry, R. P., Hageman, A. M., & Patten, D. M. (2012). Do actions speak louder than words? An empirical investigation of corporate environmental reputation. *Accounting, Organizations and Society, 37*(1), 14–25. https://doi.org/10.1016/j.aos.2011.12.001

Cho, C. H., & Patten, D. M. (2007). The role of environmental disclosures as tools of legitimacy: A research note. *Accounting, Organizations and Society, 32*(7–8), 639–647.

Cho, C. H., & Patten, D. M. (2013). Green accounting: Reflections from a CSR and environmental disclosure perspective. *Critical Perspectives on Accounting, 24*(6), 443–447. https://doi.org/10.1016/j.cpa.2013.04.003

Cho, C. H., Roberts, R. W., & Patten, D. M. (2010). The language of US corporate environmental disclosure. *Accounting, Organizations and Society, 35*(4), 431–443.

Chotiyanon, P. (2018). *Becoming a business partner—A lifelong self-orienting process*. Grenoble: DBA, Grenoble École de Management.

Chotiyanon, P., & Joannidès de Lautour, V. (2018). *The changing role of the management accountants—Becoming a business partner*. London: Palgrave Macmillan.

Cleeren, K., Dekimpe, M., & Van Heerde, H. J. (2017). Marketing research on product-harm crises: A review, managerial implications, and an agenda for future research. *Journal of the Academy of Marketing Science, 45*(5), 593–615.

Coetzee, C. M., & van Staden, C. J. (2011). Disclosure responses to mining accidents: South African evidence. *Accounting Forum, 35*(4), 232–246. https://doi.org/10.1016/j.accfor.2011.06.001

Cohen, M. (2019). *The fight against Monsanto's Roundup: The politics of pesticides*. New York: Skyhorse.

Col, B., & Patel, S. (2016). Going to haven? Corporate social responsibility and tax avoidance. [journal article]. *Journal of Business Ethics*. https://doi.org/10.1007/s10551-016-3393-2.

Cole, S. E. (2018). *Fallout: The shocking true story of suffering, corporate greed, and a young lawyer's fight for justice*. New York: 2605 Media LLC.
Collier, P. M. (2005). Governance and the quasi-public organization: A case study of social housing. *Critical Perspectives on Accounting, 16*(7), 929–949.
Cooper, C., Coulson, A., & Taylor, P. (2011). Accounting for human rights: Doxic health and safety practices—The accounting lesson from ICL. *Critical Perspectives on Accounting, 22*(8), 738–758. https://doi.org/10.1016/j.cpa.2011.07.001
Cooper, C., Taylor, P., Smith, N., & Catchpowle, L. (2005). A discussion of the political potential of social accounting. *Critical Perspectives on Accounting, 16*(7), 951–974.
Cooper, S. M., & Owen, D. L. (2007). Corporate social reporting and stakeholder accountability: The missing link. *Accounting, Organizations and Society, 32*(7–8), 649–667.
Courtney, R., Marnoch, G., & Williamson, A. (2009). Strategic planning and performance: An exploratory study of housing associations in Northern Ireland. *Financial Accountability & Management, 25*(1), 56–78.
Cragg, W. (2000). Human rights and business ethics: Fashioning a new social contract. *Journal of Business Ethics, 27*, 205–214.
Cukston, T. (2013). Bringing tropical forest biodiversity conservation into financial accounting calculation. *Accounting, Auditing & Accountability Journal, 26*(5), 688–714.
Dambrin, C., & Lambert, C. (2008). Mothering or auditing? The case of two Big Four in France. *Accounting, Auditing & Accountability Journal, 21*(4), 474–506.
Dambrin, C., & Lambert, C. (2012). Who is she and who are we? A reflexive journey in research into the rarity of women in the highest ranks of accountancy. *Critical Perspectives on Accounting, 23*(1), 1–16. https://doi.org/10.1016/j.cpa.2011.06.006
Dankbaar, B. (1997). Lean production: Denial, confirmation or extension of sociotechnical systems design? *Human Relations, 50*(5), 567–583.
Dann, G., & Haddow, N. (2008). Just doing business of doing just business: Google, Microsoft, Yahoo! and the business of censoring Chian's Internet. *Journal of Business Ethics, 79*, 219–234.
Darnall, N., Seol, I., & Sarkis, J. (2009). Perceived stakeholder influences and organizations' use of environmental audits. *Accounting, Organizations and Society, 34*(2), 170–187.
Daum, J. (2002). *Intangible assets and value creation*. London: Wiley.
Day, N. E. (1994). Designing and management compensation and benefits programs. In R. D. Herman (Ed.), *The Jossey-Bass handbook of nonprofit leadership and management* (pp. 557–590). San Francisco: Jossey-Bass Publishers.
de Haas, M., & Algera, J. A. (2002). Demonstrating the effect of the participative dialogue: Participation in designing the management control system. *Management Accounting Research, 13*(1), 41–69.

de Villiers, C., Rinaldi, L., & Unerman, J. (2014). Integrated reporting: Insights, gaps and an agenda for future research. *Accounting, Auditing & Accountability Journal, 27*(7), 1042–1067.

De Waal, A., & Orcotoma-Escarente, G. (2011). Does the application of corporate social responsibility support a high performance organisation in achieving better results? The case of mining multinationals in Peru. *International Journal of Sustainable Strategic Management, 3*(1), 33–49.

Degli Antoni, G., & Marzetti, G. V. (2019). Recycling and waste generation: An estimate of the source reduction effect of recycling programs. *Ecological Economics, 161*, 321–329.

Déjean, F., & Martinez, I. (2009). Environmental disclosure and the cost of equity: The French case. *Accounting in Europe, 6*(1), 57–80.

del Carmen Triana, M., Wagstaff, M. F., & Kim, K. (2012). That's not fair! How personal value for diversity influences reactions to the perceived discriminatory treatment of minorities. *Journal of Business Ethics, 111*, 211–218.

Dragu, I.-M., & Tiron-Tudor, A. (2013). The integrated reporting initiative from an institutional perspective: Emergent factors. *Procedia—Social and Behavioral Sciences, 92*, 275–279. https://doi.org/10.1016/j.sbspro.2013.08.672

Du, S., & Viera, E. T., Jr. (2012). Striving for legitimacy through corporate social responsibility: Insights from oil companies. *Journal of Business Ethics, 110*(4), 413–427.

Efferin, S. (2002). *Management control system, culture, and ethnicity: A case of Chinese Indones*. PhD, University of Manchester, Manchester.

Elsbach, K. D., & Sutton, R. I. (1992). Acquiring organizational legitimacy through illegitimate actions: A marriage of institutional and impression management theories. *Academy of Management Journal, 35*(4), 699–738. https://doi.org/10.2307/256313

Engels, A. (2009). The European Emissions Trading Scheme: An exploratory study of how companies learn to account for carbon. *Accounting, Organizations and Society, 34*(3–4), 488–498.

Esping-Andersen, G. (1999). *Social foundations of postindustrial economies*. Oxford: Oxford University Press.

Ezzamel, M., & Willmott, H. (1993). Corporate governance and financial accountability in the UK public sector. *Accounting, Auditing & Accountability Journal, 6*(3), 109–132.

Fama, E., & Jensen, M. (1983a). Agency problems and residual claims. *Journal of Law and Economics, 26*(2), 327–349.

Fama, E., & Jensen, M. (1983b). Separation of ownership and control. *Journal of Law and Economics, 262*, 301–325.

Fan, J., Yung, K.-C., & Pecht, M. (2015). Predicting long-term lumen maintenance life of LED light sources using a particle filter-based prognostic approach. *Expert Systems with Applications, 42*(5), 2411–2420.

Farndale, E., Scullion, H., & Sparrow, P. (2010). The role of the corporate HR function in global talent management. *Journal of World Business, 45*(2), 161–168.
Fearfull, A., & Kamenou, N. (2006). How do you account for it?: A critical exploration of career opportunities for and experiences of ethnic minority women. *Critical Perspectives on Accounting, 17*(7), 883–901.
Fleischman, R. K., Oldroyd, D., & Tyson, T. N. (2011). The efficacy/inefficacy of accounting in controlling labour during the transition from slavery in the United Stated and British West Indies. *Accounting, Auditing & Accountability Journal, 24*(6), 718–750.
Flower, J. (2014). The International Integrated Reporting Council: A story of failure. *Critical Perspectives on Accounting, 27*(1), 1–17.
Foucault, M. (1966). *Les mots et les choses.* Paris: Gallimard.
Foucault, M. (1969). *L'archéologie du savoir.* Paris: Gallimard.
Foucault, M. (1972). *History of madness.* London: Routledge.
Foucault, M. (1975). *Surveiller et punir.* Paris: Gallimard.
Frankental, P. (2011). No accounting for human rights. *Critical Perspectives on Accounting, 22*(8), 762–764.
Freeman, R. E. (2010). *Stakeholder theory: The state of the art.* Cambridge: Cambridge University Press.
Frías-Aceituno, J. V., Rodríguez-Ariza, L., & García-Sánchez, I. M. (2013). Is integrated reporting determined by a country's legal system? An exploratory study. *Journal of Cleaner Production, 44*, 45–55. https://doi.org/10.1016/j.jclepro.2012.12.006
Frigessi di Rattalma, M. (2019). *The Dieselgate—A legal perspective.* London: Springer.
García-Sánchez, I.-M., Rodríguez-Ariza, L., & Frías-Aceituno, J.-V. (2013). The cultural system and integrated reporting. *International Business Review, 22*(5), 828–838. https://doi.org/10.1016/j.ibusrev.2013.01.007
Gémes, A. (2015). *New business models for electric utility companies: An imperative for change.* Berlin: AV Akademikerverlag.
Gibson, K. (2000a). Accounting as a tool for Aboriginal dispossession: Then and now. *Accounting, Auditing & Accountability Journal, 13*(3), 289–306.
Gibson, K. (2000b). The moral basis of stakeholder theory. *Journal of Business Ethics, 26*, 245–257.
Giddens, A. (1985). *The constitution of society.* London: Verso.
Giesy, J. G., Dobson, D., & Solomon, K. R. (2000). Ecotoxicological risk assessment for Roundup® herbicide. In G. W. Ware (Ed.), *Reviews of environmental contamination and toxicology* (Vol. 167, pp. 35–120). New York: Springer.
Goddard, A., & Assad, M. J. (2006). Accounting and navigating legitimacy in Tanzanian NGOs. *Accounting, Auditing & Accountability Journal, 19*(3), 377–404.
Graafland, J. J. (2008). Sourcing ethics in the textile sector: The case of C&A. *Business Ethics: A European Review, 11*(3), 282–294.

Gray, R. (1992). Accounting and environmentalism: An exploration of the challenge of gently accounting for accountability, transparency and sustainability. *Accounting, Organizations and Society, 17*(5), 399–425.

Gray, R. (2002a). Of messiness, systems and sustainability: Towards a more social and environmental finance and accounting. *The British Accounting Review, 34*(4), 357–386.

Gray, R. (2002b). The social accounting project and accounting organizations and society privileging engagement, imaginings, new accountings and pragmatism over critique? *Accounting, Organizations and Society, 27*(7), 687–708.

Gray, R. (2006). Social, environmental and sustainability reporting and organisational value creation?: Whose value? Whose creation? *Accounting, Auditing & Accountability Journal, 19*(6), 793–819.

Gray, R. (2010). Is accounting for sustainability actually accounting for sustainability…and how would we know? An exploration of narratives of organisations and the planet. *Accounting, Organizations and Society, 35*(1), 47–62.

Gray, R. (2013a). Back to basics: What do we mean by environmental (and social) accounting and what is it for?—A reaction to Thornton. *Critical Perspectives on Accounting, 24*(6), 459–468.

Gray, R. (2013b). Back to basics: What do we mean by environmental (and social) accounting and what is it for?—A reaction to Thornton. *Critical Perspectives on Accounting, 24*(6), 459–468. https://doi.org/10.1016/j.cpa.2013.04.005

Gray, R. (2010). Is accounting for sustainability actually accounting for sustainability…and how would we know? An exploration of narratives of organisations and the planet. *Accounting, Organizations and Society, 35*(1), 47–62.

Gray, R., Bebbington, J., & Collison, D. (2006). NGOs, civil society and accountability: Making the people accountable to capital. *Accounting, Auditing & Accountability Journal, 19*(3), 319–348.

Gray, R., & Collison, D. (2002). Can't see the wood for the trees, can't see the trees for the numbers? Accounting education, sustainability and the public interest. *Critical Perspectives on Accounting, 13*(5–6), 797–836.

Gray, R., Dey, C., Owen, D., Evans, R., & Zadek, S. (1997). Struggling with the praxis of social accounting: Stakeholders, accountability, audits and procedures. *Accounting, Auditing & Accountability Journal, 10*(3), 325–364.

Gray, R., & Gray, S. J. (2011). Accountability and human rights: A tentative exploration and a commentary. *Critical Perspectives on Accounting, 22*(8), 781–789.

Gray, R., Kouhy, R., & Lavers, S. (1995). Corporate social and environmental disclosure—A review from the literature and a longitudinal study of the UK disclosure. *Accounting, Auditing & Accountability Journal, 8*(2), 47–77.

Gray, R., & Laughlin, R. (2012). It was 20 years ago today Sgt Pepper, Accounting, Auditing & Accountability Journal, green accounting and the Blue Meanies. *Accounting, Auditing & Accountability Journal, 25*(2), 228–255.

Gray, R., Owen, D., & Maunders, K. (1988). Corporate social reporting: Emerging trends in accountability and the social contract. *Accounting, Auditing & Accountability Journal, 1*(1), 6–20.

Green, W., & Cheng, M. (2019). Materiality judgments in an integrated reporting setting: The effect of strategic relevance and strategy map. *Accounting, Organizations & Society, 73*, 1–14.

Grosser, K., & Moon, J. (2008). Developments in company reporting on workplace gender equality?: A corporate social responsibility perspective. *Accounting Forum, 32*(3), 179–198. https://doi.org/10.1016/j.accfor.2008.01.004

Gueslin, A. (Ed.). (1999). *Les hommes du pneu—Les ouvriers MIchelin (1940–1980)*. Paris: Les Éditions de l'Atelier / Les Éditions Ouvrières.

Gumbrell-McCormick, R., & Hyman, R. (2013). *Trade unions in Western Europe: Hard times, hard choices*. Oxford: Oxford University Press.

Hammond, T., Clayton, B. M., & Arnold, P. J. (2009). South Africa's transition from apartheid: The role of professional closure in the experiences of black chartered accountants. *Accounting, Organizations and Society, 34*(6–7), 705–721.

Hammond, T., Clayton, B. M., & Arnold, P. J. (2012). An "unofficial" history of race relations in the South African accounting industry, 1968–2000: Perspectives of South Africa's first black chartered accountants. *Critical Perspectives on Accounting, 23*(4/5), 332–350. https://doi.org/10.1016/j.cpa.2011.10.005

Hampel, C. E., & Tracey, P. (2016). How organizations move from stigma to legitimacy: The case of Cook's travel agency in Victorian Britain. *Academy of Management Journal*. https://doi.org/10.5465/amj.2015.0365

Hansen, A. (2010). Nonfinancial performance measures, externalities and target setting: A comparative case study of resolutions through planning. *Management Accounting Research, 21*(1), 17–39.

Harcourt, S., & Harcourt, M. (2002). Do employers comply with civil/human rights legislation? New evidence from New Zealand job application forms. *Journal of Business Ethics, 35*, 207–221.

Harjoto, M., & Jo, H. (2011). Corporate governance and CSR nexus. *Journal of Business Ethics, 100*(1), 45–67. https://doi.org/10.1007/s10551-011-0772-6

Hefln, F., & Wallace, D. (2017). The BP oil spill: Shareholder wealth effects and environmental disclosures. *Journal of Business Finance & Accounting, 44*(3–4), 337–374.

Helfaya, A., & Moussa, T. (2017). Do board's corporate social responsibility strategy and orientation influence environmental sustainability disclosure? UK evidence. *Business Strategy and the Environment*. https://doi.org/10.1002/bse.1960

Henriksen, T., Dahlback, A., Larsen, S., & Moan, J. (1990). Ultraviolet-radiation and skin cancer, effect of an ozone later depletion. *Photochemistry and Photobiology, 51*(5), 579–582.

Higgins, C., Stubbs, W., & Love, T. (2014). Walking the talk(s): Organisational narratives of integrated reporting. *Accounting, Auditing & Accountability Journal, 27*(7), 1090–1119.

Hood, C., & Scott, C. (1996). Bureaucratic regulation and new public management in the United Kingdom: Mirror-image or developments? *Journal of Law and Society, 23*, 321–345.

Hoogevorst, H. (2013). *Breaking the Boilerplate.* Paper presented at the IFRS Conferences, Amsterdam.

How, S.-M., & Alawattage, C. (2012). Accounting decoupled: A case study of accounting regime change in a Malaysian company. *Critical Perspectives on Accounting, 23*(6), 403–419. https://doi.org/10.1016/j.cpa.2012.04.007

Hughner, R. S., McDonagh, P., Prothero, A., Schultz, C. J. I., & Stanton, J. (2007). Who are organic food consumers? A compilation and review of why people purchase organic food. *Journal of Consumer Behaviour, 6*(2/3), 94–110.

Humber, J. (2002). Beyond stockholders and stakeholders: A plea for corporate moral autonomy. *Journal of Business Ethics, 36*, 207–221.

Humphrey, C., Miller, P., & Scapens, B. (1993). Accountability and accountable management in the UK public sector. *Accounting, Auditing & Accountability Journal, 6*(3), 7–29.

Hurliman, A. (2011). Household use of and satisfaction with alternative water sources in Victoria Australia. *Journal of Environmental Management, 92*(10), 2691–2697.

IIRC. (2011). Towards integrated reporting. Communicating value in the 21st century. Discussion paper. Retrieved August 10, 2012, from http://www.theiirc.org/the-integrated-reporting-discussion-paper/.

Iivonen, K., & Moisander, J. (2014). Rhetorical construction of narcissistic CSR orientation. *Journal of Business Ethics, 131*(3), 649–664.

Islam, M. A., & McPhail, K. (2011). Regulating for corporate human rights abuses: The emergence of corporate reporting on the ILO's human rights standards within the global garment manufacturing and retailing industry. *Critical Perspectives on Accounting, 22*(8), 790–810.

Jacobs, K., & Jones, K. (2009). Legitimacy in parliamentary oversight in Australia—The rise and fall of two public accounts committees. *Accounting, Auditing & Accountability Journal, 22*(1), 13–34.

Jamali, D. R., El Dirani, A. M., & Harwood, I. A. (2015). Exploring human resource management roles in corporate social responsibility: The CSR-HRM co-creation model. *Business Ethics: A European Review, 24*(2), 125–143.

Jansen, E. P., Merchant, K. A., & Van der Stede, W. A. (2009). National differences in incentive compensation practices: The differing roles of financial performance measurement in the United States and the Netherlands. *Accounting, Organizations and Society, 34*(1), 58–84.

Jarvis, J. (2011). *What would Google do?* London: Harper.

Jeacle, I. (2011). A practice of her own: Female career success beyond the accounting firm. *Critical Perspectives on Accounting, 22*(3), 288–303. https://doi.org/10.1016/j.cpa.2010.12.002

Jensen, M. (2001). Value maximization, stakeholder theory, and the corporate objective function. *Journal of Applied Corporate Finance, 14*(3), 8–21.

Jensen, M., & Meckling, W. (1976). Theory of the firm: Managerial behavior, agency costs and ownership structure. *Journal of Financial Economics, 3*(4), 305–360.

Jensen, R. E. (1990). Working within neoclassical theory and "modern theory" of finance to detect and measure monopoly power components of ex post accounting rate of return. *Critical Perspectives on Accounting, 1*(1), 69–101.

Joannidès, V., Jaumier, S., & Hoque, Z. (2015). Patterns of boardroom discussions around the accountability process in a nonprofit organisation. In Z. Hoque & L. D. Parker (Eds.), *Performance management in nonprofit organizations—Global perspectives* (pp. 234–259). London: Routledge.

Jones, A. (2016). *Climate change: The climate change agenda—World government, carbon taxes & population control (climate change, global warming, world government).* Seattle: Kindle Edition.

Jørgensen, B., & Messner, M. (2009). Accounting and strategising: A case study from new product development. *Accounting, Organizations & Society, 35*(2), 184–204.

Kaplan, R., & Norton, D. (2004). *Strategy maps: Converting intangible assets into tangible outcomes.* Boston, MA: Harvard University Press.

Khetan, S. K. (2014). *Endocrine disruptors in the environment.* New York: Wiley.

Khojastehpour, M., & Johns, R. (2014). The effect of environmental CSR issues on corporate/brand reputation and corporate profitability. *European Business Review, 26*(4), 330–339.

Kim, S. N. (2004a). Imperialism without empire: Silence in contemporary accounting research on race/ethnicity. *Critical Perspectives on Accounting, 15*(1), 95–133.

Kim, S. N. (2004b). Racialized gendering of the accountancy profession: Toward an understanding of Chinese women's experiences in accountancy in New Zealand. *Critical Perspectives on Accounting, 15*(3), 400–427.

Kim, S. N. (2008). Whose voice is it anyway? Rethinking the oral history method in accounting research on race, ethnicity and gender. *Critical Perspectives on Accounting, 19*(8), 1346–1369.

Kroc, R. (2012). *Grinding it out: The making of McDonald's.* New York: St. Martin's Paperbacks.

Krooth, R., Edelson, M., & Fukurai, H. (2015). *Nuclear tsunami: The Japanese government and America's role in the Fukushima disaster.* New York: Lexington Books.

Kuruppu, S., & Milne, M. J. (2010). Dolphin deaths, organizational legitimacy and potential employees' reactions to assured environmental disclosures. *Accounting Forum, 34*(1), 1–19. https://doi.org/10.1016/j.accfor.2009.12.001

Laine, M. (2009). Ensuring legitimacy through rhetorical changes?—A longitudinal interpretation of the environmental disclosures of a leading Finnish chemical company. *Accounting, Auditing & Accountability Journal, 22*(7), 1029–1054.

Latour, B. (1987). *Science in action*. Boston, MA: Harvard University Press.

Latour, B. (1994). Pragmatogonies… A mythical account of how humans and non-humans swap properties. *American Behavioral Scientist, 37*(6), 791–808.

Latour, B. (2004). Why has critique run out of steam? From matters of fact to matters of concern. *Critical Inquiry, 30*(2), 225–248.

Latour, B. (2005). *Reassembling the social—An introduction to Actor-Network Theory*. Oxford: Oxford University Press.

Latour, B. (2008). The Netz-works of Greek deductions. *Social Studies of Science, 38*(3), 441–459.

Latour, B. (2009). *The making of law: An ethnography of the Conseil d'État*. London: Polity Press.

Lawrence, S., & Sharma, U. (2002). Commodification of education and academic labour—Using the balanced scorecard in a university setting. *Critical Perspectives on Accounting, 13*(5–6), 661–677.

Lehman, G. (2007). The accountability of NGOs in civil society and its public spheres. *Critical Perspectives on Accounting, 18*(6), 645–669. https://doi.org/10.1016/j.cpa.2006.04.002

Li, Y., & McKernan, J. (2016). Human rights, accounting, and the dialectic of equality and inequality. *Accounting, Auditing & Accountability Journal, 29*(6), 568–593.

Lippman, S. (2008). Rethinking risk in the new economy: Age and cohort effects on unemployment and re-employment. *Human Relations, 61*(9), 1259–1292.

Locke, R., Kochan, T., Romis, M., & Qin, F. (2007). Beyond corporate codes of conduct: Work organization and labour standards at Nike's suppliers. *International Labour Review, 146*(1–2), 21–40.

Lohmann, L. (2009). Toward a different debate in environmental accounting: The cases of carbon and cost-benefit. *Accounting, Organizations and Society, 34*(3–4), 499–534.

MacKenzie, D. (2009). Making things the same: Gases, emission rights and the politics of carbon markets. *Accounting, Organizations and Society, 34*(3–4), 440–455.

Mahoney, L., & Roberts, R. W. (2007). Corporate social performance, financial performance and institutional ownership in Canadian firms. *Accounting Forum, 31*(3), 233–253.

Mäkelä, H. (2011). Social responsibilities of MNCs in downsizing operations: A Finnish forest sector case analysed from the stakeholder, social contract and legitimacy theory point of view. *Accounting, Auditing & Accountability Journal, 23*(2), 149–174.

Malik, M. (2015). Value-enhancing capabilities of CSR: A brief review of contemporary literature. *Journal of Business Ethics, 127*(2), 419–438.

Mathews, M. R. (1997). Twenty-five years of social and environmental accounting research—Is there a silver jubilee to celebrate? *Accounting, Auditing & Accountability Journal, 10*(4), 481–531.

McCann, L., Hassard, J., Granter, E., & Hyde, P. J. (2015). Casting the lean spell: The promotion, dilution and erosion of lean management in the NHS. *Human Relations, 68*(10), 1557–1577.

McPhail, K., & Adams, C. A. (2016). Corporate respect for human rights: Meaning, scope, and the shifting order of discourse. *Accounting, Auditing & Accountability Journal, 29*(6), 650–678.

McPhail, K., & Ferguson, J. (2016). The past, the present and the future of accounting for human rights. *Accounting, Auditing & Accountability Journal, 29*(4), 526–541.

McPhail, K., & McKernan, J. (2011). Accounting for human rights: An overview and introduction. *Critical Perspectives on Accounting, 22*(8), 733–737.

Mena, S., Leede, M., Baumann, D., Black, N., Lindeman, S., & McShane, L. (2010). Advancing the business and human rights agenda: Dialogue, empowerment, and constructive engagement. *Journal of Business Ethics, 93*(1), 161–188. https://doi.org/10.1007/s10551-009-0188-8

Messner, M. (2009). The limits of accountability. *Accounting, Organizations and Society, 34*(8), 918–938.

Mueller, F., & Carter, C. (2007). 'We are all managers now': Managerialism and professional engineering in UK electricity utilities. *Accounting, Organizations and Society, 32*(1–2), 181–195.

Naszalyi, P., & Slama, A. (2016). An 'adhocracy' of stakeholders, or does transforming an 'Association' into a 'Cooperative'—The case of ADSA in Essonne. *Journal of Accounting & Organizational Change, 12*(1), 8–23.

Neu, D., & Graham, C. (2004). Accounting and the holocausts of modernity. *Accounting, Auditing & Accountability Journal, 17*(4), 578–603.

Newell, P. (2012). Chapter 2—Sound, decibel and hearing. In P. Newell (Ed.), *Recording studio systems* (pp. 13–33). London: Focal Press.

Niepcel, W., & Molleman, E. (1998). Work design issues in lean production from a sociotechnical systems perspective: Neo-Taylorism or the next step in sociotechnical design? *Human Relations, 51*(3), 259–297.

O'Brien, C. M., & Dhanarajan, S. (2016). The corporate responsibility to respect human rights: A status review. *Accounting, Auditing & Accountability Journal, 29*(6), 542–567.

O'Dwyer, B., & Unerman, J. (2007). From functional to social accountability: Transforming the accountability relationship between funders and non-governmental development organisations. *Accounting, Auditing & Accountability Journal, 20*(3), 446–471.

Ogden, S. G., & Bougen, P. (1985). A radical perspective on the disclosure of accounting information to trade unions. *Accounting, Organizations and Society, 10*(2), 211–224.

Oldroyd, D., Fleischman, R. K., & Tyson, T. N. (2008). The culpability of accounting practice in promoting slavery in the British Empire and antebellum United States. *Critical Perspectives on Accounting, 19*(5), 764–784.

Orij, R. (2010). Corporate social disclosures in the context of national cultures and stakeholder theory. *Accounting, Auditing & Accountability Journal, 23*(7), 868–889.

Owen, D. L., & Lloyd, A. J. (1985). The use of financial information by trade union negotiators in plant level collective bargaining. *Accounting, Organizations and Society, 10*(3), 329–350. https://doi.org/10.1016/0361-3682(85)90023-6

Parker, L. (2011). Building bridges to the future: Mapping the territory for developing social and environmental accountability. *Social and Environmental Accountability Journal, 31*(1), 7–24.

Parker, L. (2014). Corporate social accountability through action: Contemporary insights from British industrial pioneers. *Accounting, Organizations & Society, 39*(8), 632–659.

Pasewark, W. R., Shockley, R. A., & Wilkerson, J. E. (1995). Legitimacy claims of the auditing profession vis-a-vis the behaviour of its members: An empirical examination. *Critical Perspectives on Accounting, 6*, 77–94.

Passetti, E., Bianchi, L., Battaglia, M., & Frey, M. (2017). When democratic principles are not enough: Tensions and temporalities of dialogic stakeholder engagement. *Journal of Business Ethics, 142*(3), 1–18.

Patisaul, H. B., & Belcher, S. M. (2017). *Endocrine disruptors, brain, and behavior*. Oxford: Oxford University Press.

Pavlopoulos, A., Magnis, C., & Iatridiis, G. E. (2019). Integrated reporting: An accounting disclosure tool for high quality financial reporting. *Research in International Business and Finance, 49*, 13–40.

Pérez, A. (2013). The effect of corporate associations on consumer behaviour. *European Journal of Marketing, 37*(1/2), 218–238.

Pigou, A. (1946). *The economics of welfare*. London: Transaction Publishers.

Posthuma, R., & Campion, M. (2009). Age stereotypes in the workplace: Common stereotypes, moderators, and future research directions. *Journal of Management, 35*(1), 158–188.

Power, M. (2001). Imagining, measuring and managing intangibles. *Accounting, Organizations & Society, 26*(7–8), 691–693.

Power, M. (2003). Auditing and the production of legitimacy. *Accounting, Organizations & Society, 28*(3), 379–394.

Quattrone, P. (2009). Books to be practiced: Memory, the power of the visual, and the success of accounting. *Accounting, Organizations & Society, 34*(1), 85–118.

Rahaman, A. S., Lawrence, S., & Roper, J. (2004). Social and environmental reporting at the VRA: Institutionalised legitimacy or legitimation crisis? *Critical Perspectives on Accounting, 15*(1), 35–56.

Ramirez, C. (2009a). Constructing the governable small practitioner: The changing nature of professional bodies and the management of professional accountants' identities in the UK. *Accounting, Organizations and Society, 34*(3–4), 381–408. https://doi.org/10.1016/j.aos.2008.05.004

Ramirez, C. (2009b). Constructing the small local practitioner: The changing nature of professional bodies and the management of professional accountants' identities in the UK. *Accounting, Organizations & Society, 24*, 381–408.

Rayman-Bacchus, L. (2006). Reflecting on corporate legitimacy. *Critical Perspectives on Accounting, 17*(2–3), 323–335.

Reimann, F., Ehrgott, M., Kaufmann, L., & Carter, C. R. (2012). Local stakeholders and local legitimacy: MNEs' social strategies in emerging economies. *Journal of International Management, 18*(1), 1–17.

Rensburg, R., & Botha, E. (2014). Is Integrated Reporting the silver bullet of financial communication? A stakeholder perspective from South Africa. *Public Relations Review*. https://doi.org/10.1016/j.pubrev.2013.11.016

Retief, V. E., & Villiers (de), C. (2013). The accounting profession's influence on academe: South African evidence. *Accounting, Auditing & Accountability Journal, 26*(8), 1246–1278.

Reuter, M., & Messner, M. (2015). Lobbying on the integrated reporting framework: An analysis of comment letters to the 2011 discussion paper of the IIRC. *Accounting, Auditing & Accountability Journal, 28*(3), 365–402.

Richard, S., Moslemi, S., Sipahutar, H., Benachour, N., & Seralini, G.-E. (2005). Differential effects of glyphosate and roundup on human placental cells and aromatase. *Environmental Health Perspectives, 113*(6), 716–720.

Ricœur, P. (1991). *Du texte à l'action*. Paris: Seuil.

Rupert, J., Jehn, K. A., Engen, M. L., & Reuver, R. S. M. (2010). Commitment of cultural minorities in organizations: Effects of leadership and pressure to conform. *Journal of Business and Psychology, 25*(1), 25–37. https://doi.org/10.2307/40605743

Russell, S., Milne, M., & Dey, C. (2017). Accounts of nature and the nature of accounts: Critical reflections on environmental accounting and propositions for ecologically informed accounting. *Accounting, Auditing & Accountability Journal, 30*(7), 1426–1458.

Schaltegger, S., & Burritt, R. L. (2017a). *Contemporary environmental accounting: Issues concepts and practice*. London: Routledge.

Schaltegger, S., & Burritt, R. L. (2017b). *An introduction to corporate environmental management: Striving for sustainability*. London: Routledge.

Schaltegger, S., & Csutora, M. (2012). Carbon accounting for sustainability and management. Status quo and challenges. *Journal of Cleaner Production, 36*, 1–16. https://doi.org/10.1016/j.jclepro.2012.06.024

Schaltegger, S., & Wagner, M. (2017). *Managing the business case for sustainability: The integration of social, environmental and economic performance*. London: Routledge.

Schaltegger, S., & Zvedzov, D. (2016). *Corporate carbon and climate accounting*. London: Routledge.

Scholes-Fogg, T. (2011). *What next for labour?: Ideas for a new generation*. London: Queensferry Publishers.

Sheehy, B. (2014). Defining CSR: Problems and solutions. *Journal of Business Ethics, 131*(3), 625–648.

Sikka, P. (2010). Smoke and mirrors: Corporate social responsibility and tax avoidance. *Accounting Forum, 34*(3/4), 153–168.

Skouloudis, A., Malesios, C., & Dimitrakopoulos, P. (2019). Corporate biodiversity accounting and reporting in mega-diverse countries: An examination of indicators disclosed in sustainability reports. *Ecological Indicators, 98*, 888–901.

Stewart, S. (2012). Contesting public accountability: A dialogical exploration of accountability and social housing. *Critical Perspectives on Accounting*. https://doi.org/10.1016/j.cpa.2011.12.007

Subramanian, N. (2008). Legal change and gender inequality: Changes in Muslim family law in India. *Law & Social Inquiry, 33*(3), 631–672. https://doi.org/10.2307/20108777

Suchman, M. C. (1995). Managing legitimacy: Strategic and institutional approaches. *Academy of Management Review, 20*(3), 571–610.

Suddaby, R., & Greenwood, R. (2005). Rhetorical strategies of legitimacy. *Administrative Science Quarterly, 50*(1), 35–67.

Tinker, T., & Fearfull, A. (2007). The workplace politics of U.S. accounting: Race, class and gender discrimination at Baruch College. *Critical Perspectives on Accounting, 18*(1), 123–138.

Tornikoski, C. (2011). *Expatriate compensation: A total reward perspective*. PhD, EM Lyon, Lyon.

Tremblay, M.-S., Gendron, Y., & Malsch, B. (2016). Gender on board: Deconstructing the "legitimate" female director. *Accounting, Auditing & Accountability Journal, 29*(1), 165–190.

Tyson, T. N., Fleischman, R. K., & Oldroyd, D. (2004). Theoretical perspectives on accounting for labor on slave plantations of the USA and British West Indies. *Accounting, Auditing & Accountability Journal, 17*(5), 758–778.

Unerman, J., & O'Dwyer, B. (2006a). On James Bond and the importance of NGO accountability. *Accounting, Auditing & Accountability Journal, 19*(3), 305–318.

Unerman, J., & O'Dwyer, B. (2006b). Theorising accountability for NGO advocacy. *Accounting, Auditing & Accountability Journal, 19*(3), 349–376.

Unerman, J., & O'Dwyer, B. (2008). The paradox of greater NGO accountability: A case study of Amnesty Ireland. *Accounting, Organizations & Society, 33*(7–8), 801–824.

Ungar, S. (1998). Bringing the issue back in: Comparing the marketability of the ozone hole and global warming. *Social Problems, 45*(4), 510–527.

Ungar, S. (2000). Knowledge, ignorance and the popular culture: Climate change versus the ozone hole. *Public Understanding of Science, 9*(3), 297–312.

Villiers (de), C., Chen, S., Jin, C., & Zhu, Y. (2013). *Carbon sequestered in the trees of a university campus*. Paper presented at the 7th Asia-Pacific Interdisciplinary Research in Accounting conference, Kobe, Japan.

Vise, D. A. (2008). *The Google story*. New York: Pan.

Walker, A. (1999). Combating age discrimination at the workplace. *Experimental Aging Research: An International Journal Devoted to the Scientific Study of the Aging Process, 25*(4), 367–376.

Walker, S. P. (2003). Agents of dispossession and acculturation. Edinburgh accountants and the highland clearances. *Critical Perspectives on Accounting, 14*(8), 813–853.

Weber, M. (1922). *Economy and society*. Berkeley: The University of California Press.

West, A. (2017). Multinational tax avoidance: Virtue ethics and the role of accountants. [journal article]. *Journal of Business Ethics*. https://doi.org/10.1007/s10551-016-3428-8.

Williams, R., Gero, S., Bejder, L., Calambokidis, J., Kraus, S. D., Lusseau, D., … Robbins, J. (2011). Underestimating the damage: Interpreting cetacean carcass recoveries in the context of the deepwater horizon/BP incident. *Conservation Letters, 4*(3), 228–233.

Wilmshurst, T., & Frost, G. R. (2000). Corporate environmental reporting: A test of legitimacy theory. *Accounting, Auditing & Accountability Journal, 13*(1), 10–26.

Wolff, J. E. (in press). Heaps of moles?—Mediating macroscopic and microscopic measurement of chemical substances. *Studies in History and Philosophy of Science Part A*.

Zehr, S. C. (1994). Accounting for the ozone hole: Scientific representations of an anomaly and prior incorrect claims in public settings. *The Sociological Quarterly, 35*(4), 603–619.

CHAPTER 4

The Ethics of Management Accounting: Innate or Learnt?

The aftermath of financial scandals, such as Enron or WorldCom, has called for greater ethical responsibility amongst professions. The unethical behaviour of financial managers at large and auditors more specifically has been denounced (Boyce, 2018; Hope & Wang, 2018). All of them are placed under the so-called Accounting Profession. However, management accountants' ethical concerns are left aside, as though being mere bean counters would not expose these professionals to any misconduct (Low, Davey, & Hooper, 2008). Albeit, management accountants have increasingly been presented as knowledge consultants (Saravanamuthu, 2004a) and business partners (Chotiyanon, 2018; Chotiyanon & Joannidès de Lautour, 2018). Not only do they count costs and quantities, twenty-first-century management accountants appear as full-rights managers (Lambert & Pezet, 2011).

Management accountants' ethics were discussed a long time prior to the world's biggest financial scandals and then no longer (Loeb & Cory, 1989; Woelfel, 1986). Albeit, management accountants have been exposed to ethical dilemmas like any other financial managers (Bridgman, 2010; Dowdle, 2006; Lindblom, 2007; Morales, Gendron, & Guénin-Paracini, 2014; Morales & Lambert, 2013). Their exposure to ethical dilemmas owes to two joint phenomena.

Firstly, the fact that their role consists of producing information relevant for decision-making, therefore accurate and reliable information, implies that management accountants' role is at the core of organisational life and financial management. As management accounting information is

V. Joannidès de Lautour, *Strategic Management Accounting, Volume III*, https://doi.org/10.1007/978-3-030-20157-9_4

expected to support managerial decision-making and is not supposed to be disclosed as such, it does not need to be smoothed or retreated (Chotiyanon, 2018; Chotiyanon & Joannidès de Lautour, 2018; Cianci & Kaplan, 2010; Kaplan & Johnson, 1987; Kaplan & Norton, 1996, 2000, 2004, 2006, 2008). That is, management accountants produce and internally diffuse this knowledge of organisational performance, be it good or bad.

Secondly, as financial disclosure is supposed to be fed with data originating from management accounting systems, accuracy and comprehensiveness are central. Even though management accountants do not explicitly and directly contribute to financial disclosure, their role consists of providing accounts preparers with the right data. This is where ethical dilemmas could occur, if management accountants were to diffuse false information. Whatever the reason for this is, being management accountants would be confronted with an ethical dilemma. Such a situation is not purely theoretical, since their growing role in organisations has exposed them to confidential and sensitive information, almost as much as data pertaining to corporate strategy (Funnell, 2011; Irvine, 2003; Puyou, 2018; Radcliffe, 2008).

It is therefore central to understand what management accountants' ethics encompasses and how it can be encouraged. This is what this chapter is aimed at showing. To this end, it covers three major areas of management accountants' ethics. It is first important to understand how management accounting and ethics can operate together as a community of practice. As ethical concerns cannot only be innate, issues in management accountants' education are presented.

4.1 The Management Accountant, Ethical Par Excellence?

Management accountants' ethics seems never to be questioned, as though these professionals were honest and fair in nature or unexposed to ethical dilemmas. As any other professional group, management accountants form a community of practices with its own principles and guidelines. So, does ethical behaviour form a community of practices highlighting what is acceptable and what is not? Irrespective of corporate concerns and management accountants' ethicality, these ethical prospects are an ontological construct deserving special treatment and understanding.

4.1.1 Management Accounting and Ethics as Communities of Practice

It is impossible to discuss ethics without being normative as to what is good or evil (Badiou, 2001; Lévinas, 1985). In so doing, however, one implicitly assumes that everybody agrees on these values and judgements. These are rarely made explicit whilst explicitness lies in the fact that they are forming an ethical community of practice comprehending of a habitus spread within the management accounting profession, itself operating as a community of practice.

4.1.1.1 Forming Habitus as a Community of Practice

In the introduction to a publication turning the full circle with his doctoral dissertation on Kabyle marriage and home's organising and managing, Bourdieu (1977, 1998) develops some intuitions he considers worthy of further developing for accounting. For him, a common feature of all societies and organised communities is a systematic splitting of the world into two distinct bodies which he calls *contraries* (Bourdieu, 1977, 1998). Borrowing from the tradition of structural anthropology (Levi-Strauss, 1952, 1958; Mauss, 1925) in the French version of his doctoral work, he builds upon the polysemy of this term meaning *opposed* but also *complementary*: two opposed items that aspire to being united and unified (Bourdieu, 1977, p. 89). His anthropological works reveal some eloquent pairings: heaven/earth, male/female, house's inside/outside (*e.g.* courtyard as part of what is called a house) and guest/host. On the other hand, he views incommensurable contraries as sociological artefacts and not as parts of society, *for example*, good/evil, pretty/ugly, heaven/hell (Bourdieu, 1984, 1992, 1993).

In essence, the world is dual in a twofold way (Bourdieu, 1998, p. 94). Firstly, everything has a counterpart: woman is the counterpart of man and vice versa, so is the relation between a guest and a host. Nothing exists independently of another equivalent. Secondly, the counterpart is to be returned, as nothing can be gratuitous: when a host invites someone, the guest accepts it, declining it being an offence. Later, the former guest may return the invitation to his or her host who is expected to accept it for the same reasons. A gift is always reciprocated with a counter-gift that operates as an equivalent but is often different in nature. More broadly, communities of "*practices always have double truths, which are difficult to hold together. Analysis must take note of this duality*" (Bourdieu, 1998, p. 95).

In order for these items to form a community of practice, they should in essence be united through the development of an accountancy whereby items can be labelled and recorded as their intrinsic properties and equivalent nature can be identified (Bourdieu, 1977, pp. 132–139, 1992, p. 98). World dualism is what Bourdieu calls an *objective structure* that transcends the self. This structure is also immanent to the individual as the meanings associated to its contents are contingent upon the self's worldview (Bourdieu, 1977, p. 81, 1992, p. 13).

It is obvious for Bourdieu (1977, p. 178, 1992, pp. 112–113, 1998, p. 121) that the community of practice considered aims at developing an accounting of this world dualism's uniting. The observable practice itself takes the following path. Organising and accounting for the communion of the two contraries are the ultimate goal pursued by all group members. This goal is combined with the emotions usually expressed to arrive at this *representation* of the world. For Bourdieu (1998, pp. 271–283), the utmost expression of such ultimate *representation* can be found in the Kabyle house as world reversed where inside/outside, guest/host and male/female are clearly separated but reunited through the placing of furniture. From an accounting viewpoint, such *representation* would be the ultimate statements at which we can arrive and that summarise our uniting of gift (credits) and payback (debits).

Given the ambiguity of accounts' contents and uniting's very representation, a community of practice first inculcates a *worldview* resting upon *common understandings*. In order for them to be intelligible and easily absorbable for community members, *common understandings* are actively taught through metaphors and myths presented as a consistent whole (Bourdieu, 1977, pp. 128–129, 1998, pp. 46–47). Thereby, "*agents apply the same schemes of perception and action to either situation or transfer the same ritualized sequences from one to another*" (Bourdieu, 1977, p. 13).

Such understandings are aimed at providing community members with the *logic* of the whole thing. What Bourdieu (1977, pp. 91–97) calls *logic* is the conflation of *logos* and *logical sequencing*. That is, Bourdieu sees a pre-existing common language and the subsequent capability of naming heroes, events and other artefacts as part of the *logos*. This is what enables individuals to grasp metaphors' and myths' course of actions in an intelligible way, not only for them but also for any new community member. In other words, *common understandings* relate to groups members' capability of grasping the big picture and the overall coherence of details constituting these "*sensible practices, linked intelligibly to the conditions of their enactment, and also among themselves, and therefore immediately filled with sense and rationality for every individual*" (Bourdieu, 1977, p. 66).

This ability to grasp and appropriate metaphors enables their *objectification*, which ultimately allows for *representation* (Bourdieu, 1977, pp. 72–73). Objectifying metaphors and myths consists of granting them some value as true because of their exteriority and pre-existence. The whole thing can be produced through a working theory or model applying to all group members. Bourdieu (1998) considers that heroes, facts, events as well as any other artefacts operate as *variables* in the model or *determinants* for their interrelations. From pure metaphor and myth, they can operate as a doctrine for the group. The doctrine specifies what is acceptable or not and is not supposed to be questioned. The group doctrine supposedly applies to all with no distinction and no exception.

Once metaphors and myths are appropriated and objectified, the work of *representation* can operate through the development of *nomos* (Bourdieu, 1998, p. 66): "*a tacit law of perception and practice that is at the basis of the consensus on the sense of the social world [...] the basis of common sense.*" This creating of "the *obliged affections* and *affective obligations*" (Bourdieu, 1998, p. 68) is a set of rules and routines driving people's *representing* the communion of contraries and ultimately reconciliation of world dualism. In the French version of Bourdieu (1977), the notion of *rule* has a dual meaning: it is a *norm* both issued and enforced by a higher authority (pp. 22–30) but also codified habits operating *qua* a grammar (p. 98). All of this forms what Bourdieu (1977) calls a cycle and can be summarised in Fig. 4.1 below.

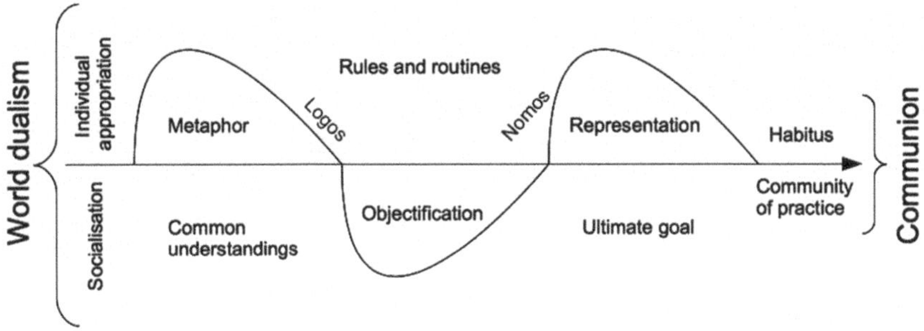

Fig. 4.1 The constitution of a habitus and community of practice (adapted from Bourdieu)

As stated by Bourdieu, a habitus is constituted when world dualism is so appropriated by group members as to be unified through a working representation upon which other community of practice's participants more or less explicitly agree. The following is a simplified version of the aforementioned figure. From totally distinct, God and mankind unite through an account of their differences, similarities and complementarities (Figs. 4.2 and 4.3).

4.1.1.2 *Ethical Management Accounting as a Habitus and a Community of Practice*

The logic of accounting, regardless of any sort of power relationships it creates, lies in the idea that the world can be categorised into *debits* and *credits* (Carruthers & Espeland, 1991; Maltby, 1997; Saravanamuthu,

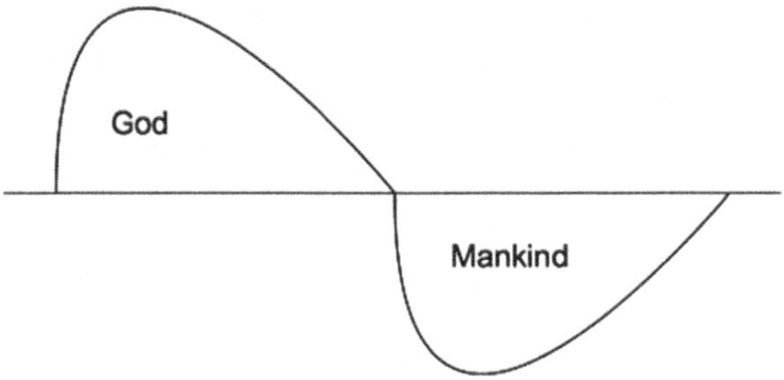

Fig. 4.2 The metaphor of world dualism

Fig. 4.3 Representation of world's unifying (the communion of male and female)

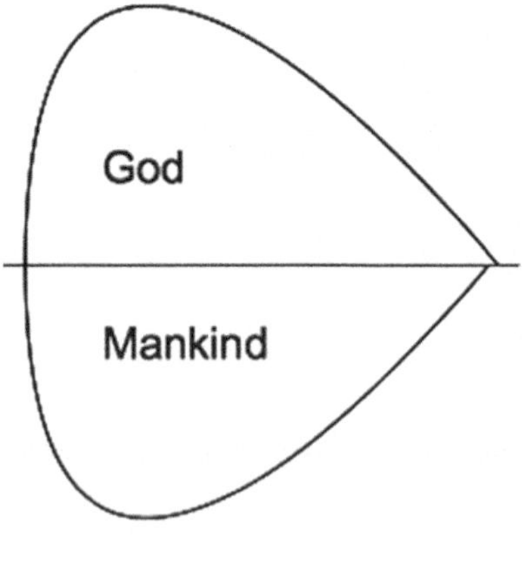

2004b, 2006). Representing gifts and use made thereof as a way of paying back funders, these are supposed to be a fair representation of one's conduct and achievements. It is through the unifying of these two distinct entities that an account appears as this fair representation at which accounting is aimed (McKernan, 2007; McKernan & Kosmala, 2004, 2007).

The ultimate goal of producing an account is to be meaningful to an Other who, reading it, can grasp the big picture as well as the detail of what I have been doing and how (Schweiker, 1993; Shearer, 2002). In order for this goal to be met, accounting rests upon common understandings regarding the oppositions and complementarities between the world's features, *for example*, assets/liabilities, investment/financing, cost/revenue, provided these items count as central to the community (Ahrens & Chapman, 2002, 2007; Ahrens & Mollona, 2007; Carter & Mueller, 2006; Chua, 2007; Jørgensen & Messner, 2010; L. D. Parker, 2002a). Accordingly, accounting is broader than the mere recording and reporting of economic transactions and financial flows but also souls and bodies (Walker, 2010), Bible reading and prayer (Jacobs & Walker, 2004), faith and action (Joannidès, 2012), indulgence and sins (Quattrone, 2004) or sacraments (Aho, 2005).

Under the purview of objectifying *debits* and *credits* in accounting, rules and routines lie in identifying gifts received for a purpose and the use made thereof (Carruthers & Espeland, 1991). Such rules and routines enable the identification of the righteous use of a gift through appropriate records. Carruthers and Espeland (1991) reason that in accounting research we tend to consider balance of credits and debits can only be observed through formal representations, that is, written records and books of accounts. This is accentuated by the idea that such records and books of accounts make conduct visible and thence controllable. Items to be accounted for are first named and then transformed into numbers through working units reflecting what should be balanced. Evaluation models and assumptions underlying the keeping of records reveal this (Quattrone, 2009). It is well accepted that the *logos* of accounting is money or any strategic working unit (Ahrens & Chapman, 2002, 2007; Jørgensen & Messner, 2010) whilst its *nomos* can be found in the principles or regulations surrounding the keeping of records (McKernan, 2007; McKernan & Kosmala, 2007). Both the *logos* and the *nomos* form a set of rules driving the representation of how *debits* and *credits* are identified, labelled and balanced. The choice thereof and exercise periodicity form a routine surrounding accounting practices (Quattrone, 2009).

4.1.1.3 Management Accounting as Ethical Habitus

Management accounting can be presented in its simplest definition as a process driven by a worldview resulting in categorising any situation into debits and credits always equalling each other (Freytag, 1855; Gambling, 1987; Hopwood, 1994; Maltby, 1997; M. Weber, 1922). For more detail, the practice of being a management accountant has been abundantly developed in prior studies (Chotiyanon, 2018; Chotiyanon & Joannidès de Lautour, 2018; Joannidès de Lautour, 2018b)

The core of accounting lies in identifying gifts received for a purpose and the use made thereof. In essence, credits and debits equal each other. The central issue is to be found in the identification of the righteous use of a gift. In accounting research, we tend to consider that balance of credits and debits can be observed only through formal representations, that is, written records and books of accounts. Items to be accounted for are first named and then transformed into numbers through working units reflecting what is expectedly balanced. Evaluation models and assumptions underlying the keeping of records reveal this. The formal representation offered by books of accounts serves to show that gifts were righteously used.

The rationale for deeds is expected to be clarified to others with fairness, the speaker being held to an "*absolute obligation to the Other*" (McKernan & Kosmala, 2004, p. 356). His or her story finds itself "*held to be understandable to others and thereby [rendering] a life intelligible and meaningful*" (Shearer, 2002, p. 545). Religious notions, justness and fairness imply that the accountable person is being constructed as a moral and responsible self, seeking to speak the truth and expecting the Other to have faith in him or her (McKernan & Kosmala, 2007; Shearer, 2002).

The financial evaluation of counterparties has colonised management accounting, because it is relatively convenient to have money as a commonly understood unit. Studying accounting in functional contexts prevents us from apprehending units other than money (Berry, 2005; Quattrone, 2004, 2009). Accordingly, if we want to approach the essence of accounting and draw on its ontology, we should depart from any economic transaction and focus on its meaning (McKernan & Kosmala, 2004, 2007; Shearer, 2002). Therefore, we are studying accounting through theological instructions in the Middle Ages, *namely* prior to the birth of the notion of capitalism.

4.1.1.4 Management Accounting and Ethics as Practice

Once a habitus is formed and has been interiorised by community members, it can be characterised as practice consisting of a bundle of *common understandings*, *routines*, *rules* and *teleoaffective structures* (Barnes, 2000; Bourdieu, 1977; Certeau (de), 1984, 1988; Coulter, 2000; Lounsbury & Crumbley, 2007; Schatzki, 2000a, 2000b, 2005).

Common understandings of how to do things are first the knowledge that *individuals* have of the way of performing actions. This knowledge can be explicit or implicit. Common understandings also encompass the interpretation people can make of knowledge and the way they can translate it into actions. However, owing to particularities of the context, practices may be altered, as common understandings might change from one actor to another (consciously or non-consciously), different rules might be issued, while ends might be emphasised differently (Schatzki, 2005, p. 475).

Management accounting's common understandings may relate to their role within the organisation: management accountants are expected to produce and diffuse relevant information for decision-making. On the other hand, ethics' common understandings consist in a collective agreement as to what is right or wrong, pretty or ugly, just or unjust. Bridging both, ethical management accounting's common understandings could be summarised as a collective agreement as to what is relevant data and must be diffused and what is not relevant information. Ethical dilemmas would occur when management accountants are not certain whether they must diffuse a certain piece of data. Professional ethics' common understandings would operate at two levels: the profession on one hand and the organisation on the other (Bayou, Reinstein, & Williams, 2011; Carnegie & Napier, 2010; McPhail, 1999; Velayutham, 2003).

Therefore, *rules* are issued to impose a normative way of doing things within the practice. Doctrines, guidelines and other norms are intentionally developed and enforced to make individuals comply with the structure's overall views through a normalised array of understandings, desires, beliefs, expectations, emotions and ultimately actions (Schatzki, 2005, p. 481). Management accounting's rules are quite intuitive, as they consist in corporate regulations and procedures to produce and diffuse information as well as to organise reporting. These rules operate as management accounting standards, such as standard costing, KPIs that need to be measured and managed or funding application procedures. Rules appear as very procedural, which leads them to be collapsed to codes of conduct when it comes to ethics (Badiou, 2001; Joannidès & McKernan, 2015). Devising the rules driving management accounting's ethics would lead to two types of codes of conduct: one for the profession and one for the organisation. This may lead to require that management accountants be affiliated to an existing professional body qualified to exert disciplinary power on them, as with legal and medical professionals (Backhof & Martin, 1991; Pratt, Rockmann, & Kaufmann, 2006).

Daily application of these rules rests upon a *habitus* consisting of the exteriorisation of interiorised knowledge through *routines*. Rules and routines specify *correct* or at least acceptable behaviour for the practice to be perpetuated. Management accounting routines could be presented as the periodicity at which reporting is done or the way budgeting or annual performance meetings are organised (M. Jensen, 2003; King, Clarkson, & Wallace, 2009; Preston, Cooper, & Coombs, 1992). Routines are probably problematic when it comes to ethics where management accountants are supposed to exert their judgement and take responsibility for their actions. Ethics' routines could simply consist of standard ways of treating dilemmas, by asking oneself one simple question: what would my mentor have done in a similar situation (Joannidès & McKernan, 2015)? Routines in ethical management accounting may simply consist in developing a mentoring system in the organisation whereby management accountants could refer to a peer, a more senior person or a committee in case of dilemmas and then decide based upon the advice they are given (Fogarty & Ravenscroft, 2000; Kram & Isabella, 1985).

This normative scheme is supplemented by *teleoaffective structures* encompassing ends and projects whether the practice is addressed and combined with the emotions usually expressed in the pursuit of that practice. Actually, as appropriations may vary, arrangements are necessary to constitute a practice: people may confront their understandings with those of others and readjust themselves accordingly until their behaviour is acceptable (Schatzki, 2000a, 2005). Teleoaffective structures underpinning management accounting pertain to the emotions mobilised towards management accountants' common goal. Traditionally, management accounting is made appealing to students and graduates, because it is presented as a profession at the intersection of strategy, operations and finance (Anthony, 1988; Anthony, Dearden, & Bedford, 1984; Joannidès de Lautour, 2018a). Teleoaffective structures in ethics could simply be summarised as the emotions driving the fact of doing the good and approaching a form of moral sanctity (Badiou, 2003; Joannidès & McKernan,

2015). Ethical management accounting's teleoaffective structures could be the idea of contributing to strategy in a way that does good to others, in particular as evidenced in social and environmental management accounting (Burritt, 2012; Cho, Guidry, Hageman, & Patten, 2012; García-de-Frutos, Ortega-Egea, & Martínez-del-Río, 2016; Russell, Milne, & Dey, 2017; Sonenshein, DeCelles, & Dutton, 2014). Some could even argue that the new roles Integrated Reporting assigns to management accountants appear as the utmost form of bridging ethics' and management accounting's teleoaffective structures (Dragu & Tiron-Tudor, 2013; Frías-Aceituno, Rodríguez-Ariza, & García-Sánchez, 2013; García-Sánchez, Rodríguez-Ariza, & Frías-Aceituno, 2013; IIRC, 2011).

4.1.2 *The Ethical Management Accountant: An Ontological Construct*

When ethical issues are discussed, it always appears that education should come first (Beggs & Dean, 2007; Floyd, Xu, Atkins, & Caldwell, 2013; May, Luth, & Schwoerer, 2014; Sigurjonsson, Arnardottir, Vaiman, & Rikhardsson, 2015; Wang & Calvano, 2015). Even though education undoubtedly plays a role in constructing ethical management accountants, this ascription rests upon the implicit assumption that ethics cannot be innate. To some extent, this resonates with our Judæo-Christian values grounded in the Original Sin and the idea that mankind in essence is incapable of exerting judgement and being ethical (Cohen, 1980; Norman, 1997). This strong assumption in fact neglects a major dimension of ethics, when associated with aesthetics: good/evil, pretty/ugly. A branch of philosophy considers that ethics precedes and accompanies the self through aesthetical constructs, thereby making ethics an ontological construct (Arendt, 1961, 1963, 1968; Badiou, 2001, 2003, 2005; Derrida, 1991, 1993, 1998, 2002, 2008; Lévinas, 1969, 1985, 1987).

4.1.2.1 *Ethics as the Construction of the Ontological Self*

The constitution of the self lies in its likes and dislikes that can be clarified through multiple sensorial encounters. This construction of likes and dislikes characterises the ontological self (Arendt, 1961, 1968). Even though two people can share some common experiences, the collection of all experiences lived by one self is proper to it and makes it different from the other. Consequently, these experiences are what constitutes self's sensitivity and personality so as to make it a conscious body. These experiences and that consciousness make the self aware of what remains inaccessible. At the same time as they constitute it, these sensorial experiences emphasise its ontological finitude: these experiences border its knowledge of the world and of itself (Arendt, 1961).

These ontological experiences of the world are of four orders: self-consciousness (Lévinas, 1969, 1987), consciousness of the others as selves (Arendt, 1961; Lévinas, 1987), the experience of God and the experience of the non-self (Lévinas, 1969, 1987), a.k.a. experience of the non-human (Latour, 1994, 2013).

The first experience constituting the self is the relationship to oneself and the discovery of oneself (Lévinas, 1969, 1987). To Lévinas, such experiences are sensorial and intimate: the self-to-be shares them with only a few people or with nobody. Sexuality, due to historical and social taboos, is the room of intimacy *par excellence* (*secrecy*) whereby the individual can express and discover himself through his five senses and the subsequent relationship to time and to life. Through sexuality, the self involves its five senses and can determine what it likes or dislikes, what matters to it and what is irrelevant. Through such preferences, the self constructs its own aesthetics. As these become more transparent, they can set its identity and form the grounds for its ethics (Foucault, 1976a, 1976b, 1984; Freud, 1905).

It is considered that sexuality is the cradle of the *eros*, that is, intimacy that makes the self a unique being. The *eros* is the collection of all sensorial experiences and as such constitutes the foundation of the ontological being. Sexuality does not necessarily mean intercourse; it however commences long before and irrespective of it. In the first place, sexuality involves and stimulates sight. The self is capable of developing a notion of visual aesthetics, by liking some shapes and colours more than others (Lévinas, 1987). It is commonly agreed that this erotic stimulation of sight involves an Other with whom one can fall in love. But, even prior to this encounter with the Other, sight is stimulated when the self is confronted with itself. The utmost form of this infatuation with oneself is to be found in Narcisse's story, as he was glazing at his own reflection in the water and bent to catch this beautiful object, fell in the water and drowned. This is how, nowadays, men and women can determine by seeing another person whether he or she is their type.

At this juncture of self-sexuality, another two senses are more abstractly developed and stimulated: hear and smell. Hear is concerned too, insofar as the individual can feel appealed or not to perceived sounds. As these cannot be grasped or fetched, it is only possible to determine whether these can actually be perceived well (volume) as well as their frequency (high or low). In the first place, irrespective of sexuality, the self can determine which of all these sounds it likes or dislikes. Sexuality, albeit, remains central to the development of this sensorial experience, Lévinas (1987) argues, since the self can do more than just like or dislike a sound. The gentleness or the softness of a voice can appear like a love potion: one abstractly becomes infatuated with a voice and wants to hear it progressively by spending more time with it. Assumedly, the sound produced during the sexual intercourse may more or less be appealing to the self, determined to continue hearing it or preferring to terminate the experience.

Philosophers Lévinas, Freud or Foucault argue this, building upon Plato's Phaedrus, who was so infatuated with Socrates that he was begging for hearing his speech repeatedly. More than the content of the teaching, what was seducing Phaeadrus was the sound of Socrates' voice. As with Narcisse and sight, an English expression represents the utmost form of hear stimulation in a sexual relation involving nobody else but the self: someone likes the sound of their own voice.

Smell is stimulated in an equally abstract manner as hearing, since the object cannot be grasped or fetched. Moreover, in otorhinolaryngology, nose and mouth are related, thereby making smell and taste twin senses. In the human, animal and vegetal world, smell acts as one feature of romancing or repulsing someone prior to the sexual relation (Diel, 1947). In the vegetal world, the smell of a flower is explicitly a sexual act whereby the sending plant expects its sexual counterpart to fertilise it. The stronger the smell is, the more sexually demanding or needing the flower is. Something similar happens in the animal world, when a female does produce a certain smell aimed at attracting males. It is exactly the same phenomenon occurring in the human world, where smell is presented as a threshold to the sexual relation (Diel, 1947; Lévinas, 1987).

I can like or not someone else's body odour and be attracted to it or repelled by it. As the self discovers fragrances, it can determine which ones it likes and which it dislikes. As body odour in the human world is not as strong as in the other two worlds, perfume and aftershave act as surrogates for it (Süskind, 1985). This can explain the fact that many advertisements for aftershave involve an odour appeal to the opposite gender: with this aftershave, you will attract all women. It is implicitly assumed that, if the sense is flattered, the relation may take place. In the opposite case, it is not certain.

Prior to puberty and sexual discovery, the infant and the toddler discover the world through their mouth: they touch objects with their tongue and their teeth. This is part of self-consciousness. In relation to smell and as a step forward to formal sexual activity, the self discovers taste (Diel, 1947). Sensuality, such as kisses, can be assimilated to a form of cannibalism: in order to subject the other, the self needs to internalise it by eating it. The kiss and other oral sexual practices express that symbolically. This oral contact with the other's body and mouth appears as a mutual absorption of each other, thereby revealing attraction to these particular tastes. The more mouth contacts the self has with the world, the more these may be perceived as likes (or dislikes). The oral contact simulates the action of eating the other and of discovering new mouth sensation.

Obviously, sexuality first involves touch: prior to and during the intercourse. By caressing one's body and then the other's, the self discovers concrete sensorial feelings. Cuddling one's teddy bear is part of this discovery, as the self spreads love. These quasi-sexual practices stimulate other nerves and muscles and bring other sensations (sexual prologue, kiss) that it can name (sweetness, warmth, cold). The utmost expression of touch in sexuality is undoubtedly when orgasm occurs (Foucault, 1976b, 1984). It brings sensations that no other action can bring as such. With puberty, when the self reaches adolescence age, it seems to be driven by these new sensorial discoveries of sexuality, often practising it in isolation. Such happens because of a physical pleasure associated with the softness of touch (Foucault, 1976b). A form of ethics can arise, since the adolescent—then the adult—must learn to domesticate and tame its sexual impulses. This is what leads to determine what practices are acceptable and what other practices are not. For long, homosexuality has been deemed unacceptable, which is no longer the case everywhere in the twenty-first century. Nowadays, what is clearly not acceptable includes molesting, abuse, paedophilia or zoophilia (Nabokov, 1955).

In addition to the discovery and the stimulation of the senses, sexuality highlights a personal and ontological relationship to time. The duration of the sexual act as well as its frequency informs on a certain relationship the self has to time. In other words, through sexuality, not only are the five senses being constructed, but also an abstract but well-informed notion of time and a definition of a preferred time horizon for the conduct of its life.

Ethics is involved in sexuality as part of ontological discovery, insofar as sexuality constructs the personal relationship of the self to the process of life and to the divine body in some sense. The finality of the sexual act is symbolically to give birth. In that respect, the act can be either explicitly or implicitly directed at that purpose (Diel, 1947; Freud, 1905, 1913; Lévinas, 1969, 1987). Implicitness or explicitness of the purpose highlights the relationship of the self to birth. It gives birth at his convenience, *for example*, at the point of time that it chooses. Sexuality informs on the wills constructed and expressed by the individual regarding the beginning of life. Similarly, the self can decide to terminate someone else's life, whereby Judæo-Christian ethics claim "thou shalt not kill". This means that ethics suggests giving birth but not taking it.

Interestingly, Freud (1913, 1927) and Lévinas (1987) reason that, in French language, the climax of the sexual act is called *little death* (petite mort—beautiful agony). The sexual act makes the self symbolically die and resurrect afterwards. This expresses its own experiences of both death and birth, which no surrogate can experience in its stead. Such experiences, by simulating death, also simulate the time when God will call the self back, that is, infinity (Lévinas, 1969, 1975). As in most religions the closest contact to God is deemed to be from death time on, approaching death is a means of enhancing one's knowledge of God. Interestingly, to Lévinas, the self seeks for the mere little death, for he can reappear and learn from that experience to constitute the living self.

Ethics continues, as any experience of the divine realm is supposed to be shared with others through witnessing. Accordingly, any Christian theologies have pointed out the necessity of witnessing for one's religious experiences, including approaching God. This would explain why solitary sexual practices have long been condemned by the church. As the self does not accompany an Other to this little death and resurrection, its solitary experience of the divine realm is perceived as a selfish experience. Ethics reaches its climax when the self shares this dual experience with someone else. In some Eastern societies, ethics' utmost form consists in witnessing to this experience before others (Leal, 2018; Mishra, 2011). Conversely, Judæo-Christian societies reject this witnessing, leaving this experience in the self's most private realm and not daring to even think about it (Foucault, 1976a; Freud, 1905).

4.1.2.2 Experiences of the Other: Communication and Languages as Cultural Constructs

Once the self has demonstrated a commencement of self-awareness or self-caring, it starts to be able to benefit from the Other in its personal construction. This construction can only be complete when likes and dislikes are confronted with the Other's (Arendt, 1961) and foremost reflection of it in the Other's eye (Lévinas, 1972, 1987, 1991). As long as it is alone, it can merely be aware of itself and of its sensorial possibilities. Alone, it is *isolated* and as such is not yet really a self. *Isolation* prevents it from being aware of its intrinsic condition. At best, sensorial experiences enable it to articulate some intuitions as to what its likes and dislikes are. Until the first encounter with the Other, this self-to-be neither makes sense of these senses nor compares them with Others' experiences. In other words, without the Other, the self cannot be; its human condition lies in its sharing and witnessing to the Other (Arendt, 1961).

The Other has three virtues that uphold the construction of the ontological self. Firstly, he mirrors its condition. Secondly, as an imperfect mirror, he reflects another, different self. From that imperfect reflection, the reflected can draw on its own characteristics (Arendt, 1961, 1968; Lévinas, 1987). Thirdly, the experience of the Other implies communication and consequently *language games* (Lévinas, 1987) that are object of common earning.

Sexuality, when not onanistic, plays that triple role: the sexual relation is a combination of two selves that discover each other's sensorial feelings. The self discovers its own senses but also those of its partner. As these feelings share the same nature (the five senses), the individual is mirrored throughout the expression of the other's senses (Lévinas, 1987). The ontological self learns how the Other expresses his own likes and dislikes. It can thereby imagine how it reacts to the Other in terms of touch, taste, smell, hear and sight. What is obvious in the sexual relation is also at work in any non-sexual relationship (Arendt, 1961, 1968): through exchanges with the Other, the self can determine aesthetical preferences. Ethics occurs as a matter of respect for this Other's differences (Arendt, 1961).

The reflected image informs the self on what it reflects. At the same time, the Other's reaction informs it on its subjective nature. Hence, two subjectivities are at work in the dual relation. The ontological self perceives itself in a given way and concludes from the confrontation with the Other that it can be perceived differently. Symmetrically, it becomes aware that it can perceive the Other differently from what the latter expects to send. Lévinas' philosophy summarises this thought by considering that the Other reflects to me who I am and who he is, without me being him or him being me. In sum, the contact to the other teaches on diversity: I am not alone and the Other's perceptions can differ from mine. This discovery of the Other and of diversity becomes part of my own ethics, as I respect them, and therefore defines myself as such. I can see the differences between us and I can define myself in this way. Ultimately, I start to be able to express what is specific to me.

Simultaneously, as the experience of the Other informs me on him or on myself, it makes me discover our ontological, human condition. Confrontation with the Other also allows me to see what we have in common (Arendt, 1961; Lévinas, 1972, 1991). These features determine what I am as a self, what we are as two selves forming a specie. Namely, I see the Other's ontological condition (access neither to my knowledge nor to my perceptions). From then on, I can discover that my own condition is limited in the same way. In the Other's limitations and actions, I can see mine and I can understand what makes us similar.

Life in concentration camps outlined that I could see my humanity and my ontology in the Other, placed in a similar condition where of humanity deprivation (Arendt, 1968). What I see as missing in the Other is exactly what I am missing. By seeing the Other, I can imagine myself in his place in any situation, because we are similar. If his spouse is murdered, my feelings are not only empathy to him but also empathy to myself for the case it would happen to me. If I rejoice because his spouse is still alive, in fact I am drawing on my own feeling if I were facing the same situation. In fact, the Other's experiences become mine in thought and subsequently part of my identity and ethics. In sum, the more I see in him, the more insights I get into my own condition.

In connection with the Other, the self must develop a language, be it that of sexuality or another form of discourse (Lévinas, 1987). Accordingly, the self develops ways of approaching the Other and communicating with him or her. Language is a mode of communication that is common to the Other and myself, as it consists of a common grammar (rules and codes of conduct), idioms and symbols (commonly shared meanings). But it also demonstrates how I address the Other. In fact, the choice of linguistic figures in the elaboration of a discourse is not neutral and highlights the identity of the speaker. At the same time, the self enriches its identity by learning a common language and accentuates its specificities in expressing itself.

At the same time as communication devices and skills constitute the self, they express its own background and eventually ethics (Lévinas, 1972). Realisations of the self have an aesthetic that relates to its sensorial likes and dislikes and informs on itself though its tolerance level for dislikes, especially those observed in the Other. Whilst sexuality remains in its intimacy, its aesthetic is communication directed at the Other and at the non-self. Be they artistic, scientific or otherwise, these realisations express the self's prior experiences and consequently what constitutes it as a self. These pieces can be considered separately or as a whole. Precisely the collection of its realisations and achievements conveys what it actually is.

4.1.2.3 Experiences of the Non-Self: Ethics and Accountability as the Culture of the Self

The non-self can be defined as anything with what the self is unable to have a sexual relationship (Lévinas, 1969, 1987). The non-self is everything that is neither the Other nor myself. The non-self has also been coined as non-human, that is, anything intangible having its own existence and strategies for life (Latour, 1994, 2008, 2013). The non-self-category is the broadest one as it embraces fauna and flora and non-living objects, such as ideas, symbols and methods. The experiences that the self has of that negatively defined object are a major part of its constitution. Even if non-selves contribute to the discovery of sensorial feelings, they do not stimulate the erotic process that activates them. Consequently, Lévinas (1972) considers that the experience of the non-self is specific.

The relationship between the self and non-selves is characterised by the responsibility of the former over the latter (Lévinas, 1969, 1985, 1987). The experiences of the non-self constitute the ethics of the self, that is, the underpinnings or its position *vis-à-vis* social topics and more generally its role within society. The self creates the non-self, until it gains its autonomy and becomes a non-self in its own rights (Latour, 1994, 1996). It is not the creation that first constitutes the self but the motivations underlying this creation, especially knowing that this non-self may well at some juncture lead to an autonomous life. The self's (moral) responsibility is first in the meaning that it gives to the non-self to-be (Lévinas, 1969, 1985, 1987). The self must justify before God and itself what it expects from the creation of the non-self. In the aftermath, it must give accounts to God and to the Other for the use it made of the non-self. As he has the ability to control the non-self, it is responsible for it to be actually what he expected it to be.

As the self is responsible for the creation and the existence of the non-self, it is also responsible for its outcomes. These can be considered other creations from the self. As such, it is also responsible for their existence. Consequently, the outcomes of the non-self are non-selves too and have no autonomous existence in the first place. Only the self was able to decide to create them or not. Responsibility is greater when the non-self becomes fully autonomous and alters the functioning of the world, *for example*, armaments and their damage to the world. Alfred Nobel has long been held responsible for dynamite and explosives he created, as they were used not only for engineering purposes but military actions. Owing to this responsibility, Nobel's ethics has led him to promote peace by enabling the awarding of a prize for those acting in favour of peace (Meyer, 1952; Pauli, 1942).

How the self constructs its own accountability and develops the way it gives an account to the Other is what constitutes its identity and thereby it as a self (Shearer, 2002). For instance, in corporate social responsibility, the self is responsible for the outcomes of the firm (non-self) and their impacts on the Other(s), that is, stakeholders (Fowles, 1993; Gray, Dey, Owen, Evans, & Zadek, 1997; Gray, Owen, & Maunders, 1988; Lehman, 2007; O'Dwyer & Unerman, 2007; L. D. Parker, 2005; Unerman & O'Dwyer, 2007). Twenty-first-century debates surrounding Artificial Intelligence and its capability of creating non-selves on its own make Lévinas' (1974) point differently valid. At some juncture, the self whence the first-order non-self originated may lose control and track of its creatures and their outcomes. This is what currently drives ethical debates around Artificial Intelligence in particular (Johnson, 2015; Matin, 2018; Sutton, Holt, & Arnold, 2016).

4.1.2.4 Construction of Systematic Individual Mental Programmes

Every individual experience contributes to the discovery of its ontology by the self. As such, they form its identity and background. As the self is connected to other selves and non-selves, these intimate (secret) experiences also condition the way it thinks and experiences the rest of the world (Lévinas, 1969, 1985, 1987). At the same time as the self knows that its intimate experiences are unknown to the Other, it is aware that it does not know the Other's experiences either. It just has no knowledge of the existence of the world. Therefore, it wonders where the world comes from and subsequently whence itself is coming, who it is and what is the meaning of life.

These apparently trivial questions actually raise major metaphysical concerns and as such operate like aporias. The self is not able to answer them in a transcendental and objective way. It can just supply approximations. In order to believe in them, it is reduced to approximating *totality*, that is, the whole. The self develops a holistic approach that makes the set of approximations coherent with each other and constitutes a global vision of the environment. At the same time, as it is not isolated in the world, it needs to make his views look likely or objective. Lévinas reasons that, in these cases, objectivity is a pure construction: the ontological self exteriorises and objectifies its own vision of the world. A way of proceeding is the development of systematic mental programmes, which are the threshold to a generalised ethics.

These systematic approximations regard *infinity* (Lévinas, 1969), *for example*, God, truth and ethics and related topics such as justice, love and democracy. Part of the ontological self is the systematic way it understands, imagines and approximates God. These systematic approximations lead to systematic perceptions. Precisely because they are systematic, these observations and conclusions operate as beliefs and characterise the self's ethics. The self believes more in his systematic thinking than in the approximations, for these remind it of its ontological condition. Thus, what is important is rather the thinking than the thought object. This is where ethics lies: In the inner approximations of totality and infinity, the self makes and which it commits itself.

Whilst beliefs consist of the way the individual sees and understands the world, these mental programmes also provide him with means to judge and appraise that world. This is what Lévinas (1969, 1987) and Arendt (1961, 1989) call *values*, central to ethics. The self does not only construct its world independently from the others. It also appraises their constructs and can adhere or not to them. Under this purview, the self can rely on critical points of its mental programmes, knowing what suits it and what does not. One step ahead, these mental programmes can also judge the subjective validity or the subjective reliability of others' values and ethics.

By understanding the intimacy of the self, its ethics could be framed. Lévinas' (1969, 1972, 1985, 1987) writings on the constitution of the self, culture and ethics were introduced as they could supplement and instance Arendt's. Therefore, the constituency of the ethics of the self was apprehended as the outcome of three experiences: oneself, the Other and the non-self. The combination of all three leads to the constitution of the sensorial perceptions (sexuality), the linguistic and communicational practices (the Other) and identity as a moral and ethical programming in progress (the non-self). At a second stage, ethics determines how the self perceives the world and the individual systematic mental programmes that uphold these perceptions and label them. Notwithstanding its specificities, the individual can share some of his or her programmes with other people.

In that respect, he or she ventures outside the ontological self and constructs the anthropological and social self, that is, the self within and towards a group sharing common values and ethics (Levi-Strauss, 1952, 1958). In that case, ethics appears as the process and the outcome of the acculturation within the group.

4.2 Educating Ethical Management Accountants

Whatever the group is, acculturation requires that implicit value should be made explicit and formally transmitted. This is simply the role education plays in raising ethical selves. Even if there is an innate dimension of ethics, the self's various sensorial preferences may also be influenced by collective notions of what is right or wrong, pretty or ugly just as good or evil. Even if ethics can be innate, it grows and becomes a form of conscience and awareness, often triggered by the environment in which one is evolving. This point is amplified by the fact that, in the twenty-first century, numerous financial, environmental or operational scandals have raised ethical questions (Beggs & Dean, 2007; Bonini & Boraschi, 2010; Marques, Dhiman, & Biberman, 2014; McMillan, 2004; Rockness & Rockness, 2005; Unerman & O'Dwyer, 2004). This suggests that ethics should be learnt and taught. In the case of management accountants, business schools have been urged to teach business ethics in their curricula (Beggs & Dean, 2007; Boyce, 2008). As the self's personal ethics is being constructed through its encounters with the Other and with non-selves, universities have a role to play in structuring these ethical issues and concerns.

4.2.1 University and Education at the Core of Management Accounting's Ethics

Major corporate scandals and business scams have been caused by savvy business leaders often with the complicity of auditors and management accountants. It is denounced that this situation owes to the grounding of accounting courses in neoclassical microeconomics domination by the imperative of profit maximisation (R. E. Jensen, 1990; Stolowy, 2005). To some extent, business schools and their teaching staff can be held responsible for those corporate scandals and profit-driven misconducts (Roca, 2008). It does seem that disciplinary teachings have overlooked of moral considerations, values and intentionality. With this model, students have been brought afar from any sense of "moral, responsibly".

4.2.1.1 Universities for the Construction of Enlightened Citizens and Professionals

With the ***advent of democracy*** characterising twenty-first-century Western societies, education has been perceived increasingly crucial to the construction of ethical selves (Badiou & Gauchet, 2016). This perceived need for more education has found a different manifestation with mass enrolment in schools and universities. Such has led to the emergence a (quasi-human) right to education (Gauchet, Blais, & Ottavi, 2016).

The utmost manifestation of this dual phenomenon can be found in the spread of MOOCs whose name is a revealer of this political agenda in itself: Massive Open Online Courses (Gauchet et al., 2016, p. 214). With massive enrolments, universities are not educating a handful of young aristocratic men and future monks. It does seem that twenty-first-century universities' purpose has been to educate youngsters. Yet, it is ambiguous whom they are serving: students or society (Gauchet et al., 2016; Gauchet, Blais, & Ottavi, 2013; Mercer, 1996).

The answer to this question is far from unanimous and reveals major political splits. A leftist approach directly inherited from postmodern thinking views universities as serving society by educating and growing enlightened citizens. Through the education and upbringing of citizens, education and universities should facilitate mobility across social classes. In contradistinction to this approach, a rightist view sees universities as serving students by helping find their place in society and obtain a (well-paid) occupation. This unfinished debate has opened for new questions, namely regarding the content of teaching and its ethicality.

The first question this split raises is that of admission and requirements for enrolment. For Gauchet et al. (2013, pp. 59–83), leftists see unconditional admission as an imperative in the construction and upbringing of enlightened citizens. This unconditionality makes admission a quasi-human right to education, raising a question as to who should bear the cost of educating citizens: the taxpayer or the self to be educated. Assumedly, anybody willing to enrol should be allowed in and attend the classes he or she chooses. This approach is vivid in continental European countries, namely France and Germany, long known for crowded lecture theatres and high failure rates at the bachelor's level (Gauchet et al., 2013). The original view backlashes by questioning whether failed students can be considered enlightened and capable of serving society… Pursuant to this approach, failure should not be viewed an individual problem confronting the student but a collective error: society failed to enlighten this student.

The opposite approach, mostly dominant in Anglo-Saxon countries or Japan, rests upon the idea that universities should select the sole students they consider capable of being successful. As a result, the vast majority of applicants may find themselves denied access to the desired education and enlightenment. Students tend no longer to choose their master or mentor, when applying for an institution. Conversely, a committee or a board makes the admission decision. Those who will be the student's master are rarely involved. Unsurprisingly, the traditional master-disciple special relationship cannot really apply in universities. As mentors and mentees do not choose each other, there is no special connection or chemistry between the two, whereby the disciple admires his or her master and follows his or her teaching. On the other hand, larger cohorts of students lead educators to have so many students that they cannot follow their individual construction and progress (Gauchet et al., 2013, 2016). The special mentor-mentee relationship based upon trust and confidence can hardly develop.

The second question manifested through these debates regarding universities' audience regards curriculum format. The question of whether curricula should be à la carte or standard is raised. As the student is placed at the core of education, he or she is more or less directly involved in the design of their own curriculum. This raises another question as to whether students should enrol in a pre-conceived programme or whether they can be considered capable of designing and building their own. Interestingly and surprisingly, Gauchet et al. (2013, 2016) stress the fact that the answer to this question does not necessarily fit within the leftist-rightist political debate. Either position belongs indifferently to one side or the other. With à la Carte curricula, the proponents of citizens' construction consider that students can choose whichever subjects they want, insofar as these will all open youngsters' mind and make them good citizens.

Almost for the opposite reason, personal development proponents see in the free choice of courses the utmost expression of the student's free will. This implicitly assumes that students or these citizens-to-be are sole knowing what is best for them. Conversely, with standard or set courses, the proponents of citizens' construction consider that society's expectations and requirements are superior. Therefore, society knows better than the individual what the community needs and is sole capable of designing curricula: an enlighten citizen *must know* certain things and acquire certain skills. By definition, the aspiring student does not know yet what is good for his or her construction. In contradistinction to this approach, personal development proponents would borrow from Signal Theory to argue that standards are necessary. Standards are what enable students to label themselves with something understandable and comparable for employers, whence the necessity of similar characteristics manifested in set curricula.

It proceeds from this observation a discussion on the need for compulsory business ethics courses in management accounting curricula. Such courses would be taught in response to previous scandals, seeking to avert a repeat thereof. If business ethics courses are compulsory, the proponents of society's authority over curricula can be fulfilled at the detriment of those claiming students' free will. This implies that business ethics education can only appear as a core course common to any business and accounting curricula.

4.2.1.2 From Developing Specialism to Ambiguous Ethics-as-Compliance

Influenced by the idea that competencies are unique and therefore highly specialised, twenty-first-century universities around the world have encouraged students to enrol in niche courses. Ultimately, their graduates have a unique command of a specific subject area and can be perceived as world experts on it. This model based on high specialisation has resulted in universities functioning in silos and in teaching being very fragmented. In some sense, this model revolutionises the twentieth-century university, where students were generalists: multiple disciplines were taught. As a result, an entire cohort of students would attend the same core courses (Gauchet et al., 2013). With the advent of highly specialised curricula, core courses' essence has been called into question. In such a context, making business ethics courses compulsory was possible in the twentieth century but is not anymore in the twenty-first century. This is what has led South African universities' students to attend classes in one subject only from the first semester of the first year and ignore neglecting all others. Through this, students would enrol in accounting detrimentally to business economics, management, marketing, HR, strategy or finance. As business ethics does not appear as a unique and bankable skill, in contradistinction to accounting skills, the need for it is not obvious. This logic seems to clash with employers' and society's needs, since this hyper-specialism and technical expertise result in graduates being relatively illiterate at formation and opinion argumentation (Retief & Villiers (de), 2013). The case of South African business schools upholds Gauchet et al.'s (2016) point that twenty-first-century universities have deviated from their original and core mission—enlightening and upbringing—as though the rightist approach to studies should prevail.

Increased specialism and technicality in university curricula have resulted in a major confusion as to what teaching and learning nowadays mean. In twentieth-century universities, masters had control over what needs to be known and in what order. In the twenty-first century, students have been placed at the centre of a university setting with their needs to be immediately fulfilled (Gauchet et al., 2013). Students have been implicitly assumed capable of knowing what is good for themselves, as though they were already enlightened citizens, which reinforces a myth that "there is no efficient learning other than the one coming from the learner, and grounded in his or her needs" (Gauchet et al., 2013, p. 115). This makes "us forget the *raison d'être* of the institution" (Gauchet et al., 2013, p. 116). The twenty-first-century university has stepwise abandoned the idea that learning is a journey and process, for "knowledge supposedly *scholarly*, precisely, has been opposed to a true culture the bourgeois class owns, and notwithstanding the simulacrum of democratisation organised by the system itself" (Gauchet et al., 2013, p. 204).

The student seeks for actionable teaching through quick wins (Gauchet et al., 2013, pp. 209–250). In order to enable this, numerous universities have engaged in teaching and assessing *skills* associated with learning goals. The introduction of these concepts and this results-oriented teaching and learning philosophy has left room for what Gauchet et al. (2013, p. 73) coin *pedagogism, namely* "a process of ideologisation" purporting scientific approaches to teaching and learning. These approaches, however, have no grounds other than the justification of education sciences' *raison d'être*. Influenced by pedagogy specialists disconnected from any other academic discipline, universities have developed in pedagogical engineering. Through this new approach, teaching focus has been placed on students' activities and outcomes. Nowadays, learning is no longer perceived as a journey towards maturity and knowledge but an occupation until getting paid employment. Pursuant to this observation, business ethics has hardly found a place in university teaching: ethics appears as a moral capability and intellectual maturity and requires time unto formation. No quick wins can really be associated with business ethics courses per se. Unless academic staff decides on students' behalf what is right or wrong, good or evil. With this, there is a risk that the original intent be perverted: whilst ethics is an inner philosophy associated with one's values, it appears as a set of rules and procedures (Badiou, 2001, 2006). In this context, there could be a confusion between ethics, compliance and conformance (Al Arabi, 2017).

According to Al Arabi (2017), conformance and compliance are grounded in systems of law or rules compelling a party to abide by certain pre-existing principles. Conformance consists of two dimensions, both of which raising a series of questions important for the understanding of ethics (Bhimani & Soonawalla, 2005; Leavitt & Maykuth, 1989; Tucker, 1962). Firstly, behind the notion of conformance lies the issuing party's authority, since there is assumedly no negotiation. The compelled party expects to be acknowledged or by the issuer as following its principles. Pursuant to this, the conforming party finds itself adapting its own procedures and ways of functioning to eventually mirror those to which they must conform. The second dimension of conformance is to be found in negative in the consequences of not conforming. When a party seeks for recognition but does not have the appropriate procedures or ways of functioning, the compelling body can ban them or impose major retribution on them (Cast, Stets, & Burke, 1999; Rai, 1975; Rupert, Jehn, Engen, & Reuver, 2010; Sandron & Hayford, 2002; Yair, 2007).

The conformance philosophy resembles the subjectification mechanisms identified in disciplinary studies (Foucault, 1975, 1984). There is no obligation to apply for recognition. Accordingly, the associated constraints must be accepted, one of those being the relinquishing of sovereignty at the benefit of an external body which eventually imposes its own way of functioning. This external body is now forced to do exactly as prescribed: it must conform to the rule it imposes on others. Because there is no obligation to join the club of conforming bodies, sanctions are dissuasive in case the applying body breaches the rules to which it is expected to conform. Where conformance is very Foucault-like is that one party transfers their own body to a third party. Not just does that third party impose rules but compels behaviour and operates as a court with no possible appeal (Forneret, 2013; Frickey, 2005; Moore, 2010; Owens & Wedeking, 2011; White Jr., 1995).

The arbitrariness underlying the notion of conformance is therefore what makes it easy to achieve: tick the right boxes and follow the right procedures. Yet, its condition of possibility lies in surrendering. Legal research stresses a lesser form of conformance: compliance. Unlike conformance, compliance does not result in abandoning and transferring sovereignty, even though norms are still imposed by third party (Cardenas, 2011; Ee, 2011; Gilliland & Manning, 2002; Greenberg, 2010; Wright,

2011). Whilst conformance leads to replicate the model to be deemed ethical, compliance results in the party under scrutiny issuing its own standards that a third party shall enforce consistently with its own agenda. All possible changes in processes and ways of functioning are the compliant body's discretion (Fasterling, 2012; McKendall, DeMarr, & Jones-Rikkers, 2002; C. Parker, 2000; J. Weber & Wasieleski, 2013).

This observation has three series of implications, one for each body and one for their relationship. Firstly, the compliant body decides on its own agenda and must prove to the third party that their revised processes and ways of functioning converge with the third party's principles. That is, the compliant body maintains full control over the compliance process (Agócs, 1997; Anderson, Welsh, Ramsay, & Gahan, 2012; Armour, Deakin, Lele, & Siems, 2009; Block, 2013; Boon, Flood, & Webb, 2005).

Secondly, the third party has supposedly issued clear minimal criteria that must be that the compliant body must meet. These criteria allegedly pertain to the core values wherewith the third party cannot compromise. This logic implies that the third party, acting as the accrediting body, should issue a to-do list and scoresheet. Compliance then eventuates when a certain score is obtained, that is, when a minimal amount of principles are not breached (Boyce, 2004; Christensen & Mohr, 1999; Rouse, Davis, & Friedlob, 1986). Students would retain from business ethics courses that they must at least do certain things to be considered ethical: they must comply with some minimal principles. This is what can be found in professional codes of conduct or codes of ethics where principles are generally so loose and ambiguous that anyone could recognise themselves therein.

Thirdly, recognition that the compliant body is ethical eventuates ex post facto and not prior to the conduct of operations. Recognition is often granted in response to obvious misuses or misconduct reported to the party whose principles may have been abused (Cardenas, 2011; Chartier, 2012; Fasterling, 2012; Latin, Tannehill, & White, 1976; McKendall et al., 2002; C. Parker, 2000; J. Weber & Wasieleski, 2013). Surprisingly, the accreditor appears as the weaker party in the relationship. Such is the case, as it almost emotionally reacts to the situation, making compliance mechanisms negative (responsive) regulations rather than positive (performative) laws (Joannidès & McKernan, 2015; McKernan, 2012; McKernan & Kosmala, 2007; McKernan & McPhail, 2012). It is no real surprise that the effect of these regulations cannot be constraining (Badiou, 2001, 2009). In fact, compliance leads to a paradoxical situation where the norms hence issued find themselves undermining their own applicability. At best, the accreditor operates *qua* an advisor on compliance that the applicant can consult or not (C. Parker, 2000).

Back to business ethics courses, the danger is that students would consider they are learning tips and hints enabling them to be ethical in any sort of situations. They would be ethical because they would tick the right box and would have done as prescribed. Be it in the greater (conformance) or lesser form (compliance), they would perceive their behaviour as ethical, because it is legally admitted as such. Through such a minimalist understanding of ethics, these courses ruin the whole purpose of teaching business ethics. In the twenty-first century, this problem has been aggravated by the skills-based approach to teaching and learning (*e.g.* serious games, Gauchet et al., 2013, p. 225). Soft and mostly hard skills are detrimental to the exercise of judgement: the reign of marks based upon purportedly objective assessment grids and criteria has enabled the rise of standards. Identifying this phenomenon, Gauchet et al. (2016) highlight the fact that all universities converge to adopting the same teaching and learning standards. The standardisation of teaching and assessing makes their institution lose its specificities in the galaxy of universities (Swanson, 2004; Bennis & O'Toole, 2005). The same textbooks are used in most institutions, course contents are alike and so are case studies and exercises (L. D. Parker, 2002b). Ultimately, business ethics appears as a toolbox with solutions for most common dilemmas.

4.2.2 *A Growing Need for Business Ethics Education*

Educating ethical people is a "moral enterprise" (Phenix, 1961). This moral enterprise can be questioned, since many people are so far from common understanding of what is good and so slow at serving what appears as right. An education is not for accumulating information but rather it is in learning to learn and being ready to make decisions and take responsibility for those. Education is supposed to make answer-able people, that is, people capable of saying "I did so, because…." It is because different people disagree on good and evil that it is crucial to teach students how to think by themselves.

4.2.2.1 Ethics as Central to Universities' Essence

Business schools' mission is not separate from that of the founding university but is a declension thereof. In a leftist scheme, the mission of a business school is to educate enlightened executives capable of thinking by themselves. This can be evidenced with Catholic universities whose is mission grounded in spirituality. One of these is Santa Clara University, whose mission statement claims: "*Santa Clara University will educate citizens and leaders of competence, conscience, and compassion to foster a more humane, just and sustainable world*" (Delbecq, 2010). Launching from such a mission statement can eventually lead to managerial integrity and morality in any organisational culture. To this end, business schools have a role to play by involving their staff in this undertaking. In this respect, the University of Navarra in Spain explicitly encourages staff

> to seek and present the truth; contribute to the academic, cultural and personal education of its students; promote academic research and healthcare activities; provide suitable opportunities for the development of its professors and employees; and carry out broad cultural outreach and social promotion work with a clear goal of service.[1]

Seemingly, these universities feel a need for being loyal to their history and purpose, as explicitly highlighted by the Catholic University of the Sacred Heart in Italy:

> Faithful to its original calling, the faculty still turns out technically and scientifically qualified graduates capable of giving an anthropological and Christian perspective to the profession, creating a work and study environment with a blend of scientific and religious visions of the world.[2]

Partaking in business education in the early 1900s, ethics was initially internalised in the business schools' mission, purpose and *raison d'être*. This inclusion could grant them legitimacy and recognition. Ethics education was part of the "point, mission and self-understanding; it was not one additional objective that business schools should have, among others" (Abend, 2013, p. 191). There was no need to treat ethics as a separate subject; rather, it was the driving force that took all its energy from early universities' overall mission. Ethics was integrated in all school activities, implicitly instilled as part of citizens-to-be's enlightenment. It does seem that this underlying principle has been called into question in the twenty-

[1] https://www.unav.edu/en/web/conoce-la-universidad/ideario-de-la-universidad.
[2] http://www.ucsc.it/our-campuses-rome#content.

first century where business ethics is explicitly in one course with its own examination (Rutherford, Parks, Canazos, & White, 2012).

At the dawn of the twentieth century, the term "business ethics" in the United States related to ethics in corporations, whereas emphasis in Europe was placed on trade and business proceeding from the Protestant work ethic (De George, 1995). Business ethics was dismissed in the first decades of the twentieth century and started to be taught in the 1970s where it started to emerge as an academic field. Business ethics education developed in the 1980s until being well established in the 1990s. Notwithstanding this non-linear spread, "ethics was constitutive of the business school project one hundred years ago" (Abend, 2013, p. 172). In this capacity, business ethics was presented as "a lens through which the whole project is conceived and implemented" (Abend, 2013, p. 172).

From 1900 to 1936, the University of California and Yale University initiated public lectures addressing ethics in business: this was considered "a major advance in terms of the legitimacy of the very claim that business ought to be conducted ethically" (Abend, 2013, p. 179). Until the 1960s, business ethics was amalgamated with business philanthropy. Only in the 1970s, business ethics started to be a matter of interest for teaching and learning purposes. Since then, a growing number of business schools have offered business ethics courses (Abend, 2013).

Notwithstanding the secularisation of society and higher education the postmoderns have claimed in the twentieth century, a growing number of universities in the twenty-first century have reclaimed their religious identities. For now, as long as this "return to what was" (Abend, 2013; Brubacher & Rudy, 2004; Calkins, 2000; Moberg & Calkins, 2001) does not see the light, business ethics courses are bound to be perpetuated. As long as "the important role of faith-based ethical systems" is underestimated, something would be absent from "frameworks for ethical business behaviour" (Epstein, 2002, p. 92). It is through the distinctiveness of religion-based "moral reasoning that should interest business ethicists concerned with methodological completeness" (Calkins, 2000, p. 347). A recent approach to teaching business ethics has called for this "moral identity" to enable students' more committing moral judgement than rule-based teaching (Gu & Neesham, 2014).

Although making business students more religious and ethical cannot happen overnight, educating them through "repetition may reinforce and crystallise religious and ethical values in their academic journey" (Chen & Tang, 2013, p. 547). Fostering forms of religiosity or spirituality can be expected "to help prepare students to consider the possibility that business endeavours, spirituality and religious commitment can be inextricable parts of a coherent life" (Epstein, 2002, p. 91). Encouraging students to actively practise their religion can be a fair way of spreading the non-procedural teaching of ethics in business curricula (Conroy & Emerson, 2004). Even though some universities reclaim these religious roots, twentieth-century secularism is such that ethics education disconnected from religion or spirituality is likely to last long. Ethics courses taught in these institutions shall convey an ethic that is contextual and necessarily contingent upon the institution itself and its students.

4.2.2.2 Re-emphasis on Ethics in Today's Accounting Curricula

Notwithstanding efforts at including ethics education in business courses, scholars are still calling for more ethics courses. These courses supposedly enhance moral efficacy and individual responsibility (May et al., 2014). Concomitantly, the corporate world, deceived with graduates, denounces ethics courses' ineffectiveness (Sigurjonsson et al., 2015). Practitioners directly and explicitly report business schools for unethical practices (Ghoshal, 2005; Gioia, 2003), as though student ethical attitudes had remained unchanged (Jewe, 2008). Alongside business courses' development, philosophical and pedagogical questions have arisen as to what should be taught and how this should be done. This reasoning was evidenced through the launch of the *Journal of Business Ethics Education* in 2004 (Bowie, De George, Fontrodona, Frederick, & Horniman, 2004; Hooker, 2004). It is not to be doubted that business school graduates must be ethical and must behave themselves. Albeit, the questions of what is ideal and how a university faculty of commerce can make this eventuate remain unanswered (Gauchet et al., 2013, 2016).

In religiously grounded university business schools, ethics education was historically day-to-day religious education. In these universities, ethical and religious values conflate. Over time, as people departed from religious teaching and prescriptions from the Church, ethics began to take on a secular appeal devoid of religious affiliations. This led to confusion and misunderstanding around the role of business schools and the status given to the teaching of ethics. In the aftermath of financial scandals and business scams, society expressed "the needs of today's and future generations were different from those of past ones" (Marques et al., 2014). A wide schism has taken place:

> Today, business schools are clearly separate from schools and departments of social work, sociology, public policy, and journalism. Today business schools focus on strategy, finance, negotiation, marketing, leadership, and organisational behaviour, and not so much on urban poverty, crime, and other social problems, charity and philanthropy, public administration, international relations, or journalism. However, in the early twentieth century a business school could be involved in several of these things at the same time... indeed an early business school could intend to train not only businessmen, but also diplomats, social workers, public servants, and journalists. (Abend, 2013, p. 182)

Paraphrasing Aristotle on the corrupt youth of his time (Celano, 2018), one could say that today's executives who fail do not because of insufficient expertise or knowledge, Rather, they fail because of insufficient morality, interpersonal skills and wisdom. In fact, "Aristotle taught that genuine leadership consisted in the ability to identify and serve the common good... It requires an education in moral reasoning" (Thomas Lindsay in Bennis and O'Toole, 2005, p. 103).

In the twenty-first century, commencing with the Enron and WorldCom scandals, business schools have responded to the latest crises by placing each time greater emphasis on ethics and corporate governance. On universities' side, business school missions have been communicated with newer and more explicit wording (Charafedine, 2011). For instance, Stanford Business School explicitly claims that "one of the four essential components of a managerial mindset is Social Impact—developing innovative effective solutions to social problems for a more just, sustainable, and healthy world" (p. 14).

Beyond isolated initiatives, a global trend has arisen: the MBA oath. This international initiative's purpose is to foster responsible value creation as a first step in embracing spirituality in business (http:/mbaoath.org). The MBA oath is aimed at making graduates of great character and leadership, not just close-minded technocrats. Confronted with the major financial scandals in which their alumni had been involved, "the Deans of Harvard and Wharton have, each for themselves, been working on rigorous revisions of their curricula" (Marques et al., 2014, p. 198). Resultantly, the Harvard MBA programme was so redesigned as to emphasising more ethics and teamwork. At the same time, the Wharton Business School launched a "doctoral programme in ethics and legal studies" (Alsop, 2006).

Outwith these apparently isolated cases, two remarks can be made. Firstly, Ivy League universities have been confronted with the issue of instilling ethics in a way that does not make it just a subject but something bigger wherewith students can identify themselves and something they can appropriate. It can be hoped that, once this approach starts being effective, other universities will follow. Secondly, search on a web browser reveals that business schools offer "conscious MBAs", "ethical MBAs" and "socially responsible MBAs". These endeavours can be driven by the intent to rebuild the "reputation of business practices in the eyes of stakeholders" (Marques et al., 2014, p. 198). All these efforts are a result of acknowledging a problem with the status quo, acknowledging that the current education in business schools needs an ethical component.

Irrespective of these numerous attempts at bringing more ethics into business and management accounting curricula, a series of questions remains unanswered. With the development of international accreditations, such as AACSB, business and accounting curricula tend to be homogenised and standardised (Rouse et al., 1986). This implies that assessment criteria also be homogenised, which bears the risk of major contradictions for business ethics education. The first contradiction lies in the risk that ethics itself be standardised through textbooks, suggesting what is right or wrong and what is good or evil. Thereby, the contingent nature of ethics is at risk of being ignored. If there is a universal, superior ethics that should impose itself to the world, it is uncertain as yet which one this should. Pretending to hold the one truth on things is what has caused totalitarianisms and wars in the twentieth century (Arendt, 1968). If a Western (European or North-American) ethics is imposed, other countries, such as Asian or Middle-Eastern countries, may not recognise themselves in these and confront these. Assuming that the first contradiction can be overcome, the second one points to issues in assessment. Whilst students' judgement capabilities are assessed, standards inevitably lead to any form of conformance or compliance. It proceeds from this a question relating to what is to be assessed and how this can be. What should assessment criteria be and how can one be sure that all students are assessed in an equal and impartial manner?

4.3 Conclusion

Management accounting appears as a profession with its own habitus and implicit rules and forms a community of practice. What makes ethics especially crucial to its functioning is that this profession is not as structured as others, such as medical, legal or chartered accountants and auditors (Backhof & Martin, 1991; Kurunmäki, 2004; Pratt et al., 2006). Unlike these other organised and structured professions, management accounting is also very heterogeneous: management accountants have very different professional backgrounds. Some come from within the accounting profession whilst others are of vocational extraction—engineers, legal professionals, pharmacists and the like (Chotiyanon, 2018; Chotiyanon & Joannidès de Lautour, 2018; Joannidès de Lautour, 2018b). As there are no formal professional or educational requirements imposing themselves, the profession is always exposed to the risk of disputable ethicality of its members.

As human beings and acknowledged professionals promoted to a management accounting position owing to their vocational competences, management accountants are expected to behave ethically. Even though it can be assumed that ethics is innate and is part of their personal construction, education matters. All told, what makes an ethical management accountant? This question may seem to be left unanswered at this stage, since no practicalities as to what should be done are suggested. This philosophical chapter elicits the idea that ethical management accounting is a habitus learnt on the job and at school.

Management accounting reports tell the story of the organisation and inform on its activities, its successes and its failures. The connection of its actions with its beliefs system, its values and its norms make these reports fair and reliable. Accounts highlight faithful conduct, hence the imperative of having reliable and trustworthy management accountants. If management is convinced by the story, supposedly decision-making can be done properly. Convincing accounts are expected to ultimately contribute to the completion of organisational mission. Management accountants' ethics can be summarised as a practice whereby they must prove their commitment to management and effective decision-making through accurate, timely and relevant information.

In sum, an ethical management accountant is foremost a capable and competent management accountant. Competency involves that management accountants should exert their judgement and discernment regarding the numbers they produce. In particular, in relation to cost accounting and CVP analysis, management accountants should be capable of tracing the actual and most plausible reasons for a certain performance level without necessarily being contented with the surface of figures. Unfavourable labour efficiency variance does not necessarily mean that the workforce is a problem and that labour costs should be reduced. An ethical management accountant is someone capable of either discerning the most applicable causes for a situation or of admitting they cannot explain the phenomenon under scrutiny. Ethical management accountants are also professionals remaining on top of what makes their profession, namely new regulations and technologies. That is, ethical management accountants are people on whom management can actually rely upon.

As management accountants are dealing with sensitive and confidential information, part of their professional integrity consists in not disclosing or sharing outside the organisation what they observe. In particular, this implies not sharing critical information about their former employer when joining a new company, or not joining a direct competitor at a time critical for their current employer. An ethical management accountant is one on whose discretion an employer can rely upon even after they have left the organisation. This however raises a sensitive question regarding the status of whistle-blowers and the reporting of fraudulent practices. This question is outside the scope of this particular chapter but is addressed elsewhere (Fig. 4.4).

This chapter highlighted a real need for business ethics education in university business schools at the same time as we observe these courses' current limits. Such courses appear as procedural, legal or technical guidelines offered to students, oftentimes arising in response to a scandal and revealing a nevermore philosophy (Beggs & Dean, 2007; Bonini & Boraschi, 2010; Boyce, 2004, 2008, 2018; Cho, 2009; Low et al., 2008; Marques et al., 2014; McMillan, 2004; Rockness & Rockness, 2005; Stolowy, 2005; Unerman & O'Dwyer, 2004). Albeit, these business ethics courses cannot fulfil their claimed mission and fully convince students and society.

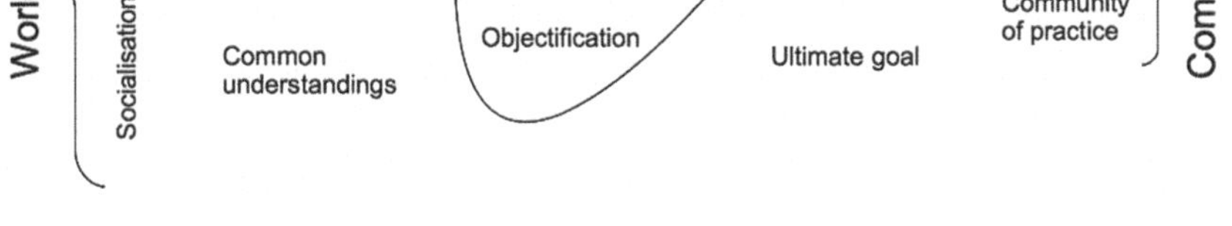

Fig. 4.4 Ethical management accounting

This leaves open two challenges that research and universities need addressing to solve this as yet unresolved contradiction. If tertiary institutions, especially business schools and faculties of commerce, claim to belong to a university, they need to return to their religious roots and thereby instil a religious economic theology into their teaching without necessarily creating specific business ethics courses. This opens three areas for future research. Firstly, not just in business ethics, but also in philosophy and education, work on the possibility of a twenty-first-century theology that would integrate university faculties and therefore curricula could be undertaken. What we here call theology may not necessarily be religious; to be inclusive, such a theology could be secular. Some more research into the core values of the essence of business schools will need to be questioned. A business school needing specific business ethics courses cannot qualify as a faculty and can therefore not belong to a university. That is, the possibility of splitting business schools from universities, as is the case of INSEAD or French Grandes Écoles (Stolowy, 2005), could be envisaged if it is found that they cannot adhere to a neo-theological model. Thirdly, as we highlight business ethics courses' weaknesses, further research would benefit from investigating what a positive ethics means and how it can be instilled into students.

Bibliography

Abend, G. (2013). The origins of business ethics in American universities. *Business Ethics Quarterly, 23*(2), 171–205.

Agócs, C. (1997). Institutionalized resistance to organizational change: Denial, inaction and repression. *Journal of Business Ethics, 16*(9), 917–931.

Aho, J. (2005). *Confession and bookkeeping—The religious, moral, and rhetorical roots of modern accounting*. New York: State University of New York Press.

Ahrens, T., & Chapman, C. S. (2002). The structuration of legitimate performance measures and management: Day-to-day contests of accountability in a UK restaurant chain. *Management Accounting Research, 13*(2), 151–171.

Ahrens, T., & Chapman, C. S. (2007). Management accounting as practice. *Accounting, Organizations and Society, 32*(1–2), 1–27.

Ahrens, T., & Mollona, M. (2007). Organisational control as cultural practice—A shop floor ethnography of a Sheffield steel mill. *Accounting, Organizations and Society, 32*(4–5), 305–331.

Al Arabi, F. (2017). *Islamic financial products and services in Western banks—Whence and whither?* Doctorate of Business Administration, Grenoble École de Management, Grenoble.

Alsop, R. (2006). Business ethics education in business schools: A commentary. *Journal of Management Education, 30*(1), 11–14.

Anderson, H., Welsh, M., Ramsay, I., & Gahan, P. (2012). The evolution of shareholder and creditor protection in Australia: An international comparison. *The International and Comparative Law Quarterly, 61*(1), 171–207. https://doi.org/10.2307/41350139

Anthony, R. N. (1988). *The management control function*. Boston, MA: Harvard Business School Publishing.

Anthony, R. N., Dearden, J., & Bedford, N. M. (1984). *Management control systems*. Homewood, IL: Irwin.

Arendt, H. (1961). *The human condition*. Chicago: The University of Chicago Press.

Arendt, H. (1963). *Eichmann in Jerusalem*. London: Penguin.

Arendt, H. (1968). *Totalitarianism: Part three of the origins of Totalitarianism*. Boston: Harvest Books.

Arendt, H. (1989). *La crise de la culture*. Paris: Folio.

Armour, J., Deakin, S., Lele, P., & Siems, M. (2009). How do legal rules evolve? Evidence from a cross-country comparison of shareholder, creditor, and worker protection. *The American Journal of Comparative Law, 57*(3), 579–629. https://doi.org/10.2307/25652658

Backhof, J. F., & Martin, C. L. J. (1991). Historical perspectives: Development of the codes of ethics in legal, medical and accounting professions. *Journal of Business Ethics, 10*, 99–110.

Badiou, A. (2001). *Ethics: An essay on the understanding of Evil*. London: Verso.

Badiou, A. (2003). *Saint Paul: The foundation of universalism*. Stanford, CA: Stanford University Press.

Badiou, A. (2005). *Metapolitics*. London: Verso.

Badiou, A. (2006). *Polemics*. London: Verso.

Badiou, A. (2009). *Theory of the subject*. London: Continuum.

Badiou, A., & Gauchet, M. (2016). *What is to be done? A dialogue on communism, capitalism, and the future of democracy*. London: Polity Press.

Barnes, B. (2000). Practice as collective action. In T. R. Schatzki, K. Knorr Cetina, & E. Savigny (von) (Eds.), *The practice turn in contemporary theory* (pp. 17–28). London: Routledge.

Bayou, M. E., Reinstein, A., & Williams, P. F. (2011). To tell the truth: A discussion of issues concerning truth and ethics in accounting. *Accounting, Organizations and Society, 36*(2), 109–124.

Beggs, J., & Dean, K. (2007). Legislated ethics or ethics education?: Faculty views in the post-Enron era. *Journal of Business Ethics, 71*(1), 15–37. https://doi.org/10.1007/s10551-006-9123-4

Bennis, W. G., & O'Toole, J. (2005). How business schools lost their way. *Harvard Business Review, 83*(5), 96–104.

Berry, A. (2005). Accountability and control in a cat's cradle. *Accounting, Auditing & Accountability Journal, 18*(2), 255–297.

Bhimani, A., & Soonawalla, K. (2005). From conformance to performance: The corporate responsibilities continuum. *Journal of Accounting and Public Policy, 24*(3), 165–174. https://doi.org/10.1016/j.jaccpubpol.2005.03.001

Block, F. (2013). Relational work and the law: Recapturing the legal realist critique of market fundamentalism. *Journal of Law and Society, 40*(1), 27–48. https://doi.org/10.2307/23354502

Bonini, S., & Boraschi, D. (2010). Corporate scandals and capital structure. *Journal of Business Ethics, 95*(2), 241–269. https://doi.org/10.1007/s10551-011-0856-3

Boon, A., Flood, J., & Webb, J. (2005). Postmodern professions? The fragmentation of legal education and the legal profession. *Journal of Law and Society, 32*(3), 473–492. https://doi.org/10.2307/3557242

Bourdieu, P. (1977). *Outline of a theory of practice*. Cambridge: Cambridge University Press.

Bourdieu, P. (1984). *Distinction: A social critique of the judgement of taste*. London: Routledge.

Bourdieu, P. (1992). *The logic of practice*. London: Polity Press.

Bourdieu, P. (1993). *The field of cultural production: Essays on art and literature*. London: Polity Press.

Bourdieu, P. (1998). *Practical reason: On the theory of action*. London: Polity Press.

Bowie, N., De George, R. T., Fontrodona, J., Frederick, W. C., & Horniman, A. (2004). What do I try to achieve by teaching business ethics? *Journal of Business Ethics Education, 1*(1), 7–28.

Boyce, G. (2004). Critical accounting education: Teaching and learning outside the circle. *Critical Perspectives on Accounting, 15*(4–5), 565–586.

Boyce, G. (2008). The social relevance of ethics education in a global(ising) era: From individual dilemmas to systemic crises. *Critical Perspectives on Accounting, 19*(2), 255–290.

Boyce, G. (2018). Accounting, ethics and human existence: Lightly unbearable, heavily kitsch. *Critical Perspectives on Accounting, 25*(3), 97–109.

Bridgman, T. (2010). Beyond the manager's moral dilemma: Rethinking the 'ideal-type' business ethics case. *Journal of Business Ethics, 94*(2), 311–322. https://doi.org/10.1007/s10551-011-0759-3

Brubacher, J. S., & Rudy, W. (2004). *Higher education in transition: A history of American colleges and universities*. New Brunswick, NJ: Transaction Publishers.

Burritt, R. L. (2012). Environmental performance accountability: Planet, people, profits. *Accounting, Auditing & Accountability Journal, 25*(2), 370–405.

Calkins, M. J. (2000). Recovering religion's prophetic voice for business ethics. *Journal of Business Ethics, 23*, 339–352.

Cardenas, S. (2011). *Conflict and compliance: State responses to international human rights pressure*. University of Pennsylvania Press.

Carnegie, G. D., & Napier, C. J. (2010). Traditional accountants and business professionals: Portraying the accounting profession after Enron. *Accounting, Organizations and Society, 35*(3), 360–376.

Carruthers, B. G., & Espeland, W. N. (1991). Accounting for rationality: Double-entry bookkeeping and the rhetoric of economic rationality. *The American Journal of Sociology, 97*(1), 31–69.

Carter, C., & Mueller, F. (2006). The colonisation of strategy: Financialisation in a post-privatisation context. *Critical Perspectives on Accounting, 17*(8), 967–985.

Cast, A. D., Stets, J. E., & Burke, P. J. (1999). Does the self conform to the views of others? *Social Psychology Quarterly, 62*(1), 68–82. https://doi.org/10.2307/2695826

Celano, A. (2018). *Aristotle's ethics and medieval philosophy: Moral goodness and practical wisdom*. Cambridge: Cambridge University Press.

Certeau (de), M. (1984). *The practice of everyday life, Volume 1*. Los Angeles: University of California Press.

Certeau (de), M. (1988). *The practice of everyday life, Volume 2—Living and cooking*. Los Angeles: University of California Press.

Charafedine, R. (2011). Notre Dame University presentation on status of business schools. In N. D. University (Ed.). Beyruth.

Chartier, G. (2012). Enforcing law and being a State. *Law and Philosophy, 31*(1), 99–123. https://doi.org/10.2307/41348268

Chen, Y., & Tang, T. (2013). The bright and dark sides of religiosity among university students: Do gender, college major, and income matter? *Journal of Business Ethics, 115*(3), 531–553.

Cho, C. H. (2009). Legitimation strategies used in response to environmental disaster: A French case study of Total SA's Erika and AZF incidents. *European Accounting Review, 18*(1), 33–62.

Cho, C. H., Guidry, R. P., Hageman, A. M., & Patten, D. M. (2012). Do actions speak louder than words? An empirical investigation of corporate environmental reputation. *Accounting, Organizations and Society, 37*(1), 14–25. https://doi.org/10.1016/j.aos.2011.12.001

Chotiyanon, P. (2018). *Becoming a business partner—A lifelong self-orienting process*. Grenoble: DBA, Grenoble École de Management.

Chotiyanon, P., & Joannidès de Lautour, V. (2018). *The changing role of the management accountants—Becoming a business partner*. London: Palgrave Macmillan.

Christensen, A. L., & Mohr, R. M. (1999). Nonprofit lobbying: Museums and collections capitalization. *Financial Accountability & Management, 15*(2), 115–133. https://doi.org/10.1111/1468-0408.00077

Chua, W. F. (2007). Accounting, measuring, reporting and strategizing—Re-using verbs: A review essay. *Accounting, Organizations and Society, 32*(4–5), 487–494.

Cianci, A. M., & Kaplan, S. E. (2010). The effect of CEO reputation and explanations for poor performance on investors' judgments about the company's future performance and management. *Accounting, Organizations and Society, 35*(4), 478–495.
Cohen, J. (1980). Original sin and the evil inclination: A Polemicit's appreciation of human nature. *The Harvard Theological Review, 73*(3/4), 495–520.
Conroy, S., & Emerson, T. (2004). Business ethics and religion: Religiosity as a predictor of ethical awareness among students. *Journal of Business Ethics, 50*, 383–396.
Coulter, J. (2000). Human practices and the observability of the 'macro-social'. In T. R. Schatzki, K. Knorr Cetina, & E. Savigny (von) (Eds.), *The practice turn in contemporary theory* (pp. 29–41). London: Routledge.
De George, R. T. (1995). *Business ethics* (4th ed.). Englewood Cliffs: Prentice Hall.
Delbecq, A. L. (2010). Organisational compassion: A litmus test for a spiritually centered university culture. *Journal of Management, Spirituality & Religion, 7*(3), 241–249.
Derrida, J. (1991). *Given time. I, Counterfeit money*. Chicago: University of Chicago Press.
Derrida, J. (1993). *Aporias: Dying—Awaiting (one another at) the "limits of truth" (mourir—s'attendre aux "limites de la vérité")*. Stanford, CA: Stanford University Press.
Derrida, J. (1998). *Monolingualism of the other, or, the prosthesis of origin*. Stanford, CA: Stanford University Press.
Derrida, J. (2002). *Ethics, institutions, and the right to philosophy*. Lanham, MD: Rowman & Littlefield.
Derrida, J. (2008). The laws of reflection: Nelson Mandela in admiration. In P. Kamuf & E. Rottenberg (Eds.), *Psyche—Invention of the other* (Vol. 2, pp. 63–86). Stanford, CA: Stanford University Press.
Diel, P. (1947). *Psychology of motivation* (2002 ed.). London: Hunter House.
Dowdle, M. W. (Ed.). (2006). *Public accountability—Designs, dilemmas and experiences*. Cambridge: Cambridge University Press.
Dragu, I.-M., & Tiron-Tudor, A. (2013). The integrated reporting initiative from an institutional perspective: Emergent factors. *Procedia—Social and Behavioral Sciences, 92*, 275–279. https://doi.org/10.1016/j.sbspro.2013.08.672
Ee, C. (2011). *Compliance by design: IT controls that work*. IT Governance Ltd.
Epstein, M. E. (2002). Religion and business—The critical role of religious traditions in management education. *Journal of Business Ethics, 38*, 91–96.
Fasterling, B. (2012). Development of norms through compliance disclosure. *Journal of Business Ethics, 106*(1), 73–87.
Floyd, A. L., Xu, F., Atkins, R., & Caldwell, C. (2013). Ethical outcomes and business ethics: Towards improving business ethics education. *Journal of Business Ethics, 117*, 753–776.

Fogarty, T., & Ravenscroft, S. (2000). Making accounting knowledge: Peering at power. *Critical Perspectives on Accounting, 11*(4), 409–431.

Forneret, M. (2013). Pulling the trigger: An analysis of circuit court review of the "Prosecutor Bar". *Columbia Law Review, 113*(4), 1007–1050. https://doi.org/10.2307/23491835

Foucault, M. (1975). *Discipline and punish*. New York: Vintage Books.

Foucault, M. (1976a). *History of sexuality: 1. Introduction*. New York: Vintage Books.

Foucault, M. (1976b). *History of sexuality: 2. The use of pleasure*. New York: Vintage Books.

Foucault, M. (1984). *History of sexuality: 3. The care of the self*. New York: Vintage Books.

Fowles, A. J. (1993). Changing notions of accountability: A social policy view. *Accounting, Auditing & Accountability Journal, 6*(3), 97–108.

Freud, S. (1905). *Three essays on the theory of sexuality*. New York: Basic Books.

Freud, S. (1913). *Totem et tabou* (2001 ed.). Paris: Petite bibliothèque Payot.

Freud, S. (1927). *L'avenir d'une illusion* (2004 ed.). Paris: Presses Universitaires de France.

Freytag, G. (1855). *Soll und Haben*. Berlin: Weichert.

Frías-Aceituno, J. V., Rodríguez-Ariza, L., & García-Sánchez, I. M. (2013). Is integrated reporting determined by a country's legal system? An exploratory study. *Journal of Cleaner Production, 44*, 45–55. https://doi.org/10.1016/j.jclepro.2012.12.006

Frickey, P. P. (2005). Getting from Joe to Gene (McCarthy): The avoidance canon, legal process theory, and narrowing statutory interpretation in the early Warren Court. *California Law Review, 93*(2), 397–464. https://doi.org/10.2307/3481460

Funnell, W. (2011). Keeping secrets? Or what government performance auditors might not need to know. *Critical Perspectives on Accounting, 22*(7), 714–721.

Gambling, T. (1987). Accounting for rituals. *Accounting, Organizations & Society, 12*(4), 319–329.

García-de-Frutos, N., Ortega-Egea, J. M., & Martínez-del-Río, J. (2016). Anti-consumption for environmental sustainability: Conceptualization, review, and multilevel research directions. [journal article]. *Journal of Business Ethics*. https://doi.org/10.1007/s10551-016-3023-z

García-Sánchez, I.-M., Rodríguez-Ariza, L., & Frías-Aceituno, J.-V. (2013). The cultural system and integrated reporting. *International Business Review, 22*(5), 828–838. https://doi.org/10.1016/j.ibusrev.2013.01.007

Gauchet, M., Blais, M.-C., & Ottavi, D. (2013). *Pour une philosophie politique de l'éducation*. Paris: Fayard/Pluriel.

Gauchet, M., Blais, M.-C., & Ottavi, D. (2016). *Transmettre, apprendre*. Paris: Fayard/Pluriel.

Ghoshal, S. (2005). Bad management theories are destroying good management practices. *Academy of Management Learning & Education, 4*, 75–91.
Gilliland, D. I., & Manning, K. C. (2002). When do firms conform to regulatory control? The effect of control processes on compliance and opportunism. *Journal of Public Policy & Marketing, 21*(2), 319–331. https://doi.org/10.2307/30000744
Gioia, D. A. (2003). Teaching teachers to teach corporate governance differently. *Journal of Management & Governance, 7*, 255–262.
Gray, R., Dey, C., Owen, D., Evans, R., & Zadek, S. (1997). Struggling with the praxis of social accounting: Stakeholders, accountability, audits and procedures. *Accounting, Auditing & Accountability Journal, 10*(3), 325–364.
Gray, R., Owen, D., & Maunders, K. (1988). Corporate social reporting: Emerging trends in accountability and the social contract. *Accounting, Auditing & Accountability Journal, 1*(1), 6–20.
Greenberg, M. D. (2010). *Directors as guardians of compliance and ethics within the corporate citadel: What the policy community should know*. RAND Corporation.
Gu, J., & Neesham, C. (2014). Moral identity as leverage point in teaching business ethics. *Journal of Business Ethics, 124*(3), 527–536.
Hooker, J. (2004). Introducing the Journal of Business Ethics Education—JBEE. *Journal of Business Ethics Education, 1*(1), 3–6.
Hope, O.-K., & Wang, J. (2018). Management deception, big-bath accounting, and information asymmetry: Evidence from linguistic analysis. *Accounting, Organizations & Society, 70*(Oct.), 33–51.
Hopwood, A. G. (1994). Accounting and everyday life: An introduction. *Accounting, Organizations and Society, 19*(3), 299–301.
IIRC. (2011). Towards integrated reporting. Communicating value in the 21st century. Discussion paper. Retrieved August 10, 2012, from http://www.theiirc.org/the-integrated-reporting-discussion-paper/.
Irvine, H. (2003). Trust me! A personal account of confidentiality issues in an organisational research project. *Accounting Forum, 27*(1), 111–131.
Jacobs, K., & Walker, S. P. (2004). Accounting and accountability in the Iona Community. *Accounting, Auditing & Accountability Journal, 17*(3), 361–381.
Jensen, M. (2003). Paying people to lie: The truth about the budgeting process. *European Financial Management, 9*(3), 379–406.
Jensen, R. E. (1990). Working within neoclassical theory and "modern theory" of finance to detect and measure monopoly power components of ex post accounting rate of return. *Critical Perspectives on Accounting, 1*(1), 69–101.
Jewe, R. D. (2008). Do business ethics courses work? The effectiveness of business ethics education: An empirical study. *Journal of Global Business Issues, 2*(1), 1–6.
Joannidès, V. (2012). Accounterability and the problematics of accountability. *Critical Perspectives on Accounting, 23*(3), 244–257.

Joannidès, V., & McKernan, J. (2015). Ethics: From negative regulations to fidelity to the event. In P. O'Sullivan, N. Allington, & M. Esposito (Eds.), *The philosophy, politics and economics of finance in the 21st century—From hubris to disgrace* (pp. 310–331). London: Routledge.

Joannidès de Lautour, V. (2018a). *Strategic management accounting—Volume I: Aligning strategy, operations and finance*. London: Palgrave Macmillan.

Joannidès de Lautour, V. (2018b). *Strategic management accounting—Volume II: Beyond the numbers*. London: Palgrave Macmillan.

Johnson, D. (2015). Technology with no human responsibility? *Journal of Business Ethics, 127*(4), 707–715.

Jørgensen, B., & Messner, M. (2010). Accounting and strategising: A case study from new product development. *Accounting, Organizations & Society, 35*(2), 184–204.

Kaplan, R., & Johnson, T. (1987). *Relevance lost: Rise and fall of management accounting*. Boston, MA: Harvard University Press.

Kaplan, R., & Norton, D. (1996). *The balanced scorecard: Translating strategy into action*. Boston, MA: Harvard University Press.

Kaplan, R., & Norton, D. (2000). *The strategy-focused organization: How balanced scorecard companies thrive in the new business environment*. Boston, MA: Harvard University Press.

Kaplan, R., & Norton, D. (2004). *Strategy maps: Converting intangible assets into tangible outcomes*. Boston, MA: Harvard University Press.

Kaplan, R., & Norton, D. (2006). *Alignment: How to apply the balanced scorecard to corporate strategy*. Boston, MA: Harvard University Press.

Kaplan, R., & Norton, D. (2008). *Execution premium. Linking strategy to operations for competitive advantage*. Boston, MA: Harvard University Press.

King, R., Clarkson, P. M., & Wallace, S. (2009). Budgeting practices and performance in small healthcare businesses. *Management Accounting Research, 21*(1), 40–55.

Kram, K. E., & Isabella, L. A. (1985). Mentoring alternatives: The role of peer relationships in career development. *Academy of Management Journal, 28*(1), 110–132. https://doi.org/10.2307/256064

Kurunmäki, L. (2004). A hybrid profession—The acquisition of management accounting expertise by medical professionals. *Accounting, Organizations & Society, 29*, 327–347.

Lambert, C., & Pezet, E. (2011). The making of the management accountant, becoming the producer of truthful knowledge. *Accounting, Organizations and Society, 36*(1), 10–30. https://doi.org/10.1016/j.aos.2010.07.005.

Latin, H. A., Tannehill, G. W., & White, R. E. (1976). Remote sensing evidence and environmental law. *California Law Review, 64*(6), 1300–1446. https://doi.org/10.2307/3480040

Latour, B. (1994). Pragmatogonies… A mythical account of how humans and non-humans swap properties. *American Behavioral Scientist, 37*(6), 791–808.

Latour, B. (1996). *Aramis or the love of technology.* Boston, MA: Harvard University Press.

Latour, B. (2008). The Netz-works of Greek deductions. *Social Studies of Science, 38*(3), 441–459.

Latour, B. (2013). *An inquiry into modes of existence: An anthropology of the moderns.* Boston, MA: Harvard University Press.

Leal, J. (2018). *Tantrism: Sex magic for the soul.* London: Lulu.com.

Leavitt, N., & Maykuth, P. L. (1989). Conformance to attorney performance standards: Advocacy behavior in a maximum security prison hospital. *Law and Human Behavior, 13*(2), 217–230. https://doi.org/10.2307/1393745

Lehman, G. (2007). The accountability of NGOs in civil society and its public spheres. *Critical Perspectives on Accounting, 18*(6), 645–669. https://doi.org/10.1016/j.cpa.2006.04.002

Levi-Strauss, C. (1952). *Race et histoire* (2005 ed.). Paris: Gallimard.

Levi-Strauss, C. (1958). *Anthropologie structurale* (Vol. 1 & 2). Paris: Plon.

Lévinas, E. (1969). *Totality and infinity.* Pittsburgh: Duquesne University Press.

Lévinas, E. (1972). *Humanism of the other* (N. Poller, Trans.). Chicago: University of Illinois Press.

Lévinas, E. (1974). *Otherwise than being or beyond essence.* Pittsburgh: Duquesne University Press.

Lévinas, E. (1975). *God, death and time* (B. Bergo, Trans.). Stanford, CA: Stanford University Press.

Lévinas, E. (1985). *Ethics and infinity.* Pittsburgh: Duquesne University Press.

Lévinas, E. (1987). *Time and the other* (R. A. Cohen, Trans.). Pittsburgh: Duquesne University Press.

Lévinas, E. (1991). *Entre nous: Thinking-of-the-other* (M. Smith & B. Harshav, Trans.). New York: Continuum.

Lindblom, L. (2007). Dissolving the moral dilemma of whistleblowing. *Journal of Business Ethics, 76*(4), 413–426. https://doi.org/10.1007/s10551-006-9291-2

Loeb, S. E., & Cory, S. N. (1989). Whistleblowing and management accounting: An approach. *Journal of Business Ethics, 8*(12), 903–916.

Lounsbury, M., & Crumbley, E. (2007). New practice creation: An institutional perspective on innovation. *Organization Studies, 28*(7), 993–1012.

Low, M., Davey, H., & Hooper, K. (2008). Accounting scandals, ethical dilemmas and educational challenges. *Critical Perspectives on Accounting, 19*(2), 222–254.

Maltby, J. (1997). Accounting and the soul of the middle-class: Gustav Freytag's *Soll und Haben. Accounting, Organizations & Society, 22*(1), 69–87.

Marques, J. F., Dhiman, B., & Biberman, J. (2014). Teaching the un-teachable: Storytelling and meditation in workplace spirituality courses. *Journal of Management Change, 33*(3), 196–217.

Matin, K. (2018). Ethical implications and accountability of algorithms. *Journal of Business Ethics*, 1–16. https://doi.org/10.1007/s10551-018-3921-3
Mauss, M. (1925). *Essai sur le don. Forme et raison de l'échange dans les sociétés archaïques*. Paris: Presses Universitaires de France.
May, D. R., Luth, M. T., & Schwoerer, C. E. (2014). The influence of business ethics education on moral efficacy, moral meaningfulness, and moral courage: A quasi-experimental study. *Journal of Business Ethics, 124*(1), 67–80.
McKendall, K., DeMarr, B., & Jones-Rikkers, C. (2002). Ethical compliance programs and corporate illegality: Testing the assumptions of the corporate sentencing guidelines. *Journal of Business Ethics, 37*(4), 367–383.
McKernan, J. F. (2007). Objectivity in accounting. *Accounting, Organizations and Society, 32*(1–2), 155–180.
McKernan, J. F. (2012). Accountability as aporia, testimony and gift. *Critical Perspectives on Accounting, 23*(3), 258–278.
McKernan, J. F., & Kosmala, K. (2004). Accounting, love and justice. *Accounting, Auditing & Accountability Journal, 17*(3), 327–360.
McKernan, J. F., & Kosmala, K. (2007). Doing the truth: Religion—Deconstruction—Justice, and accounting. *Accounting, Auditing & Accountability Journal, 20*(5), 729–764.
McKernan, J. F., & McPhail, K. (2012). Accountability and accounterability. *Critical Perspectives on Accounting, 23*(12), 177–182.
McMillan, K. P. (2004). Trust and the virtues: A solution to the accounting scandals? *Critical Perspectives on Accounting, 15*(6–7), 943–953.
McPhail, K. (1999). The threat of ethical accountants: An application of Foucault's concept of ethics to accounting education and some thoughts on ethically educating for the other. *Critical Perspectives on Accounting, 10*(6), 833–866.
Mercer, G. (1996). The global citizenship MBA orientation program: Action learning at the University of Michigan Business School. *Journal of Business Ethics, 15*(1), 111–120.
Meyer, E. P. (1952). *Dynamite and peace the story of Alfred Nobel*. London: Little Brown & Company.
Mishra, K. (2011). *Kashmir Saivism: The central philosophy of tantrism*. London: Indica Books.
Moberg, D. J., & Calkins, M. J. (2001). Reflection in business ethics: Insights from St. Ignatius' spiritual exercises. *Journal of Business Ethics, 33*, 250–270.
Moore, D. H. (2010). Do US Courts discriminate against treaties? Equivalence, duality and non-self-execution. *Columbia Law Review, 110*(8), 2228–2294. https://doi.org/10.2307/27896321
Morales, J., Gendron, Y., & Guénin-Paracini, H. (2014). The construction of the risky individual and vigilant organization: A genealogy of the fraud triangle. *Accounting, Organizations and Society, 39*(3), 170–194. https://doi.org/10.1016/j.aos.2014.01.006

Morales, J., & Lambert, C. (2013). Dirty work and the construction of identity. An ethnographic study of management accounting practices. *Accounting, Organizations & Society, 38*(3), 228–244.

Nabokov, W. (1955). *Lolita*. New York: Vintage Books.

Norman, A. (1997). Regress and the doctrine of epistemic original sin. *The Philosophical Quarterly, 14*(189), 477–494.

O'Dwyer, B., & Unerman, J. (2007). From functional to social accountability: Transforming the accountability relationship between funders and non-governmental development organisations. *Accounting, Auditing & Accountability Journal, 20*(3), 446–471.

Owens, R. J., & Wedeking, J. P. (2011). Justices and legal clarity: Analyzing the complexity of US Supreme court opinions. *Law & Society Review, 45*(4), 1027–1061. https://doi.org/10.2307/41475243

Parker, C. (2000). The ethics of advising on regulatory compliance: Autonomy or interdependence? *Journal of Business Ethics, 28*(4), 339–351.

Parker, L. D. (2002a). It's been a pleasure doing business with you: A strategic analysis and critique of university change management. *Critical Perspectives on Accounting, 13*(5–6), 603–619.

Parker, L. D. (2002b). Twentieth-century textbook budgetary discourse: Formalisation, normalization and rebuttal in an Anglo-Saxon environment. *European Accounting Review, 11*(2), 291–313.

Parker, L. D. (2005). Social and environmental accountability research: A view from the commentary box. *Accounting, Auditing & Accountability Journal, 18*(6), 842–860.

Pauli, H. E. (1942). *Alfred Nobel: Dynamite king, architect of peace*. London: L.B. Fischer.

Phenix, H. P. (1961). *Education and the common good*. New York: Harpers & Brothers.

Pratt, M. G., Rockmann, K. W., & Kaufmann, J. B. (2006). Constructing professional identity: The role of work and identity learning cycles in the customization of identity among medical residents. *Academy of Management Journal, 49*(2), 235–262. https://doi.org/10.5465/amj.2006.20786060

Preston, A. M., Cooper, D., & Coombs, R. W. (1992). Fabricating budgets: A study of the production of management budgeting in the national health service. *Accounting, Organizations and Society, 17*(6), 561–593.

Puyou, F.-R. (2018). Systems of secrecy: Confidences and gossip in management accountants' handling of dual role expectations and MCS limitations. *Management Accounting Research, 40*(Sep.), 15–26.

Quattrone, P. (2004). Accounting for God: Accounting and accountability practices in the Society of Jesus (Italy, XVI–XVII centuries). *Accounting, Organizations and Society, 29*(7), 647–683.

Quattrone, P. (2009). Books to be practiced: Memory, the power of the visual, and the success of accounting. *Accounting, Organizations & Society, 34*(1), 85–118.

Radcliffe, V. (2008). Public secrecy in auditing: What government auditors cannot know. *Critical Perspectives on Accounting, 19*(1), 99–126.

Rai, L. (1975). Pressures to conform. *Economic and Political Weekly, 10*(1/2), 16–18. https://doi.org/10.2307/4536794

Retief, V. E., & Villiers (de), C. (2013). The accounting profession's influence on academe: South African evidence. *Accounting, Auditing & Accountability Journal, 26*(8), 1246–1278.

Roca, E. (2008). Introducing practical wisdom in business schools. *Journal of Business Ethics, 82*, 607–620.

Rockness, H. O., & Rockness, J. (2005). Legislated ethics: From Enron to Sarbanes-Oxley, the impact on corporate America. *Journal of Business Ethics, 57*, 31–54.

Rouse, J., Davis, J., & Friedlob, T. (1986). The relevant experience criterion for accounting accreditation by the AACSB—A current assessment. *Journal of Accounting Education, 4*(1), 147–160.

Rupert, J., Jehn, K. A., Engen, M. L., & Reuver, R. S. M. (2010). Commitment of cultural minorities in organizations: Effects of leadership and pressure to conform. *Journal of Business and Psychology, 25*(1), 25–37. https://doi.org/10.2307/40605743

Russell, S., Milne, M., & Dey, C. (2017). Accounts of nature and the nature of accounts: Critical reflections on environmental accounting and propositions for ecologically informed accounting. *Accounting, Auditing & Accountability Journal, 30*(7), 1426–1458.

Rutherford, A. M., Parks, L., Canazos, D., & White, C. (2012). Business ethics as a required course: Investigating the factors impacting the decision to require ethics in the undergraduate business core curriculum. *Academy of Management Learning & Education, 11*(2), 174–186.

Sandron, F., & Hayford, S. R. (2002). Do populations conform to the law of anomalous numbers? *Population (English Edition, 2002), 57*(4/5), 755–761. https://doi.org/10.2307/3246664

Saravanamuthu, K. (2004a). Gold-collarism in the Academy: The dilemma in transforming bean-counters into knowledge consultants. *Critical Perspectives on Accounting, 15*(4–5), 587–607.

Saravanamuthu, K. (2004b). What is measured counts: Harmonized corporate reporting and sustainable economic development. *Critical Perspectives on Accounting, 15*(3), 295–302.

Saravanamuthu, K. (2006). Gandhian-Vedic paradigm: Theorising sustainable development. In Z. Hoque (Ed.), *Methodological issues in accounting research: Theories, methods and issues* (pp. 291–332). Melbourne, VIC: Spiramus Press.

Schatzki, T. R. (2000a). Practice mind-ed-orders. In T. R. Schatzki, K. Knorr Cetina, & E. Savigny (von) (Eds.), *The practice turn in contemporary theory* (pp. 42–55). London: Routledge.

Schatzki, T. R. (2000b). Practice theory. In T. R. Schatzki, K. Knorr Cetina, & E. Savigny (von) (Eds.), *The practice turn in contemporary theory* (pp. 1–14). London: Routledge.

Schatzki, T. R. (2005). The sites of organizations. *Organization Studies, 26*(3), 465–484.

Schweiker, W. (1993). Accounting for ourselves: Accounting practices and the disclosure of ethics. *Accounting, Organizations & Society, 18*(2–3), 231–252.

Shearer, T. (2002). Ethics and accountability: From the for-itself to the for-the-other. *Accounting, Organizations and Society, 27*(6), 541–573.

Sigurjonsson, T. O., Arnardottir, A. A., Vaiman, V., & Rikhardsson, P. (2015). Managers' views on ethics education in business schools: An empirical study. *Journal of Business Ethics, 130*(1), 1–13.

Sonenshein, S., DeCelles, K. A., & Dutton, J. E. (2014). It's not easy being green: The Role of self-evaluations in explaining support of environmental issues. *Academy of Management Journal, 57*(1), 7–37. https://doi.org/10.5465/amj.2010.0445

Stolowy, H. (2005). Nothing like the Enron affair could happen in France (!). *European Accounting Review, 14*(2), 405–415.

Süskind, P. (1985). *Perfume: The story of a murderer.* London: Penguin Classics.

Sutton, S. G., Holt, M., & Arnold, V. (2016). "The reports of my death are greatly exaggerated"—Artificial intelligence research in accounting. *International Journal of Accounting Information Systems, 22*(Sep.), 60–73.

Swanson, D. (2004). The buck stops here: Why universities must reclaim business ethics education. *Journal of Academic Ethics, 2*(1), 43–61.

Tucker, S. (1962). Restitution: Quasi-Contract: Non-conformance with state building contractors licensing statute as basis for denial of restitution. *Michigan Law Review, 60*(6), 823–827. https://doi.org/10.2307/1286784

Unerman, J., & O'Dwyer, B. (2004). Enron, WorldCom, Andersen et al.: A challenge to modernity. *Critical Perspectives on Accounting, 15*(6–7), 971–993.

Unerman, J., & O'Dwyer, B. (2007). The business case for regulation of corporate social responsibility and accountability. *Accounting Forum, 31*(4), 332–353.

Velayutham, S. (2003). The accounting profession's code of ethics: Is it code of ethics or a code of quality assurance? *Critical Perspectives on Accounting, 14*(4), 483–503.

Walker, S. P. (2010). Child accounting and 'the handling of human souls'. *Accounting, Organizations and Society, 35*(6), 628–657.

Wang, L. C., & Calvano, L. (2015). Is business ethics education effective? An analysis of gender, personal ethical perspectives, and moral judgment. *Journal of Business Ethics, 126*(4), 591–602.

Weber, J., & Wasieleski, D. M. (2013). Corporate ethics and compliance programs: A report, analysis and critique. *Journal of Business Ethics, 112*(4), 609–626.

Weber, M. (1922). *Economy and society*. Berkeley: The University of California Press.

White, W. H., Jr. (1995). Foreign law, politics & litigants in US Courts: A discussion of issues raised by Transportes Aereos Nacionales, S. A. v. de Brenes. *The University of Miami Inter-American Law Review, 27*(1), 161–202. https://doi.org/10.2307/40176362

Woelfel, C. J. (1986). Standards of ethical conduct for management accountants. *Journal of Business Ethics, 5*(5), 365–371.

Wright, S. (2011). *PCI DSS: A practical guide to implementing and maintaining compliance* (3rd ed.). London: IT Governance Ltd.

Yair, G. (2007). Existential uncertainty and the will to conform: The expressive basis of Coleman's rational choice paradigm. *Sociology, 41*(4), 681–698. https://doi.org/10.2307/42857031

CHAPTER 5

Ethical and Accountable Management Accounting: Mission Impossible?

Academe, society and the accounting profession all call for greater business ethics and accountability. Management accountants, as any other actors, are expected to play a role in this construction of an ethical, reliable and accountable organisation. Albeit, it seems that business ethics research oscillates between two schools of thought: one claiming the possibility of coining universally applicable ethical rules (*e.g.* codes of conduct), and one claiming the very subjectivity of ethics (postmoderns). Those two schools have been presented as having no common denominator, but their topic—ethics. Yet, Alain Badiou rejects this artificial divide by arguing that the very immanent dimension of ethics (subjectivity) is the starting point for its transcendence (universalism). In so saying, Badiou challenges the assumptions made by either school of thought, reasoning contemporary discourses on ethics have been resting on three fallacies and averted ethics from happening. In order not to fall into the trap he is denouncing, he proposes the conditions of possibility for ethics: fidelity to the truth event. Thus far, his influence on business ethics research has been very little (Joannidès & McKernan, 2014; Pérezts & Picard, 2014), probably because he is giving the hope that positive ethics is possible (Joannidès & McKernan, 2014). Ethics, accountability, responsibility and transparency have traditionally been presented as not to be dissociated. Literally read, accountability consists of making oneself "tell-able", that is, account-able (Garfinkel, 1967; Roberts & Scapens, 1985; Shearer, 2002):

V. Joannidès de Lautour, *Strategic Management Accounting, Volume III*, https://doi.org/10.1007/978-3-030-20157-9_5

> any setting organizes its activities to make its properties as an organized environment of practical activities detectable, countable, recordable, reportable, tell-a-story-about-able, analyzable—in short *accountable*. (Garfinkel, 1967, p. 33, emphasis in original)

The capability of telling a story about one's day-to-day activities can be summarised as the bundle of understandings and teleoaffective structures shaped by rules guiding the "*giving and demanding of reasons for conduct*" (Roberts & Scapens, 1985, p. 447). In fact, some people are legitimate to make demands over the conduct of others and seek reasons for actions taken, which raises three questions: to whom is one accountable, for what and by which means? In other words, how can accountability be a practice?

The subject is then constituted as answer-able, that is, as one who must be able to give evidence of the reasonableness of his or her actions to a community of others. Narrative as well as the giving and receiving of accounts have been recognised as central to the development of moral agency and the rendering of "*life intelligible and meaningful*" (Shearer, 2002, p. 545). Concern for truth, fairness and justice in accountability is intensified when the moral aspect of the practice is emphasised and when accountability is associated with an "*absolute obligation to the Other*" (McKernan & Kosmala, 2004, p. 356), that is, an open-ended obligation imposing itself on everybody, such as justice or love (*op. cit.*, p. 329). The accountable person is presented as a moral and responsible self, seeking to witness the truth, so that others have faith in him or her. Traditionally, such truth and fairness can be found in stockholders and investors basing decisions upon faith in financial disclosure (McKernan & Kosmala, 2007, p. 743).

Accountability implies relationships between people and raises the question of *to whom* accounts of oneself should be directed (Schweiker, 1993; Shearer, 2002). Accounts are owed to "others", and an "absolute other" respectively acting as principals and Higher-Principals, holding "supreme" authority over the organisation and its members (Laughlin, 1996).[1] Consistent with the moral foundations of accountability, the

[1] Depending on the institution, the Higher-Principal can be the community of stockholders or capital markets (listed companies), donors (registered charities) or taxpaying citizens (public sector organisations). Although customers, clients and suppliers are key actors in organisational life, they are considered neither resource providers nor ultimate account demanders. Accountability to them takes on a different form, called *stakeholder accountability*,

Higher-Principal may demand accounts proving the appropriateness of resource use in relation to agreed purposes.

This applies to top managers with respect to the finance providers and markets who meet at annual general meetings and other events. On these occasions, such managers take instruction, directly from their Higher-Principals and subsequently render accounts to them. Organisational authorities are considered to have the legitimacy to define policy and doctrine reflecting the requirements of the Higher-Principal and to compel people to conduct themselves accordingly. In this capacity, managers can command other members to make the conduct of operations coherent. This then forms hierarchic accountability characterised by managers imposing accounting records as the privileged form of account (Roberts, 1991, p. 359). People are obliged to follow prescribed procedures when accounting for conduct in order to facilitate superiors' control of accounts and behaviour. When accounts of conduct are given to a hierarchic superior, prescriptions from the organisation management control system are followed in day-to-day accountability (Ahrens & Chapman, 2002). Thence, numerical figures can provide the Higher-Stakeholder with a visual, memorisable representation of how resources are used in the conduct of business operations. These accounting records are coupled with words that, in the worst case, merely label them and, in the best case, make sense of them to tell an intelligible story (Quattrone, 2009). In face-to-face meetings with investors, comments on numerical figures are demanded from accountable managers: questions are asked and satisfactory answers are expected (Roberts, Sanderson, Barker, & Hendry, 2006, p. 283).

This call for greater accountability and ethics leaves a series of questions unanswered: what do ethics and accountability mean and imply? How can they be practised in corporate day-to-day life outside mere incantations and codes of conduct? More broadly, how can ethics and accountability be conceived of in positive terms? Owing to these questions, this chapter sets out to address a possible ontological misunderstanding pertaining to ethics and accountability by first highlighting their aporetic nature and the reasons for the difficulty in enabling them. Building upon these contradictions, this chapter suggests ways of overcoming these limits and problematics of both ethics and accountability as well as implications for management accounting.

and constitutes a step towards Higher-Stakeholder accountability (Collier, 2008; Cooper & Owen, 2007).

5.1 Contemporary Ethics as a Quadruple Contradiction

Calls for more ethics or greater accountability are almost systematically articulated after an occurrence of a major scandal, because this situation has caused damage to some victims. Accordingly, the people in charge are wanted, because "they must be accountable," one often hears. The current debate on ethics "*amounts to a genuine nihilism, a threatening denial of thought as such*" (Badiou, 2001, p. 3). Such a strong claim makes him denounce in his works the triple contradiction of ethics, be it regulatory or subjective: the contradiction of victimisation, the contradiction of universalism and the contradiction of the Other. Similarly, and unsurprisingly, accountability's essence also appears as contradictory.

5.1.1 The Contradiction of Victimisation

The first problem pertaining to ethics is such that "*we must reject the ideological framework of 'ethics' and concede nothing to the negative and victimary definition of man*" (Badiou, 2001, p. 16). Victimisation is an unresolved contradiction resting upon a twofold contradiction: victims' human nature and the legitimacy of legalised ethics.

5.1.1.1 The Contradiction of the Victim's Human Nature

This first contradiction of Western approaches to ethics, including business ethics, lies in an incapability of devising positive and anticipatory ethics. Ethical claims and good intentions are systematically a response to a situation collectively perceived as evil without ever appearing as upfront proclaiming of the good. For Badiou (2001, p. 10), ethical guidelines are thence looking towards the past and suggesting "nevermore", which is the case because "*it is easier to establish consensus regarding what is evil rather than regarding what is good*". This presupposes that evil is that from which good can be derived without having an existence per se. For Badiou (2001), there proceeds from this evil dominating ethical discourses a body of self-evident principles capable of imposing themselves. Ethics is then grounded in the idea of consensual law-making concerning human beings in general, as mortal victims and potential victims, through a demarcation of the evil that might be done to them, according to a certain conception of their human essence and universal interests.

As human beings decide on what is ethical and what is not, a new contradiction is conveyed. They are the weak to be protected and the agents of their own protection concurrently as though they had two ontologies: a being and a non-being (Badiou, 2007). Therefore, Badiou (2001, p. 12) is concerned that this regulative ethics makes victims of its subjects, it casts them as essentially victims and potential victims of evil: whilst ethics proclaims the moral superiority of man and woman, it denies their essence as precisely "*something other than a mortal being*".

The observation that this victim is to be protected and rescued is particularly problematic in the case of business where the economy, markets and Capitalism themselves are presented as what is threatened and in need of protection through codes of ethics, codes of conduct as well as good or best practices (Badiou, 2008, 2012b). In his lectures, he pinpoints another two yet unresolved contradictions highlighted by such ambiguities surrounding victimisation. Firstly, free market economy and Capitalism appear as the weak that need international collective protection on behalf of human rights. Yet, it is commonly agreed that the fall of the Berlin Wall in 1989 and the collapse of the USSR in 1991 have marked the free market economy and Capitalism as the strongest in the Cold War (Boltanski & Chiapello, 2006; Chiapello & Fairclough, 2002). Badiou therefore warns against ethics which would miss its target and would protect the stronger in the name of the weak. Secondly, needs for protecting the free market economy and Capitalism implicitly supports Marx's argument that Capitalism is likely to collapse under the logic of its internal weaknesses and contradictions. Yet, its proponents, falling into a Ricardian tradition, would agree that free market economy's and Capitalism's self-regulation is the condition of their success.

5.1.1.2 The Contradiction of Legitimate Legalised Ethics

Those negative responses are to be found in our Judæo-Christian roots where the Ancient Testament specified the Jewish Law and *rules* for everyday life (Badiou, 2003, 2012b). Initially, rules were 613 in number and covered all aspects of life, 365 being prohibitive laws (and as many retributions), whereas the remaining 248 were affirmative (Urbach, 1979). The rabbinic literature, such as synthesised by Urbach (1979), explains that every day brings its new temptation to be resisted only by a strict *Do-Not.* On the other hand, the whole man stands in the service of God, each part of his body being entrusted with the execution of its respective functions (Urbach, 1979, pp. 355–361). Then, David came and reduced these commandments to 11, Isaiah to 6, Micah to 3, Isaiah to 2 and lastly Amos and Habakkuk to one, being positive but less acknowledged: "*seek the Lord and live by faith*".

As a result, this negative response appears as "*part of what prohibits any idea, any coherent project of thought, settling for overlaying unthought and anonymous situations with mere humanitarian prattle*" (Badiou, 2001, pp. 32–33). This is how we often have professional regulations issued and enforced by professional bodies through codes of ethics specifying that good is what is *not* dishonest and does *not* contradict laws and regulations (Backhof & Martin, 1991; Brooks, 1989; Gaumnitz & Lere, 2002; Preston, Cooper, Scarbrough, & Chilton, 1995; Savan, 1989; Tweedie, Dyball, Hazelton, & Wright, 2013; White & Montgomery, 1980). Based on those premises, Badiou (2001, p. 38) observes that, in responding to atrocities and scandals, ethical principles are the manifestation of Western conceptions of what is evil and good (non-evil), and the imposing of our Western approach to what is normal and abnormal (the Law).

In sum, contemporary ethics is characterised by a major shortcut: once evil is specified and regulations are issued, complacently complying with them becomes ethical behaviour. Notwithstanding, we still ignore what is good, other than non-evil. We still do not know what a right for good is and not a right for non-evil. From then on, how can we ascertain "*the possibility of the impossible [...] against the ethics of living-well*" (Badiou, 2001, p. 39) is an ethics that can act as a life-driver beyond the weak-as-victim's protecting?

5.1.2 *The Contradiction of Universal Ethics*

Discussions surrounding ethics have long opposed the idea that there are superior moral principles that should indistinctively apply to everybody and the idea that ethics is foremost subjective. In fact, universal ethics and therefore ethical ethics so to speak appear as another two contradictions.

5.1.2.1 The Contradiction of Superior Universal Principles

Ethics' universalism rests upon certain self-evident principles claimed to be superior to others and therefore supposed to apply universally. Some of these principles, notes Badiou (2001, p. 14), can be found in free market economy and Capitalism but also democracy, each of them being imposed on societies whence they were absent. In the name of those ethical principles, the proponents of ethics speak for the world but deny individuals and the specificity of their respective situations. Since the collapse of the USSR, free market economy and Capitalism have been brought into the former Soviets; albeit, individuals' economic circumstances have worsened (Badiou, 2012a; Carrère d'Encausse, 1992, 2000, 2011). Likewise, in the name of democracy, the West has "freed" Iraq from Saddam Hussein's dictatorship. Bringing "democracy" into the country has resulted in the population undergoing chaos, quasi civil war and a new dictatorship arising (Badiou, 2004, 2012b). In either situation, in the name of universal principles, the Western ideology has colonised the rest of the world. The rise of the Islamic State in this region has emerged as a critique of the Western ethics consisting of authoritatively imposing a certain form of democracy on the weak (Badiou, 2012a, 2012b). Badiou highlights that it is then considered ethical to oppress people for their own good (non-evil), as though it were ethical to adopt an unethical behaviour and means when such is done in the name of ethics!

What Badiou (2009) develops in the political realm also applies to the economic realm: "*in our situation, that of Capital, the reign of number is thus the reign of the unthought slavery of numericality itself*" (Badiou, 2008, p. 213). In business, such is at stake when ethics is uttered in the name of free market economy, Capitalism or capital markets efficiency, is often presented as the layperson investing his or her savings (putting his or her savings where? Investing his or her savings?) Concurrently, that layperson is denied any right to express himself or herself regarding corporate policy. Prior to the critique articulated by Badiou, a similar stance was already vivid in Labour Process-informed discourses: these companies relocate work to exploit cheap labour for the sake of those laypeople's wealth who invested in them (Allsop & Calveley, 2009; Bryer, 2006; Carter & Tinker, 2006; Wray-Bliss, 2002). These critics denounce the idea that it is ethical to protect markets and investors but not individuals constituting them (Miller & O'Leary, 1994).

5.1.2.2 The Contradiction of Ethical Ethics

Nobody would publicly reject the idea of protecting the weak. Those universal principles eventually exclude, expel or hold in deep contempt those who protect the weak and disagree, (It looks like here you are repeating the same meaning of the two sentences?) because these universal ethical concerns purport to be objectively superior (Badiou, 2001, pp. 13–14). In fact, by denying anyone the fundamental right to disagree, the Western approach to ethics de facto appears as the non-democratic rejection and muting of any opponents to its "universal" project. This is especially vivid in the case of the Arab Spring, where those who have not supported calls for democracy in the Middle East, such as Russia or China, have been denounced as supporters of evil (Badiou, 2012a, 2012b).

If ethics has a universal reach, ethical indignations should apply to any evil situation (Badiou, 2001, 2003). Yet, such is not quite the case, "universal" ethics being just selective of who deserves protection and those who do not. Still with the Arab Spring example, Badiou (2012b) shows that the purported universal democracy principle has led the West to protect opponents to the Syrian regime. In so doing, just one category of rebels has been accredited as worthy victims whilst those who are calling for Jihad and the constitution of an Islamic Republic have been muted and fought. From a purely Western perspective, highlights Badiou (2012a, 2012b), this is no real surprise: it is ethical to support and protect democracy's proponents. Yet, this situation reveals two unresolved contradictions. Firstly, in the name of universal ethics, the West calls and fights for democracy in one particular country, ignoring those whose situation is not deemed as severe. Secondly, in the name of ethics one distinguishes between those deserving to be protected and those who do not. All in all, Badiou (2001, 2012b) considers that, in their essence, Western approaches to ethics makes it lose its universal reach.

Corporate social responsibility (CSR), *qua* business ethics' heyday (Crane & Matten, 2016), seem to fall into this trap where not all stakeholders are considered equally deserving of protection. This is particularly vivid in the fact that different companies or different industries will emphasise different stakeholders (Sheehy, 2015; Vallentin, 2015). Even worse is where a company promotes the wellbeing of one particular stakeholder, *for example*, employees, and relocates numerous activities to countries where labour is cheaper, as with international companies operating in Bangladesh (Falkenberg & Falkenberg, 2009). Here, CSR appears as the utmost discrimination within the same company where Western employees deserve protection whilst others do not. Ethically, this designates today a principle that governs how we relate to the "what is going on" as a vague way of regulating our commentary on historical situations (Badiou, 2001, p. 2).

5.1.3 The Contradiction of the Other

As a consequence, the contradiction of victimisation and universalism leads to the contradiction of an ethics of the Other. This Other, as an extension of what our Judæo-Christian roots prescribe, is incarnated by Lévinas' philosophy and is full of as yet unresolved contradictions.

5.1.3.1 The Contradiction of the I in the Eye

The victimising of mankind and subsequent imperative to protect and rescue suffering minorities is underpinned by the idea that I see myself in the face of the Other. I am an other and in turn the other is myself (Lévinas, 1972, 1987, 1991). This ethics of the Other, ultimately becomes a matter of responding to the other as a victim, of seeing oneself in that victim, and not doing evil to the other, not killing, not harming, not doing what I would not like the other to do to me (Lévinas, 1985). Therefore, Badiou (2001, p. 30) strongly rejects this ethics of the Other that "*designates above all the incapacity, so typical of the contemporary world, to name and strive for a Good.*" For Badiou, this ethic of the Other is self-dismissive; it loses its universality as it is essentially individualistic. Whilst supposedly addressed to the Other, that form of ethics is eventually addressed to me and what I need, so I prevent any harm from happening to me nor do I feel guilty. This means, this form of ethics is purely selfish as I care about myself under the pretext of caring for this Other. This is implicitly what publications applying Legitimacy Theory to CSR practices emphasise: those contribute to enhancing corporate legitimacy within society, not to gratuitously caring for the Other (Castelló & Lozano, 2011; Du & Viera Jr., 2012; Iivonen & Moisander, 2014; Sitaoja, 2006).

5.1.3.2 The Contradiction of Ontological Fullness

Recognising the Other would not be problematic if we really accorded him or her some ontological fullness. Speaking of the universal Other robs the other of substance and reality (Badiou, 2001, pp. 20–23). Who is this Other? Is he or she what I think the average Other would be? Is he or she an incarnation of me or anyone else? All told, that notion of the Other seems to have been so over-extensively applied that anyone differing from me in one way or another is other. Unsurprisingly, instead of eventually speaking for a universal Other, ethical discourses address everybody who is other than me, that is, not a single Other but multiple ones. In acknowledging not one Other but multiple others, that ethic "*amounts to 'recognition of the other' [...] or to the 'ethics of differences' [...] or to multiculturalism. Or simply to good old-fashioned 'tolerance' which consists of not being offended by the fact that others think and act differently from you*" (p. 20). At the same time, "*the self-declared apostles of ethics and of the 'right to difference' are clearly horrified by any vigorously sustained difference*" (p. 24).

Good and ethical are the simple recognition of this Other as someone I can be. Simultaneously, acknowledging his or her difference allows me to claim my own difference to get differentiated treatment. As Badiou (2001) puts it, the Lévinassian ethics of the Other is very individualistic, selfish and narcissistic. Whence, "*the whole ethical predication based upon recognition of the other should be purely and simply abandoned*" (p. 25).

The question of tolerance to diversity under all its forms has lately been central to business ethics (del Carmen Triana, Wagstaff, & Kim, 2012; Pless & Maak, 2004). Yet, in such situations, as stressed by del Carmen Triana et al. (2012), promoting diversity has led to stigmatising groups under the pretext of protecting them. Hence, in the ethical name of gender equality, females have been treated like a minority, whilst they represent 52% of the world population. This means these ethics of the Other lead to considering groups of others incapable of being by themselves, which denies them ontological fullness: they are incomplete human beings (Badiou, 2001). This problem takes us back to the fallacy of human rightism.

5.1.4 Accountability as Contradiction, Testimony and Gift

Many call for more or greater accountability, albeit it seems giving an account is not always possible. Even though it were possible to give an account of everything to every interested party, this would raise the question of whether this really makes sense and to whom in fact it does. In other words, accountability as a principle undoubtedly has its merits but may in practice be difficult if not impossible to satisfactorily discharge. The accountability relationship is intrinsically limited, which makes answers to apparently simple questions very difficult to articulate, probably because of an ontological and linguistic impossibility.

5.1.4.1 Three Intrinsic Limits to Accountability

Three lines of questioning regarding the difficulties of operationalising accountability are especially relevant to the concerns of this chapter. One is informed by Judith Butler's (2005) work and questions whether accountability is always unambiguously desirable (Messner, 2009). Another study influenced by Butler discusses the pertinence of amalgamating accountability and transparency, and calls for intelligent accountability (Roberts, 2009). Finally, a Derridean approach investigates whether and how accountability can be in its essence compatible with the construction of the moral and responsible self (McKernan, 2011).

Accountability might not always be desirable because of three limits the accountable person cannot always overcome (Messner, 2009). Firstly, the accountable self is *opaque* and is not always capable of reflecting on its deeds and their rationale. It is not always capable of relating its actions to a purpose: sometimes no intelligible reason can be given, limiting the production of verbal or numerical accounts. For example, a bricklayer cannot systematically count each brick. To do so would be exhausting and overwhelming, therefore he or she cannot quantify his or her actions; likewise, he or she cannot always explain his or her gestures when bricklaying. Secondly, forcing the giving of an account *exposes* the accountable person to violence exerted by others—by the Higher-Principal, peers or superiors whose demands for good reasons for conduct might sound like an interrogation. This becomes equally difficult because these others are also *opaque*, meaning the accountable individual does not know exactly what they want of him or her. If my understanding of the other's expectations is mistaken, an account of myself cannot be fully intelligible to him or her, even though it may be a fair representation of the perception I have of myself. Conversely, I may believe I fully understand what the other wants of me and be compelled to distort my account to make it intelligible. Therefore, I may produce an account which is not a fair representation of how I perceive the events I am reporting. The third limit occurs when the other is other than the Higher-Principal, when the accountability relationship, instead of being direct, becomes *mediated*. In this situation, accounts are given to an intermediary between the Higher-Principal and me. The role and status of the intermediary principal as well as my accounts in the relationship to the Higher-Principal remain unclear. Mediation might lead to tensions for the accountable person de facto compelled to satisfy possible contradictory demands. For instance, an employee commenting on his or her performance does not always know who will appraise him or her—the Higher-Principal or his or her direct manager. Also, the employee does not always understand the role of his or her evaluation in creating value for the Higher-Principal.

The three limits to giving an account of oneself highlighted by Butler (2005) lead Roberts (2009) to stress that amalgamating accountability and transparency form part of the problematic inherent to accountability. Whilst the giving of an account supposedly contributes to the construction of the moral person, the need for transparency is based on the assumption that one, the accountable self, always finds oneself as "*already guilty in the face of*" the Other (p. 959). Guilt implies suspicion and presents accountability as a mechanism whereby the individual has to prove that he or she is being fair on the mediating other. Transparency, argues Roberts, is not a synonym for fairness, justness and morals but often distorts these, so accountability is unduly reduced to compliance with ethical guidelines (*e.g.* codes of conduct or reporting standards). Concerns about transparency result in dismissing morals and account giving as an individual practice. Therefore, Roberts suggests that returning to what one's conscience orders would give rise to intelligent accountability.

In his reflections on the ontology of accountability based on Derrida's treatment of contradictions, McKernan (2011) sets out to demonstrate that, in essence, the publicity pursuant to accountability cannot succeed in constructing the moral or responsible person, although giving an account is meant to enable this. When accountability is amalgamated with business ethics, the individual is expected to behave in accordance with social prescriptions rather than with moral principles guiding his or her own conscience. He or she cannot assume his or her own responsibility, since accounting already states what is right or wrong in his or her stead. Accountability holds an unresolved contradiction: the morality of decisions implied by individual conduct is undermined, rather than supported, by the giving of an account. The morality of decisions cannot explicitly fit with any pre-established format: accounting standards or management control systems do not enable us to identify whether a record has a moral foundation. Yet, such records are supposed to contribute to constructing the moral person. This contradiction is accentuated by the fact that appraising the adequacy of conduct with orders given by one's conscience falls into the domain of individual secrecy and is not supposed to be shared with others, unless, of course, the individual chooses to testify openly to his or her understanding of the higher authority's requirements. Instruments of mediation (*e.g.* records and accounting standards) therefore make the self-account-able before others yet un-response-able before the Higher-Principal.

The problematics of accountability regarding *to whom* one should give an account consists of the following unanswered questions. Why should an Other, aside from the Higher-Principal, demand an account from me? In turn, why should I respond to the demands by this other if I am responsible before the Higher-Principal? Seemingly, the limits identified by Messner (2009), the ambiguities stressed by Roberts (2009), and the aporetic nature of accountability, as contended by McKernan (2011), constrain the operationalisation of individual account giving. Accountability emerges as an unreachable ideal.

5.1.4.2 The Problematics of Accountability

Traditionally, Agency Theory approaches have claimed that the principal was legitimate to make such demands in situations characterised by information asymmetry. Supposedly, the principal is identifiable and but ignores what the agent does. Therefore, accounting, reporting, auditing and management control systems have been implemented (Broadbent, Dietrich, & Laughlin, 1996; Gendron, Cooper, & Townley, 2001; Laughlin, 1996). However, the principal cannot always be easily identified, in particular when he is multiple, *for example*, stockholders as a group. Hence, intermediary people are commissioned to operate as substitutes, which Laughlin (1996) calls intermediary principals, who ultimately give meta-accounts to the Higher-Principal.

In any organisation, the difficulty of knowing in person or being in a direct relationship with the Higher-Principal leads to accountability being mediated through other "others" and through the organisation itself.[2] Subordinates are unlikely to have a direct relation to stockholders enabling them to relate their actions to the exact return investors might expect (Alawattage & Wickramasinghe, 2009). In contrast to conventional organisational contexts, a religious setting in its essence challenges this idea: supposedly, believers have a direct relationship to God through prayer. In the absence of a direct relationship with the Higher-Principal, others operate as surrogates in hierarchic accountability. In day-to-day life

[2] In day-to-day activities, *socialising* accountability operates as a substitute for hierarchic accountability. Peers and other group members operate as the wardens of organisational doctrine and demand reasons for conduct they expect to be consistent with what the Higher-Stakeholder is supposed to require. Peers serve as surrogates for the Higher-Stakeholder, exerting lateral controls. Socialising accountability appears as a soft form of hierarchic accountability (Roberts, 1996, 2001).

these issues raise new questions pointing to the "problematics" of practising such composite accountability.[3]

In fact, the need for intermediary principals reveals the inappropriateness of agency theory-based approaches, as the Higher-Principal is unbeknown to people at the bottom of the organisation. Likewise, his expectations and requirements cannot be known, which neutralises the information asymmetry hypothesis. Indeed, neither the principal nor the agent knows who the other is as well as what he expects and does. This results in a situation characterised by reciprocal non-information symmetry. Nonetheless, the notion of people/institutions legitimate to make demands calls for insights from practice theories.

As the organisation is a practice, itself comprised of sub-practices, accountability should be regarded as a nexus including managers, employees and all other stakeholders (Cooper & Owen, 2007). Thence, any party is legitimate to demand reasons for conduct and accounts thereof. In doing so, they are legitimate substitutes for a Higher-Stakeholder, who is not commissioning them. Ultimately, accounts are given to the unknowledgeable and unbeknown Higher-Stakeholder incarnated by knowledgeable intermediary substitutes. Given that these latter take the Higher-Stakeholder's rights and duties, they enter into a relation, which can be called subrogation. Hence, organisational managers and members, any external stakeholders and the individual himself are surrogates, as Fig. 5.1 below summarises.

Owing to the impossible direct relationship between the Higher-Stakeholder and the individual, no accounts can be demanded or given. However, surrogates intervene and demand reasons for conduct based on their very concerns, which are arguably part of the Higher-Stakeholder's. Arguably, the Higher-Stakeholder has expectations and requirements unbeknown to the layperson in the organisation. Accountability as a prac-

[3] Etymologically speaking, a ***problem*** is an object sent forward (πρω-βλεμα). This notion is therefore generally understood to mean that an object sent forward can never be reached. Endeavours to approach it ultimately result in it being pushed further forward. By extension, the notion of ***problematics*** encompasses ideas: sending an idea forward means that this idea is subject to debate and controversy. The notion of ***problematics*** is very suggestive of the impossibility of giving any definitive answer, making the object sent forward unanswerable. The impossibility of answering such questions led Plato to conceive of the notion of ***contradiction*** as an unanswerable question. Nowadays, a ***contradiction*** is understood to be an irresolvable contradiction or logical disjunction. This is the sense Spinoza and his followers drew in the seventeenth century from the term's original meaning.

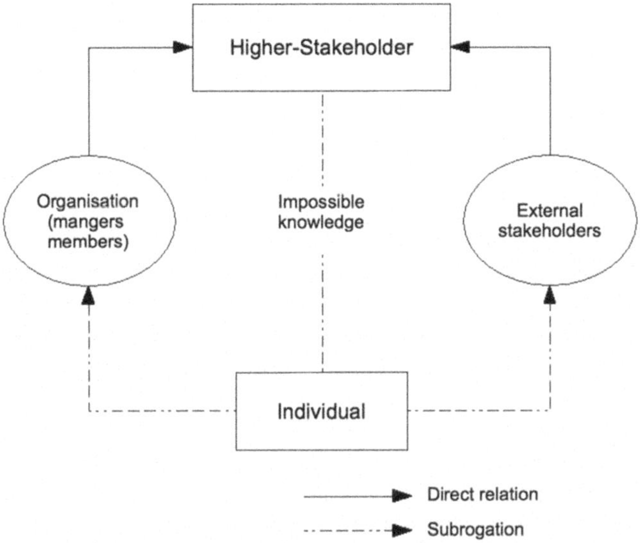

Fig. 5.1 On the Higher-Stakeholder being subrogated in the three realms

tice then consists of translating these at the various levels in such a way that, ultimately, the individual at the bottom can conduct himself consistently. To this end, the Higher-Stakeholder commissions organisational managers can demand their subordinates reasons for conduct. In doing so, they subrogate the Higher-Stakeholder to whom they ultimately render accounts. *Qua* his surrogates, they are legitimate to approximate his expectations and requirements and make it the rule for conduct within the practice.

Likewise, other external stakeholders, such as customers, suppliers or public authorities are in a given relationship legitimate to demand accounts. Again, they act as surrogates for the Higher-Stakeholder whose expectations and requirements they may approximate. Indeed, giving them an account is part of giving one to the Higher-Stakeholder, this being a way of fulfilling his (unbeknown) expectations and requirements. Lastly, the individual, at the bottom of the practice, approximates the requirements of the intermediary stakeholders to whom he or she has to give practical reasons for conduct. On the other hand, conduct itself is dictated through approximations of the Higher-Stakeholder's expectations and requirements. Effectively, commitment to value creation suggests that the individual conducts himself in a manner consistent with what he approximates as the Higher-Stakeholder's very expectations. Ultimately, in practice, how the individual conducts himself reveals how he has subrogated the Higher-Stakeholders and other intermediaries commissioned by him. In sum, accountability "*systems and their implications [a]re subject to a continuous process of interpretation and re-interpretation*" (Ahrens & Chapman, 2002, p. 166).

In this subrogation-approximation cascade, what is observable is a practice of social ontologies, such as approached by Schatzki (2000). Indeed, the threefold notion of practice he observes is hereby applied at every single relationship within the practice. In sum, accountability as a practice rests upon the organising of multiple ontologies (Law, 1996).

5.1.4.3 A Linguistic and Cultural Impossibility

To overcome the linguistic misunderstanding leading to defining accountability as account-giving, responsibility or transparency, it is crucial to explicate its whence and whither in English language. Tocqueville observes that the term *accountability* appears for the first time in English language in sermons given by the American pastors at the time of the Independence War. Since the Independence Declaration, American society has been founded on the sanctified notion of Freedom. Indeed, the first colonists and settlers were trying to escape and flee from Church oppression as undergone in Europe. Jointly, American society has been resting on what is now known as "The American Dream": make a fortune, provided that one's qualities and capabilities allow for it (Parsons & Platt, 1983).

Within such a socio-political context where everyone is encouraged to develop and advance their own capabilities, accountability is defined as follows. First of all, it is an *ability* to give and *account* of one's conduct's justness (McKernan & Kosmala, 2004; Roberts & Scapens, 1985). American Society is built on values and norms defining what is expected of its members in their capacity as citizens, family members, community members and professionals (Parsons, 1982, 1991). The United States is cemented in the pattern of *rights* and *obligations* regulating community expectations (Parsons & Shils, 2001). Hence, accountability appears as an imperative of justification. Accountability thereby relates to the obligation on anybody and on organisations to prove the justness of their conduct before the community of others. Rights' and obligations' reciprocity are delineated in forms of "mutual accountability".

Any means of proof are available to the one who finds himself or herself accountable. These means include trials by an authorised person or institution—whence the notion of *authority*—(Jacobs & Walker, 2004; Joannidès, 2012; Joannidès & Jaumier, 2013; Roberts et al., 2006) but also any bureaucratically standardised and formalised means, such as nowadays' accounting (Quattrone, 2009; Roberts & Scapens, 1985; Scapens & Roberts, 1993). Hence, accountability can be hierarchic and addressing this Other authorised to trial me. It can be socialising, directed at peers in our social interactions; or it can be individualising, just addressing myself to make sense of one's own actions (Roberts, 1991).

Accountability systems are the counterpart of a democratic society in which decision-making power is effectively exercised by citizens who have an absolute right to information's comprehensiveness and publicity (Tocqueville (de), 1835). Democracy is enabled through social structures within which citizens can assess the actions of their leaders but also can appoint or dismiss them. A major implication of this observation is that such structures reach outside the mere political power as theorised by Lincoln—"Power of People for People by People"—This latter motto is in reality only a manifestation of accountability, amongst other forms.

Any decision-maker, as well as any citizen, must be in a capacity of giving to those who demand it, a fair account of their actions, and they are also prohibited from discussing the grounds of such a request. Although this condition of accountability could be in some foreign contexts perceived as a trespassing of freedom, it is a constituting feature thereof within American Society. This paradox can be cleared through the notion of "agency", other concept unique to English language. In the notion of "agency", although actors operate within given social structures, they keep intact their freedom of action in any circumstances they are facing (Emirbayer & Mische, 1998; Kim, 2003). Such an "agency" capability rests upon the constant and permanent distancing between the individual and his various roles in society (Bourricaud, 1977). Just as individuals' embedding in social structures enables them to exercise their *agency*, accountability manifests itself to them as a practicality of their (American) identity's reflexive construction.

Thus, in accountability, the possibility offered to others to assess people and their actions results in conduct's absolute transparency. What could appear to a non-American observer, especially a French one, as a panoptic deviance of American Society, seeks to guarantee equality of chances amongst people as well as to facilitate judgement and decision-making

(Parsons & Platt, 1983). Through the reflexivity it enables, accountability must be understood as pertaining to the construction of a free individual (Hayek, 1979).

Now that these notions have been refreshed, it is time to insist on the central place accountability has within American Society. It is common, especially within the critical accounting literature, to denounce the influence played by Capitalism on the collapsing of accountability into mere (financial) reporting procedures, thereby neglecting justification's moralising dimension (Kamuf, 2007; McKernan & McPhail, 2012). In passing, also some North-American business thinkers deplore this corruption of accountability, unjustly narrowed down to accounts of performance (Simons, 2005). Yet, the grounds of accountability remain very vivid within North-American Society. Nowadays, when a situation is deemed iniquitous, it is not unusual to hear about the alleged guilty ones: "They must be accountable!" All in all, although many have been denouncing the financialisation of social relations (McKernan, 2012; Roberts, 2009), accountability as a political project and object has remained central and almost unchanged within American Society (Parsons & Platt, 1983).

It is because accountability relates to a given political order that it is difficult to comprehend outside an Anglo-Saxon context. It is for the same reason that it can lead to resistance in countries where Anglo-Saxon leaders endeavour to impose it, such as France (Joannidès, 2012; Kamuf, 2007). Already in 1835, Tocqueville intuited that accountability would probably not be exportable as it is to France or other European countries, precisely because it relates to the specificities of American Society and Democracy.

5.2 Mission Possible: Ethics and Accountability as Positive

Calls for greater ethics or more ethical and accountable practices and behaviours are articulated in reaction to major scandals. As such, ethics and accountability appear as the delayed negative response to the worst that could happen. For this simple reason, both ethics and accountability can only be discharged in a procedural way, such as Ethical codes (Avshalom & Rachman-Moore, 2004; Dienhart, 1995; Schwartz, 2000) of Codes of conduct (Avshalom & Rachman-Moore, 2004; Gordon & Miyake, 2001; White & Montgomery, 1980). As such, ethics and accountability appear as the response seen in negative terms to a problem but not as a positively conceived project.

5.2.1 Positive Ethics as the Reunion of Totality and Infinity

After Western approaches to ethics and accountability have been dismissed, a few questions arise: how can ethics be viewed positively as doing the good? What are the conditions of possibility for universal ethics? Answer to these questions can be found in Badiou's (2003) exploring of Saint Paul's journey as the founder of Christian ethics whereby the universal and the specific appear as ethics' inseparable ontological two facets.

5.2.1.1 Ethics as the Reunion of the Universal and the Specific

Notwithstanding relativist ontologies claiming ethics is only subjective and can therefore not be transcendental, it can be argued an absolute truth exists, and therefore absolute and universal principles underlying ethics could apply (Badiou, 2001, 2003). To him, such principles are not to be found in any conception of what is good or evil, but in something superior and neither questionable nor disputable. For him, ethics' universalism lies in the irrational and non-intellectualised appropriation by the individual of such universal principles. It is not because such principles are superior that they can forge ethics but because they are interiorised by those whose conduct they are guiding. To Badiou (2003), our Western societies have over-emphasised the Decalogue and its prohibitive nature at the expense of the Gospels. Whilst the Decalogue is inspired by the Jewish Law (the Torah and the Mishnah) expressed in negative the Gospel appears as a positive approach to ethics.

Ethical conduct to God and mankind lies in faithful commitment to an absolute truth by which Christians abide. This absolute truth is to be found in a two-facet event: the death of Jesus on the Cross and the miracle of his resurrection three days later (Badiou, 2003, p. 63). Any Christian takes these two statements for true because its *only "proof" lies precisely in its having been declared by a subject* [Paul] (Badiou, 2003, p. 5). The apostle shows us that truth *is eventual, or of the order of what occurs, it is singular. It is neither structural, nor axiomatic, nor legal* (p. 14). In other words, ethics rests not upon commandments, orders or regulations but on the admission that "*Christ is precisely incalculable*" (Badiou, 2003, p. 50), which is decisively emphasised in Cor. II.12.I-II.

The very originality of Badiou's view of ethics lies in that it finds its foundations in that event that can neither be proved nor told fairly. Telling it would just make it unbelievable. That Christ-based ethics is therefore a set of "*unutterable utterances*", *only experience by the subject who has been visited by miracle* (Badiou, 2003, p. 51), that is, by the one who has encountered the event (Badiou, 2007, p. 232). Grounded in subjectivity and an individual encounter with the event (Badiou, 2003, p. 66, p. 103), the event causing the truth should be potentially reiterated (Badiou, 2009, p. 10). Pursuant to this claim, "*faith cannot be confused with mere private conviction [...] The real of faith is an effective declaration, which, with the word 'resurrection', utters that life and death are not ineluctably distributed as they are in the 'old man'*" (Badiou, 2003, p. 88). This means the truth event is perpetuated through the action of witnessing to it before the rest of the world at all times, because *without fidelity, that declaration is useless* (Badiou, 2003, p. 91).

All told, ethics, according to Badiou is what reunites the absolute and the universal together with the individual. It is the exterior disruptive event, unquestionable and undisputable, that causes people to believe in it and appropriate it. Ethics then appears as the constant and steady fairness that reunion of the universal and the particular, made possible through fidelity to the event.

5.2.1.2 Ethics as the Offshoot of a Disruptive Event

Ethics cannot impose itself on the world on the grounds of purported universal ex nihilo principles that would suddenly be accepted by people and applicable (Badiou, 2003). He agrees that ethics is a response to something happening in the world. Whilst conventional Western approaches to ethics see it as the response to a negative event Badiou (2001, 2003) views it as a fundamental altering of the world's ordering and functioning. To be comprehended and accepted by human understanding, any form of ethics rests upon a profound disruptive event. Central to Badiou's philosophy is the notion of the event, that is, something that may "*happen in certain times and places, which, unlike the minor contingencies of everyday life, rupture with the established order of things*" (Levi, 1991, p. xxvii). Accordingly, an event, which is at the origins of ethics, cannot be a general concern or idea:

> The event is attached, in its very definition, to the point in which the historicity of the situation is concentrated. Every event has a site which can be singularized in the historical situation [...] It is not because the site exists in the situation that there is an event. But, *for* there to be an event, there must be the local determination of a site. (Badiou, 2007, pp. 178–179)

Altering the world order of functioning in the future, the event must be locatable in space and time and its actors must be identifiable. An event is generally past (Jesus' death and resurrection) but can be a future promise (the return of the Messiah in Judaism). For Badiou, the temporal disconnection of the event from present time is central, since it requires a form of belief in something that is not making our day-to-day life. This is how he considers Jesus Christ was not admitted as the saviour when he first launched his movement. With neither hindsight nor formal expectations, he could not be seen at that time as the saviour and even less as God's son. All told, the event is not an end but the beginning of a new world: *the event has not come to prove something; it is pure beginning* (Badiou, 2003, p. 49).

As a result, in his lectures and public appearances, Badiou often warn that the Global Financial Crisis and global warming are not events and cannot be the basis for twenty-first century's ethics. These are too general and generic concerns that cannot be precisely located in space and time. At best, there can be anecdotal situations looking like an event, such as polar bears falling from ice blocks in the Arctic to express global warming. Rather, a major characteristic of the event as foundational to ethics for Badiou (2007, p. 206) is that it must be nameable "*inasmuch as it is named* e_x, *the event is clearly* this *event*" (Badiou, 2007, p. 206). In naming this event such, one acknowledges its singularity and extraordinarities. This is what can make it disruptive.

The two conditions proposed by Badiou (2007), that is, singularity in space and time and rupture with the order of the world in which it happens, make the event a transgression of an established order (Badiou, 2003). Jesus Christ died after the new church he founded had been prohibited, calling the functioning of Judaism into question and threatening the Roman Empire. Those who believed in the gospel of God's love and forgiveness as spread by Jesus were prosecuted by the order of Pilate, Jesus (and then Paul) being the leader of an illegal faction (Badiou, 2003, p. 27). Whence, Badiou (2003, 2007, 2009) explains, the event is necessarily transgression. It is because it transgresses the order of the world in which it happens that an event is remarkable, recallable and commits people to its truth.

In sum, an event appears as a breakthrough in space and time and gives birth to issues requiring a solution: "*events happen in certain times and places, which, unlike the minor contingencies of everyday life, rupture with the established order of things*" (Levi, 1991). As such, the event to Badiou does put ourselves outside our comfort zone and leads us to question the meaning and direction of our everyday life conduct. This event's first merit is that it leads us to ponder why we have always been doing this or that, why our way of living has been deemed just and whether this was right. Ethics can commence on those grounds through fidelity to the event.

5.2.1.3 Ethics as Fidelity to the Event and Its Apostle

Ethics lies in fidelity to the event admitted as true in its disruptive and moral nature. Under this purview, the event must be incarnated by an *apostle* (Badiou, 2003, p. 45), a harbinger uttering and witnessing to the event itself. In other words, to Badiou (2007, p. 329) fidelity to the event "*is the work of a militant*" and definitely has a political dimension. This political dimension consists of acting as a role model, even in hard times, without ever losing faith in the person who caused the event. Whilst this person has characteristics above humanity, notwithstanding a human nature, and is someone one could imitate, he or she is the sole capable of bearing this ethical fidelity to the event.

In our Western world, ethics appears as fidelity to the event of Jesus' crucifixion and resurrection as witnessed to by Saint Paul (Badiou, 2001, 2003, 2007). Jesus Christ's overall message was appropriated by Saint Paul who had never seen him but had a direct revelation of this truth by God (see Acts). Since Paul had this revelation and has believed in Jesus' death and resurrection, he has authored every single epistle making the New Testament. In those, he has set the bases for Christian ethics across congregations around the Mediterranean Sea. What is common to all these epistles is that believing implies fidelity to one's conversion to Jesus' new church (Badiou, 2003, pp. 17–18), and new birth through faith. Fidelity then consists of symbolically reiterating Jesus resurrection (Badiou, 2003, p. 45, p. 60).

All told, ethics is caused by a disruptive event witnessed to by a militant who becomes its main harbinger. It is so because this apostle manages to have others converted and iterating his own activity as a role model that the core message associated with the event can be interiorised by individuals and diffused at the same time. Once it is appropriated, the event must be uttered and shared with others who appropriate to and keep disseminating it. Onwards this truth is being uttered as external to the witness and universal. As new witnesses spread the word, they increasingly make reference to what the person causing the event did and how this apostle would react if confronted with a similar situation.

Therefore, the apostle or the militant "*must be accountable only for what others see and hear, which is to say, his declaration*" (Badiou, 2003, p. 51). The militant is accountable to those who made the event happen (to Jesus and later on Saint Paul) by steadily reminding of event contemporaneity and pertinence (Levi, 1991, pp. xxv–xxvi; Badiou, 2003, pp. 60–61, pp. 99–100).

As they are harbingers of the event, fidelity commits them to ensuring its perpetuation (and reiteration) in its aftermath. This must be shown in their daily conduct whereby, confronted with dilemmas, they are expected to ponder what Jesus would have done in a similar situation and to behave themselves accordingly. If nobody speaks for the event, this latter will fade as though it had never happened, the world continuing evolving on its own. This point is backed with the argument that Jesus Christ's resurrection would have been ignored if no Christians had spoken for it (Badiou, 2007, p. 26). And this, continues Badiou, denies that the event is miraculous and over-human nature. Badiou (2007) calls this a paradox but seems to relate to an aporetic accountability of the apostle before the event.

The apostle is also accountable to the audience they are addressing. He or she is expected to share this unutterable utterance and the depth of event's implications with others who have not yet been exposed to it. Therefore, as with Jesus and then Paul, they must deploy a sort of *narrative accountability* (Ricœur, 1955, 1991). Here, telling the ineffable is the utmost difficulty confronting them. Rather than just telling the event, later apostles are to conduct a life faithful to the truth event and speaking for itself, being fair heirs of those who made the event happen in the past and organised its aftermath. In other words, as with the dissemination of the truth, apostolic accountability lies in witnessing to the event and its changing of our lives since it happened. Failing to behave oneself in accordance with what I think the actor in the event would have done in a similar situation denies it its ethical significance. If nobody eventually abides by the event and makes it part of their day-to-day life, this event is not worthy of any consideration.

In this dual form of fidelity to the event, the apostle is to be a faithful person, that is, someone believing in the truth of the event with no proof or evidence, just accepting that the gospel it bears will change the order of things for good. Such is the case of Christians committed to Jesus Christ's resurrection (Badiou, 2009, p. 51).

In sum, in *lieu* of being a set of prohibitions or prescriptions, forms of business ethics would appear as fidelity to the event, as delineated in the subsequent sub-sections.

5.2.1.4 What Would My Mentor Have Done in the Same Situation?
Man should be viewed not as a victim but as an agent capable of overcoming the mortal condition. If he or she cannot do it by himself or herself, ethics lies in the providing of assistance towards this. Evil should be identified from our capability of doing good and not vice versa. Humbly, rather than dealing with good or evil in general, particular situations should be taken into consideration with voice given to those individuals for whom ethics must speak. Universal claims are full of contradictions, especially that of backing and feeding a phenomenon's hubris at the same time as it is disgraced. There cannot be one ethic applying universally but contextualised ethics of one particular aspect of life which, because it is specific, can apply to all situations it embraces. Lastly, ethics is only possible as fidelity to the trespassing event witnesses to as true.

In sum, in case of an ethical dilemma, the concerned actor should ask himself or herself what the hero of the event would have done in a similar situation. Business ethics, according to Badiou's philosophy, is possible under the following conditions.

The triple contradiction characterising contemporary Western approaches to ethics, as highlighted by Badiou (2001, 2003, 2007) results in the impossibility of claiming a universal business ethics applying to every single type of situation and actor. To Badiou, what can make ethics universal is its unconditional application within a specific situation, because "*ethics does not exist. There is only the ethic-of (of politics, of love, of science, of art)*" (Badiou, 2001, p. 27). A common mistake consists in a failure to recognise that there is no ethics "in general", rather "*there is only a particular kind of animal, convoked by certain circumstances to become*" concerned by ethics (Badiou, 2001, p. 40).

Pursuant to this, in essence, there can be no universal ethic that would wonderfully apply to all situations and be pertinent to all sorts of dilemmas. Even though situations can look similar, they are too different in nature to be unified and governed by one universal ethic. As a consequence, business ethics cannot exist as such. At best, there can be an ethic of a certain type of practice; however, it seems that the multiplicity of situations rather opens for an ethic of each of those (*e.g.* an ethic of financial advice to people, companies; an ethic of payroll, an ethic of product placing).

Such a situated ethic of a certain business concern or practice can occur only if a disruptive event with positive consequences occurs at a certain time and place. Badiou's philosophy warns us against a situated ethic that would arise subsequent to a scandal or any negative event. Business ethics codes or principles tend to arise in such negative aftermaths without bearing much hope other than that of "nevermore" (Bonini & Boraschi, 2010; Low, Davey, & Hooper, 2008; Stolowy, 2005).

Financial scandals, such as WorldCom and Enron, or anything like the 2015 Dieselgate cannot appear as ethics' grounds. Rather, an ethic of the automotive industry could find its grounds in the advent of a reliable and affordable environment-friendly car, *as per* Tesla's lead product. Outside the mere energy feed challenge it raises, this car disrupts automakers' technologies, production modes and approach to a vehicle (García-de-Frutos, Ortega-Egea, & Martínez-del-Río, 2016; Hoi, Wu, & Zhang, 2016). Likewise, the advent of a self-driven car, as tested by Google, would be disruptive of ethical decision-making, since the owner would no longer be the one making a choice when confronted with a dilemma (García-de-Frutos et al., 2016; Poczter & Jankovic, 2014). Subsequently, other manufacturers and clientele would refer to this disruption to characterise what is an acceptable vehicle and what is not. To date, Håkan Samuelsson, the Volvo Cars CEO, had declared that he would follow the move initiated by Google and Tesla and commercialise exclusively electric cars in 2017 (past tense) and bring to the market self-driven cars in 2019 for which the company would take full responsibility in case of road incidents (http://www.volvocars.com/au/about/innovations/intellisafe/autopilot).

The event must be impersonated by a character whose courage and braveness would show the rest of the world that they were right to fight their battles and promote their own views. Whilst in Badiou's philosophy, this character appears in the person of Jesus Christ this should be one character associated with the situation in which the event occurs. This is the condition under which ethics could be consistent with Badiou's other prescriptions. As there can, to him, only be an ethic of something, there needs to be an event and a person. By claiming Jesus Christ and Saint Paul, Badiou (2001, 2003) suggests this character is a human body or at least a person.

This would mean that, in the case of an ethic of the automotive industry, the person should necessarily be Elon Musk (Tesla) or Larry Schmidt (Google). These contemporary heroes are those through which disruption could happen and through which a certain message of hope can be disseminated. Yet, to Badiou (2001, 2003) what grants them this moral authority is that they are modern times' prophets, whose vocation is not to tell others what to do.

To Badiou, Jesus Christ's ethics has diffused because of his main apostle, Saint Paul, who has confidently and faithfully spread the word, even without meeting the saviour in person. Jesus Christ's ethics has been made possible because his word has been appropriated by other human beings claiming fidelity to the event of his death and resurrection for cleansing our sins. Therefore, as with the automotive industry, Elon Musk or Larry Schmidt could not have this dual identity of prophets and apostles. If we consider them prophets, another automaker could be their harbinger (*e.g.* Volvo).

5.2.2 *Accountability as a Political Agenda*

Once the origins of its contemporary forms are understood accountability can also happen: the 1787 US Declaration of Independence and Constitution whereby a new society with a new social and moral contract was to be constructed. For the first time in history, accountability could appear as a positive societal project. The American Revolution appeared as the disruptive event breaching the established social order leading to the Declaration of Independence. Its apostles were the Founding Fathers to whom it is still abundantly referred to nowadays in case of political dilemmas (Tocqueville (de), 1835). This constructive political agenda can with no doubt be applied to business and management accountants. As US Society, this possibility of accountability could be grounded in pluralism, minority protection and diversity management, the interplay between responsibility and liability, and ultimately a form of publicity.

5.2.2.1 Democratic Pluralism and Plural Accountability

American Society's first characteristic lies in acknowledging and taking account of "plural voices" (Tocqueville (de), 1835, T.I. loc. 3712). Depending on their Prussian, Irish, Scottish, Catholic, Protestant or Jewish origins, American citizens do not have the same expectations or aspirations. Consequently, they do not demand the same type of accounts on their leaders. In return, they expect to be able to give an account of their own conduct in a form meaningful to them in particular. In this respect, one should remember that "*millions of men march altogether to the same horizon point: their language, their religion, their customs and habits differ; their goal is common*" (Tocqueville (de), 1835, T.II loc.1982, emphasis added). Therefore, Tocqueville (T.III loc.1074) reminds us that "there is no good language without clear terms" and observes deep distrust from American Society vis-à-vis experts. Those latter, by developing their own language, speak in a jargon unintelligible to citizens. Thence such a uniform linguistic apparatus is unanimously rejected, for it does not allow informed judgement. A contemporary example can lie in the notion of "embedded value" well-known to insurance companies reporting on their activities but certainly not to citizens reading these reports (Knights & Vurdubakis, 1993; Patten, 2002). As a requirement from American Society, a single and technical language is strongly prohibited (Kaspi, 2008; Parsons & Platt, 1983). Unsurprisingly, political accountability imposes that contents and modes of account giving be as varied as the body of organisational stakeholders (Brown, 2009; Brown, Dillard, & Hopper, 2015; Dillard & Roslender, 2011; Gallhofer, Haslam, & Yonekura, 2015). Such pluralistic voices are expressed as follows.

Public authorities have the right to demand accounts of tax payments, employment preservation or territory occupation. A factory's neighbourhood is in the capacity of demanding accounts of damages caused to fauna and flora. Customers can expect an account of irreproachable product quality or, if needed, a working customer service fixing the problem in case the company is not required to publicly justify itself (*e.g.* Volkswagen after the diesel scandal was revealed). Such can be the meaning of defect product recall policies accompanied with technical details explicating the origin of the problem (Hsu & Lawrence, 2016; Laufer & Jung, 2010; Magno, 2012; Potter, Murray, Lawson, & Graham, 2012). For their part, suppliers are given the inalienable right to expect contract honouring as well as the perfect transparency of how it is honoured by the client. Lastly, employees also have an absolute right to information relating to the impact of corporate decisions on work conditions (Ogden & Bougen, 1985; Owen & Lloyd, 1985). This peculiar social contract is what allows Brown (2009), Dillard and Roslender (2011), Brown et al. (2015) as well as Gallhofer et al. (2015) to explain the rise of social and environmental reporting in the United States in the late nineties. According to them, CSR disclosure, just like any annual report, is the utmost accountability response to the imperative of making public intelligible information taking account of citizens' own concerns.

5.2.2.2 Accountability, Minority Protection and Diversity Management

A direct consequence of pluralism recognition lies in the treatment of the minority by the majority, and this is politically as well as societally. Although democracy implies that minorities should abide by the majority's wills and decisions, "*what is then a majority taken collectively, just an individual with opinions and most often interests contrary to those of another individual called minority?*" (Tocqueville (de), 1835, T.II loc. 1448). These groups "are in a minority and need to be assured all rights be protected in order for theirs to be freely exercised" (T.II loc. 2141). It thereby appears necessary to counter "the majority's omnipotence" perceived as "such a great peril" for American Society (T.II loc. 376). Specific rights are granted to claimed and recognised minorities, in order for them to emancipate from what Tocqueville (T.II loc. 403) calls the tyranny of the majority; those "*who form the minority unite, first to count themselves and weaken the majority's moral empire*". In the name of equality of chances, protecting minorities' rights and encouraging them to claim those are at the core of the American consensus (Parsons & Platt, 1983). In order for this to be enabled, minorities systematically have a say on collective decisions that could affect them.

It is what led to the creation and institutionalisation of the status of minority shareholders ("minority interests" in consolidation accounting). Correlatively, minority stakeholders' protection has been central to accountability processes in the United States since the launch of the earliest stock exchanges and the concomitant rise of associations representing and defending minority interests (Galbraith, 1994). Any decision affecting a minority must be preceded by an impact study whilst a possible compensation for the damage caused by majority's fulfilment to the minority (Siekkinen, 2016).

Outside minority stockholders, any minority can congregate within an association and thereby be protected. It is from this minority voices' taking into consideration in accountability processes that numerous interest groups representing them towards decision makers develop. In large US companies, it is not unusual to see institutions representing African-American or Latin American minorities. Management decisions affecting these minorities are systematically submitted to their representatives who can negotiate arrangements or compensations (Guillén, 1994). In such negotiations, the company is required to prove that these minority interests have been taken into account. Failing to meet that obligation of proving is subject to court prosecution on behalf of those spoiled minorities, as disposed in the Constitution's Sixth and Fourteenth amendments.

When not one but several minorities whose interests are to be taken into account and protected, the company eventually finds itself obliged to organise and manage diversity (Bender, 2004, 2007). Tocqueville notes that diversity is mostly ethnic (Irishmen, Scots, Prussians, Italians, First Nations) and religious (Catholics, Protestants, Jews). In the twenty-first century, those minorities are those "unusual actors"—minorities based on gender, sexual orientation, social background, religion, race or ethnicity (Annisette, 2003, 2008; Annisette & Trivedi, 2013). In the United States, an organisation that would put at danger any of these minorities' interest, be it for the good of the majority, would be expected to publicly justify the opportunity of doing so and would be obligated to clarify how damages inflicted to minorities are being fixed or compensated (Guillén, 1994).

All this has two series of consequences. Firstly, organisational actors are required to self-declare their belonging to one or several minorities. In countries other than Anglo-Saxon, doing so would be considered an oddity whilst such is done in order to have minorities' rights and claims protected. It is under this purview that job applicants are asked their race or ethnicity, religion, gender and sometimes sexual orientation. Secondly, once minorities have been identified and accounted for across the country, it is not unusual that companies be imposed quotas, so that national cultural diversity be embraced and fully represented. Pursuant to minorities' protection, affirmative action measures are taken, with HR directors expected to prove to State government their effort on this matter (Kalev, Dobbin, & Kelly, 2006).

5.2.2.3 Accountability, Responsibility and Liability

Pursuant to the Declaration of Independence, an additional notion is implicitly associated with accountability: liability in its legal sense. Directors do have obligations and "*do not need their subordinates' permission to fulfil them, and they cannot escape them without being held liable*" (Tocqueville (de), 1835, T.I loc. 1069).

American Society calls for an obligation to account for what has been done for the common good (country, shareholders, stakeholders). Failing to fulfil this obligation to give an account commits the individual's or organisation's liability. The dismissal of leaders rests upon the fact that they periodically engage their responsibility and liability. In the case their actions would not have succeeded to meet the expected results, they find themselves in a position of justifying why such is the case. It is then on the grounds of justification persuasiveness that American citizens decide to renew or not their managers and leaders.

Thus, accountability must allow to hold actors responsible (response-able) for their actions, that is, the compulsory ability to answer any questions about those without giving any prejudice of operating mechanisms (McKernan, 2012; Roberts, 2009). If the individual fails to provide an answer at all, or if this latter does not prove convincing, his liability[4] is then engaged. That is, a moral debt vis-à-vis the whole of society is accounted for, which needs to be paid off. Not repaying this moral debt is considered an offence against Society and is therefore subject to prosecution and sanctions (McPhail & McKernan, 2011; Roberts et al., 2006). The managing body is assessed on its capacity to create value, be it financial, social or environmental or justification as to why they did not succeed (Cho, Roberts, & Patten, 2010; Gray, 2013; Hoffman, 1999; Mouck, 1999; Roberts et al., 2006). For instance, the oil spill incurred by British Petroleum in 2010 provoked by the explosion of the Deepwater Horizon platform followed by the controversial management of its consequences rapidly led to the CEO's dismissal and replacement (Lin-Hi & Blumberg, 2011).

In American Society, "*each person is taught to take responsibility for his or her own actions*" (Tocqueville (de), 1835, T.II loc.1861) through two mechanisms enabling to identify with great precision for what he or she is effectively responsible and can be held liable (Guillén, 1994).

Firstly, everybody's role within society in general and in particular within the organisation is more clearly defined. A clear and precise mandate is given to each actor who is therefore authorised to act only within these boundaries: "*it is entrusted to a small assembly where his responsibility and liability are divided and his action is exercised*" (Tocqueville (de), 1835, T.IV loc.2997). Trespassing on the terms is always problematic, for it becomes almost impossible to retrace the chain of responsibility. It is then as impossible to identify one particular person's responsibility and the way his or her liability can be confronted. This is what could explain that, in the name of accountability, job descriptions in American businesses be very precise and detailed as to the employee's tasks and duties (Organ, 1997; Weldon & Gargano, 1988). This is also what could explain that leaders' mandates have a term and can be periodically revoked by shareholders (Roberts et al., 2006). All this significantly differs from what can occur in contexts foreign to accountability, such as France where job

[4] This legal notion of liability embraces moral concerns discussed in the critical accounting literature on assets and liabilities or debits and credits.

descriptions are not very detailed and where employees can make their job boundaries evolve as experience increases (Lubatkin, Lane, Collin, & Very, 2005). In such situations, employee's responsibility is difficult to trace, hence his or her liability cannot be confronted.

Accountability implies a second mechanism enabling responsibility's identifying. This mechanism appears as a consequence of the first one and manifests itself in stringent, clear if not rigid procedures aimed at protecting each person's rights. Through handbooks of procedures, codes of conduct and other covenants, the entire chain of responsibility and liability can be traced, so that "*the county will never be responsible for the sheriff's actions*" (Tocqueville, T.I loc.3764). It is thence not a surprise that method bureaus, Taylorism or Fordism arose and developed in the United States (Smith & Meiksins, 1995), and this prior to seeking to rationalise, routinise or optimise modes of production (Parker & Ritson, 2011)

5.2.2.4 Accountability's Inevitable Publicity

Tocqueville notes that, in the name of protecting citizens in a position of giving an account of themselves, accountability procedures are always made public and accompanied with counterbalancing powers and institutions. These latter, acknowledged by the Constitution's Sixth Amendment, are supposed to guarantee that account giving and justification processes be impartial and independent to effectively contribute to the common good: "*therefore, every year, new plans are discussed before municipal assemblies or before State parliament, and then reproduced by newspapers, which excite universal interest as well as citizens' zeal*" (Tocqueville (de), 1835, T.I loc. 2817).

Since then, media has been expected to relay those mechanisms by which a leader must give an account to the American people or a citizen to the community. In the name of Democracy, it has been expected that independent newspapers would offer an impartial account of public matters (National Politics section) but also of private issues (other types of sections). Nowadays, accountability's publicity consists of media appearances of those expected to give an account of their actions (Parsons & Platt, 1983). For instance, Mark Zuckerberg was trialled by the US Congress on numerous occasions regarding issues in privacy raised by Facebook and the event was live-broadcasted on national TV channels.

Conversely, in other countries foreign to the notion of accountability, such as France, privacy and reputation are guaranteed and protected by the Constitution. Correlatively, absolute transparency, as imposed by

North American accountability and Democracy is strongly and unanimously rejected in France. Prior to Larry Page's trial before the Congress of the United States, Eric Schmidt (Google co-founder and Larry Page's business partner) was invited to the French President's Élysée House to explain—not justify—his company's fiscal optimisation system. Not only was this meeting not broadcasted, it was just elicited in some specialists' newsfeeds (Gardels, 2013).

5.3 Conclusion

In a world dominated by economic constraints, the accountable self must give evidence of its commitment to creating financial value for stockholders (Shearer, 2002, pp. 565–566). In reaction to neoclassical economists (*e.g.* Jensen) who restrict value to monetary surpluses,[5] proponents of welfare economics (*e.g.* Sen) broaden the notion to include social and environmental dimensions (Gray, 2002b, 2010).[6] Accounts are driven by the obligation to prove commitment to value creation (Simons, 2005) and the need to prevent from self-interest pursuit (*viz.* agency theory). Traditionally, as she notes, value creation has been understood for stockholders, neglect of stakeholders being claimed because they are not concerned by the corporate value maximisation function (Jensen, 2001). De facto, such narrow approaches to accountability have left no room for non-listed companies.

Within the organisation, value takes differentiated forms related to what counts as strategic (Ahrens & Chapman, 2002, 2007; Ahrens & Mollona, 2007; Jørgensen & Messner, 2010; Messner, 2009). Once such value has been commonly understood, subordinates are expected to provide managers with management accounting figures, which can also comprise of non-financial data. As part of the organisational management control system, these data are produced and circulated following the organisational standards and procedures. In a private sector organisation, such figures can address costs and income, number of units produced or sold, per unit value, inventory or delivery velocity. In public sector organisations and non-profits, management accounting figures can inform on the same issues as well as value for society, that is, welfare produced

[5] For these economists, the absence of maximisation functions makes non-financial accountability irrelevant.

[6] For instance, social value can be the welfare produced for society in general or parts of it. One measure of environmental value can be reductions in greenhouse gas emissions.

(Bebbington & Gray, 2001; Gray, 2002a, 2002b; Gray, Dey, Owen, Evans & Zadek, 1997; Unerman & O'Dwyer, 2007).

It is no secret that measuring value relies heavily on the calculative dimension of accounting.[7] Numerical figures give a visual, memorisable representation of resources and their use to create value. However, such numbers do not suffice to provide an understanding of what has been undertaken and why. Consequently, they are coupled with words that, at worst, label them and, at best, make sense of them (Quattrone, 2004, pp. 657–658, 2009, p. 86). In sum, while numbers and calculations are used to record conduct and value, words serve to convey an intelligible story. Such is the case in annual reports where balance sheets, profit-and-loss accounts and cash-flow statements presenting business activities in financial terms are complemented with texts explaining strategy, operations and future projects and prospects (McKernan & Kosmala, 2004, p. 342). Likewise, in face-to-face meetings with investors, comments on numerical figures are demanded from accountable managers: questions are asked and satisfactory answers are expected (Roberts et al., 2006). Narrative accountability is directed at those who listen to and believe in (accounting) stories. For this reason, the speaker is held to an "*absolute obligation to the Other*" (McKernan & Kosmala, 2004, p. 356): he or she should tell a fair story of commitment to value creation that would be intelligible to any interested party.

Bibliography

Ahrens, T., & Chapman, C. S. (2002). The structuration of legitimate performance measures and management: Day-to-day contests of accountability in a U.K. restaurant chain. *Management Accounting Research, 13*(2), 151–171.

Ahrens, T., & Chapman, C. S. (2007). Management accounting as practice. *Accounting, Organizations and Society, 32*(1–2), 1–27.

Ahrens, T., & Mollona, M. (2007). Organisational control as cultural practice—A shop floor ethnography of a Sheffield steel mill. *Accounting, Organizations and Society, 32*(4–5), 305–331.

[7] To explain how calculations dominate accountability discourse, Quattrone (2004) shows how monks in the Society of Jesus used to quantify the lives of their flock. They accounted for souls through sacraments, sins and subsequent indulgences. These were valued at a price set by the clergy to remit offences against God.

Alawattage, C., & Wickramasinghe, D. (2009). Weapons of the weak: Subalterns' emancipatory accounting in Ceylon tea. *Accounting, Auditing & Accountability Journal, 22*(3), 379–404.

Allsop, D., & Calveley, M. (2009). Miners' identity and the changing face of the labour process within the UK coal mining industry. *Qualitative Research in Accounting & Management, 6*(1/2), 57–69.

Annisette, M. (2003). The colour of accountancy: Examining the salience of race in a professionalisation project. *Accounting, Organizations and Society, 28*(7–8), 639–674.

Annisette, M. (2008). Race and ethnicity. In J. R. Edwards & S. P. Walker (Eds.), *The Routledge companion to accounting history* (pp. 451–469). London: Routledge.

Annisette, M., & Trivedi, V. U. (2013). Globalization, paradox and the (un)making of identities: Immigrant Chartered Accountants of India in Canada. *Accounting, Organizations & Society, 38*(1), 1–29.

Avshalom, A., & Rachman-Moore, D. (2004). The methods used to implement an ethical code of conduct and employee attitudes. *Journal of Business Ethics, 54*(3), 225–244. https://doi.org/10.1007/s10551-004-1774-4

Backhof, J. F., & Martin, C. L. J. (1991). Historical perspectives: Development of the codes of ethics in legal, medical and accounting professions. *Journal of Business Ethics, 10*, 99–110.

Badiou, A. (2001). *Ethics: An essay on the understanding of evil.* London: Verso.

Badiou, A. (2003). *Saint Paul: The foundation of universalism.* Stanford, CA: Stanford University Press.

Badiou, A. (2004). Fragments of a public diary on the American war against Iraq. *Contemporary French and Francophone Studies, 8*(3), 223–238.

Badiou, A. (2007). *Being and event.* London: Continuum International Publishing.

Badiou, A. (2008). *Number and numbers.* Cambridge: Polity Press.

Badiou, A. (2009). *The logics of worlds: Being and event II.* London: Continuum.

Badiou, A. (2012a). *Philosophy for militants (Pocket communism).* London: Verso.

Badiou, A. (2012b). *The rebirth of history.* London: Verso.

Bebbington, J., & Gray, R. (2001). An account of sustainability: Failure, success and a reconceptualization. *Critical Perspectives on Accounting, 12*(5), 557–588.

Bender, A.-F. (2004). Égalité professionnelle ou gestion de la diversité? *Revue Française de Gestion, 151*(4), 205–217.

Bender, A.-F. (2007). L'approche diversité dans les pays anglo-saxons et en France. In I. Barth & C. Falcoz (Eds.), *Le management de la diversité—enjeux, fondements et pratiques* (pp. 215–232). Paris: L'Harmattan.

Boltanski, L., & Chiapello, E. (2006). *The new spirit of capitalism.* London: Verso.

Bonini, S., & Boraschi, D. (2010). Corporate scandals and capital structure. *Journal of Business Ethics, 95*(2), 241–269. https://doi.org/10.1007/s10551-011-0856-3

Bourricaud, F. (1977). *L'individualisme institutionnel: Essai sur la sociologie de Talcott Parsons*. Paris: Presses Universitaires de France.

Broadbent, J., Dietrich, M., & Laughlin, R. (1996). The development of principal-agent, contracting and accountability relationships in the public sector: Conceptual and cultural problems. *Critical Perspectives on Accounting, 7*(3), 259–284.

Brooks, L. J. (1989). Ethical code of conduct: Deficient in guidance for the Canadian accounting profession. *Journal of Business Ethics, 71*, 117–129.

Brown, J. (2009). Democracy, sustainability and dialogic accounting technologies: Taking pluralism seriously. *Critical Perspectives on Accounting, 20*(3), 313–342.

Brown, J., Dillard, J., & Hopper, T. (2015). Accounting, accountants and accountability regimes in pluralistic societies: Taking multiple perspectives seriously. *Accounting, Auditing & Accountability Journal, 28*(5), 626–650. https://doi.org/10.1108/AAAJ-03-2015-1996

Bryer, R. (2006). Accounting and control of the labour process. *Critical Perspectives on Accounting, 17*(5), 551–598.

Butler, J. (2005). *Giving an account of oneself*. Fordham: Fordham University Press.

Carrère d'Encausse, H. (1992). *La gloire des nations ou la fin de l'Empire soviétique*. Paris: LGF.

Carrère d'Encausse, H. (2000). *La Russie inachevée*. Paris: Fayard.

Carrère d'Encausse, H. (2011). *La Russie entre deux mondes*. Paris: Pluriel.

Carter, C., & Tinker, A. M. (2006). Critical accounting and the labour process. *Critical Perspectives on Accounting, 17*(5), 525–528.

Castelló, I., & Lozano, J. M. (2011). Searching for new forms of legitimacy through corporate responsibility rhetoric. *Journal of Business Ethics, 100*, 11–29.

Chiapello, E., & Fairclough, N. (2002). Understanding the new management ideology: A transdisciplinary contribution from critical discourse analysis and new sociology of capitalism. *Discourse & Society, 13*(2), 185–208.

Cho, C. H., Roberts, R. W., & Patten, D. M. (2010). The language of US corporate environmental disclosure. *Accounting, Organizations and Society, 35*(4), 431–443.

Collier, P. M. (2008). Stakeholder accountability: A field study of the implementation of a governance improvement plan. *Accounting, Auditing & Accountability Journal, 21*(7), 933–964.

Cooper, S. M., & Owen, D. L. (2007). Corporate social reporting and stakeholder accountability: The missing link. *Accounting, Organizations and Society, 32*(7–8), 649–667.

Crane, A., & Matten, D. (2016). *Business ethics: Managing corporate citizenship and sustainability in the age of globalization*. Oxford, UK: Oxford University Press.

del Carmen Triana, M., Wagstaff, M. F., & Kim, K. (2012). That's not fair! How personal value for diversity influences reactions to the perceived discriminatory treatment of minorities. *Journal of Business Ethics, 111*, 211–218.

Dienhart, J. (1995). Rationality, ethical codes, and an egalitarian justification of ethical expertise: Implications for professions and organizations. *Business Ethics Quarterly, 5*, 419–450.

Dillard, J., & Roslender, R. (2011). Taking pluralism seriously: Embedded moralities in management accounting and control systems. *Critical Perspectives on Accounting, 22*(2), 135–147.

Du, S., & Viera, E. T., Jr. (2012). Striving for legitimacy through corporate social responsibility: Insights from oil companies. *Journal of Business Ethics, 110*(4), 413–427.

Emirbayer, M., & Mische, A. (1998). What is agency? *American Journal of Sociology, 103*(4), 962–1023.

Falkenberg, A., & Falkenberg, J. (2009). Ethics in international value chain networks: The case of Telenor Bangladesh. *Journal of Business Ethics, 90*, 355–369.

Galbraith, J. K. (1994). *L'argent*. Paris: Folio.

Gallhofer, S., Haslam, J., & Yonekura, A. (2015). Accounting as differentiated universal for emancipatory praxis: Accounting delineation and mobilisation for emancipation(s) recognising democracy and difference. *Accounting, Auditing & Accountability Journal, 28*(5), 846–874. https://doi.org/10.1108/AAAJ-08-2013-1451

García-de-Frutos, N., Ortega-Egea, J. M., & Martínez-del-Río, J. (2016). Anti-consumption for environmental sustainability: Conceptualization, review, and multilevel research directions. *Journal of Business Ethics*. https://doi.org/10.1007/s10551-016-3023-z

Gardels, N. (2013). Governance after the end of power. *New Perspectives Quarterly, 30*(3), 2–7.

Garfinkel, H. (1967). *Studies in ethnomethodology*. Englewood Cliffs, NJ: Prentice Hall.

Gaumnitz, R. B., & Lere, C. J. (2002). Contents of codes of ethics of professional business organizations in the United States. *Journal of Business Ethics, 35*, 35–49.

Gendron, Y., Cooper, D., & Townley, B. (2001). In the name of accountablity: State auditing, independence and new public management. *Accounting, Auditing & Accountability Journal, 14*(3), 278–310.

Gordon, K., & Miyake, M. (2001). Business approaches to combating bribery: A study of codes of conduct. *Journal of Business Ethics, 34*, 161–173.

Gray, R. (2002a). The social accounting project and Accounting Organizations and Society Privileging engagement, imaginings, new accountings and pragmatism over critique? *Accounting, Organizations and Society, 27*(7), 687–708.

Gray, R. (2002b). Of messiness, systems and sustainability: Towards a more social and environmental finance and accounting. *The British Accounting Review, 34*(4), 357–386.

Gray, R. (2010). Is accounting for sustainability actually accounting for sustainability…and how would we know? An exploration of narratives of organisations and the planet. *Accounting, Organizations and Society, 35*(1), 47–62.

Gray, R. (2013). Back to basics: What do we mean by environmental (and social) accounting and what is it for?—A reaction to Thornton. *Critical Perspectives on Accounting, 24*(6), 459–468.

Gray, R., Dey, C., Owen, D., Evans, R., & Zadek, S. (1997). Struggling with the praxis of social accounting: Stakeholders, accountability, audits and procedures. *Accounting, Auditing & Accountability Journal, 10*(3), 325–364.

Guillén, M. (1994). *Models of management : Work, authority, and organization in a comparative perspective*. Chicago: University of Chicago Press.

Hayek, F. v. (1979). *The road to Serfdom*. London: Routledge.

Hoffman, A. J. (1999). Institutional evolution and change: Environmentalism and the US chemical industry. *Academy of Management Journal, 42*(4), 351–371.

Hoi, C. K., Wu, Q., & Zhang, H. (2016). Community social capital and corporate social responsibility. *Journal of Business Ethics*. https://doi.org/10.1007/s10551-016-3335-z

Hsu, L., & Lawrence, B. (2016). The role of social media and brand equity during a product recall crisis: A shareholder value perspective. *International Journal of Research in Marketing, 33*(1), 59–77. https://doi.org/10.1016/j.ijresmar.2015.04.004

Iivonen, K., & Moisander, J. (2014). Rhetorical construction of narcissistic CSR orientation. *Journal of Business Ethics*. In press.

Jacobs, K., & Walker, S. P. (2004). Accounting and accountability in the Iona Community. *Accounting, Auditing & Accountability Journal, 17*(3), 361–381.

Jensen, M. (2001). Value maximization, stakeholder theory, and the corporate objective function. *Journal of Applied Corporate Finance, 14*(3), 8–21.

Joannidès, V. (2012). Accounterability and the problematics of accountability. *Critical Perspectives on Accounting, 23*(3), 244–257.

Joannidès, V., & Jaumier, S. (2013). De la démocratie en Amérique du Nord à l'accountability à la française. Comprendre les origines sociopolitiques de l'accountability. *Revue Française de Gestion, 237*(8), 99–116.

Joannidès, V., & McKernan, J. (2014). Ethics: From negative regulations to fidelity to the event. In P. O'Sullivan (Ed.), *From hubris to disgrace: The philosophy, politics and economics of finance in the 21st century* (pp. 310–331). London: Routledge.

Jørgensen, B., & Messner, M. (2010). Accounting and strategising: A case study from new product development. *Accounting, Organizations & Society, 35*(2), 184–204.

Kalev, A., Dobbin, F., & Kelly, E. (2006). Best practices or best guesses? Assessing the efficacy of corporate affirmative action and diversity policies. *American Sociological Review, 71*(4), 589–617.

Kamuf, P. (2007). Accounterability. *Textual practice, 21*(2), 251–266.

Kaspi, A. (2008). *Comprendre les États-Unis d'aujourd'hui*. Paris: Poche.

Kim, K. (2003). *Order and agency in modernity: Talcott Parsons, Erving Goffman, and Harold Garfinkel*. Albany: State University of New York Press.

Knights, D., & Vurdubakis, T. (1993). Calculations of risk: Towards an understanding of insurance as a moral and political technology. *Accounting, Organizations and Society, 18*(7–8), 729–764. https://doi.org/10.1016/0361-3682(93)90050-G

Laufer, D., & Jung, J. M. (2010). Incorporating regulatory focus theory in product recall communications to increase compliance with a product recall. *Public Relations Review, 36*(2), 147–151. https://doi.org/10.1016/j.pubrev.2010.03.004

Laughlin, R. (1996). Principals and higher-principals: Accounting for accountability in the caring professions. In R. Munro & J. Mouritsen (Eds.), *Accountability: Power, ethos and the technologies of managing* (pp. 225–244). London: International Thomson Business Press.

Law, J. (1996). Organizing accountabilities: Ontology and the mode of accounting. In R. Munro & J. Mouritsen (Eds.), *Accountability: Power, ethos and the technologies of managing* (pp. 283–306). London: International Thomson Business Press.

Levi, P. (1991). *If this is a man*. London: Abacus.

Lévinas, E. (1972). *Humanism of the other* (N. Poller, Trans.). Chicago: University of Illinois Press.

Lévinas, E. (1985). *Ethics and infinity*. Pittsburg: Duquesne University Press.

Lévinas, E. (1987). *Time and the other* (R. A. Cohen, Trans.). Pittsburgh: Duquesne University Press.

Lévinas, E. (1991). *Entre nous: Thinking-of-the-other* (M. Smith & B. Harshav, Trans.). New York: Continuum.

Lin-Hi, N., & Blumberg, I. (2011). The relationship between corporate governance, global governance, and sustainable profits: Lessons learned from BP. *Corporate Governance: An International Review, 11*(5), 571–584.

Low, M., Davey, H., & Hooper, K. (2008). Accounting scandals, ethical dilemmas and educational challenges. *Critical Perspectives on Accounting, 19*(2), 222–254.

Lubatkin, M. H., Lane, P. J., Collin, S., & Very, P. (2005). Origins of corporate governance in the USA, Sweden and France. *Organization, 26*(6), 867–888.

Magno, F. (2012). Managing product recalls: The effects of time, responsible vs. opportunistic recall management and blame on consumers' attitudes. *Procedia—Social and Behavioral Sciences, 58*, 1309–1315. https://doi.org/10.1016/j.sbspro.2012.09.1114

McKernan, J. (2011). Deconstruction and the responsibilities of the accounting academic. *Critical Perspectives on Accounting, 22*(7), 198–713.

McKernan, J. F. (2012). Accountability as contradiction, testimony and gift. *Critical Perspectives on Accounting, 23*(3), 258–278.

McKernan, J. F., & Kosmala, K. (2004). Accounting, love and justice. *Accounting, Auditing & Accountability Journal, 17*(3), 327–360.

McKernan, J. F., & Kosmala, K. (2007). Doing the truth: Religion deconstruction justice, and accounting. *Accounting, Auditing & Accountability Journal, 20*(5), 729–764.

McKernan, J. F., & McPhail, K. (2012). Accountability and accounterability. *Critical Perspectives on Accounting, 23*(12), 177–182.

McPhail, K., & McKernan, J. (2011). Accounting for human rights: An overview and introduction. *Critical Perspectives on Accounting, 22*(8), 733–737.

Messner, M. (2009). The limits of accountability. *Accounting, Organizations and Society, 34*(8), 918–938.

Miller, P., & O'Leary, T. (1994). Accounting, "economic citizenship" and the spatial reordering of manufacture. *Accounting, Organizations and Society, 19*(1), 15–43.

Mouck, T. (1999). Financial reporting, democracy and environmentalism: A critique of the commodification of information. *Critical Perspectives on Accounting, 6*(6), 535–553.

Ogden, S. G., & Bougen, P. (1985). A radical perspective on the disclosure of accounting information to trade unions. *Accounting, Organizations and Society, 10*(2), 211–224.

Organ, D. W. (1997). Organizational citizenship behavior: It's construct clean-up time. *Human Performance, 10*(2), 85–97.

Owen, D. L., & Lloyd, A. J. (1985). The use of financial information by trade union negotiators in plant level collective bargaining. *Accounting, Organizations and Society, 10*(3), 329–350. https://doi.org/10.1016/0361-3682(85)90023-6

Parker, L., & Ritson, P. (2011). Rage against the dying of the light: Lyndall Urwick's scientific management. *Journal of Management History, 17*(4), 379–398.

Parsons, T. (1982). The hierarchy of control. In L. H. Mayhew (Ed.), *Talcott Parsons on institutions and social evolution: Selected writings* (pp. 157–172). Chicago: The University of Chicago Press.

Parsons, T. (1991). *The social system.* London: Routledge.

Parsons, T., & Platt, G. M. (1983). American values and American society. In T. Parsons (Ed.), *On institutions and social evolution* (pp. 327–338). Chicago: The University of Chicago Press.

Parsons, T., & Shils, E. (2001). Values, motives and systems of action. In T. Parsons & E. Shils (Eds.), *Toward a general theory of action: Theoretical foundations for the social sciences* (pp. 47–275). New Brunswick: Transaction Publishers.

Patten, D. M. (2002). Give or take on the internet: An examination of the disclosure practices of insurance firm web innovators. *Journal of Business Ethics, 26*, 247–259.

Pérezts, M., & Picard, S. (2014). Compliance of comfort zone? The work of embedded ethics in performing regulations. *Journal of Business Ethics*. In press.

Pless, N. M., & Maak, T. (2004). Building an inclusive diversity culture: Principles, processes and practice. *Journal of Business Ethics, 54*, 129–147.

Poczter, S. L., & Jankovic, L. M. (2014). The Google car: Driving toward a better future? *Journal of Business Case Studies, 10*(1), 7–14.

Potter, A., Murray, J., Lawson, B., & Graham, S. (2012). Trends in product recalls within the agri-food industry: Empirical evidence from the USA, UK and the Republic of Ireland. *Trends in Food Science & Technology, 28*(2), 77–86. https://doi.org/10.1016/j.tifs.2012.06.017

Preston, A., Cooper, D., Scarbrough, D. P., & Chilton, R. C. (1995). Changes in the code of ethics of the US accounting profession, 1917 and 1988: The continual quest for legimating. *Accounting, Organizations & Society, 20*, 507–546.

Quattrone, P. (2004). Accounting for God: Accounting and accountability practices in the Society of Jesus (Italy, XVI–XVII centuries). *Accounting, Organizations and Society, 29*(7), 647–683.

Quattrone, P. (2009). Books to be practiced: Memory, the power of the visual, and the success of accounting. *Accounting, Organizations & Society, 34*(1), 85–118.

Ricœur, P. (1955). *Histoire et vérité*. Paris: Seuil.

Ricœur, P. (1991). *Du texte à l'action*. Paris: Seuil.

Roberts, J. (1991). The possibilities of accountability. *Accounting, Organizations and Society, 16*(4), 355–368.

Roberts, J. (1996). From discipline to dialogue: Individualizing and socialising forms of accountability. In R. Munro & J. Mouritsen (Eds.), *Accountability: Power, ethos and the technologies of managing* (pp. 40–61). London: International Thomson Business Press.

Roberts, J. (2001). Trust and control in Anglo-American systems of corporate governance: The individualizing and socialising effects of processes of accountability. *Human Relations, 54*(12), 1547–1582.

Roberts, J. (2009). No one is perfect: The limits of transparency and an ethic for 'intelligent' accountability. *Accounting, Organizations and Society, 34*(8), 957–970.

Roberts, J., Sanderson, P., Barker, R., & Hendry, J. (2006). In the mirror of the market: The disciplinary effects of company/fund manager meetings. *Accounting, Organizations and Society, 31*(3), 277–294.

Roberts, J., & Scapens, R. (1985). Accounting systems and systems of accountability—Understanding accounting practices in their organisational contexts. *Accounting, Organizations and Society, 10*(4), 443–456.

Savan, B. (1989). Beyond professional ethics: Issues and agendas. *Journal of Business Ethics, 8*, 179–185.

Scapens, R. W., & Roberts, J. (1993). Accounting and control: A case study of resistance to accounting change. *Management Accounting Research, 4*(1), 1–32.
Schatzki, T. R. (2000). Practice theory. In T. R. Schatzki, K. K. Cetina, & E. Savigny (von) (Eds.), *The practice turn in contemporary theory* (pp. 1–14). London: Routledge.
Schwartz, M. (2000). Why ethical codes constitute an unconscionable regression. *Journal of Business Ethics, 23*, 173–184.
Schweiker, W. (1993). Accounting for ourselves: Accounting practices and the disclosure of ethics. *Accounting, Organizations & Society, 18*(2–3), 231–252.
Shearer, T. (2002). Ethics and accountability: From the for-itself to the for-the-other. *Accounting, Organizations and Society, 27*(6), 541–573.
Sheehy, B. (2015). Defining CSR: Problems and solutions. *Journal of Business Ethics, 131*(3), 625–648.
Siekkinen, J. (2016). Value relevance of fair values in different investor protection environments. *Accounting Forum, 40*(1), 1–15. https://doi.org/10.1016/j.accfor.2015.11.001
Simons, R. (2005). *Levers of organization design: How managers use accountability systems for greater performance and commitment.* Boston: Harvard University Press.
Sitaoja, M. E. (2006). Value priorities as combining core factors between CSR and reputation—A qualitative study. *Journal of Business Ethics, 68*, 91–111.
Smith, C., & Meiksins, P. (1995). System, society and dominance effects in cross-national organisational analysis. *Work, Employment and Society, 9*(2), 241–267.
Stolowy, H. (2005). Nothing like the Enron affair could happen in France (!). *European Accounting Review, 14*(2), 405–415.
Tocqueville (de), A. (1835). *Democracy in America: And two essays on America.* London: Penguin Classics.
Tweedie, D., Dyball, M. C., Hazelton, J., & Wright, S. (2013). Teaching global ethical standards: A case and strategy for broadening the accounting ethics curriculum. *Journal of Business Ethics, 115*(1), 1–15.
Unerman, J., & O'Dwyer, B. (2007). The business case for regulation of corporate social responsibility and accountability. *Accounting Forum, 31*(4), 332–353.
Urbach, E. (1979). *The sages, their beliefs and concepts.* Jerusalem: The Magnes Press, The Hebrew University.
Vallentin, S. (2015). Governmentalities of CSR: Danish government policy as a reflection of political difference. *Journal of Business Ethics, 127*(1), 33–47.
Weldon, E., & Gargano, G. M. (1988). Cognitive loafing—The effects of accountability and shared responsibility on cognitive effort. *Personality and Social Psychology Bulletin, 14*(1), 159–171.
White, B. J., & Montgomery, R. (1980). Corporate codes of conduct. *California Management Review, 23*, 80–87.
Wray-Bliss, E. (2002). Abstract ethics, embodied ethics: The strange marriage of Foucault and positivism in labour process theory. *Organization, 9*(1), 5–39.

Conclusion

This volume sets out to discuss ethical issues surrounding management accounting. The five chapters developed a different facet thereof. Chapter 1 showed how management accounting was formed during the industrial revolution as a tool for economic and social progress and has since then served any types of masters from colonisation or emancipation but also military strategy or even the Shoah. Chapter 2 explicitly discussed management accountants' ontological construction. Its starting point was the ambiguity surrounding two notions often used in management research: trust and confidence. Chapter 3 addressed issues in social and environmental reporting. In so doing, this chapter brought unusual economic theory into accounting research: welfare economics. Thereby, fresher insight could be brought into management accounting research, enabling to ponder what good and evil mean and how they can be measured. Chapter 4 questioned the innate or learnt nature of ethics and raised the question of how necessary it is to teach management accounting students ethics courses. Chapter 5 endeavoured to turn the full circle by questioning the possibility of ethics in management accounting, namely because this notion bears numerous questions and contradictions bound to make it difficult to happen at all.

By addressing all these issues, I am very conscious that some others, still very important to management accounting's ethics, have been left aside. I see four in particular that have not been discussed in this volume: whistle-

V. Joannidès de Lautour, *Strategic Management Accounting, Volume III*, https://doi.org/10.1007/978-3-030-20157-9

blowing, the reliance paradigm, tone at the top and spirituality. None of these issues has formally been overlooked but addressed implicitly or indirectly.

Whistle-blowing was not treated as such, but related issues may transpire from discussions revolving around identifying what is good and what is evil. But it is true that issues in reporting an evil situation were not elicited. I can ascribe this to the fact that, being French and writing on the Shoah, I see there is always an ambivalence *vis-à-vis* the reporting of a situation perceived as unjust. During World War II, many French people reported people as Jews, because governmental authorities encouraged them to do so. Since then, reporting and issues relating to whistle-blowing have always been cautiously apprehended. Almost on purpose, I did not address this particular issue of whistle-blowing.

I did not say anything on the reliance paradigm, although it is increasingly central to the investor-investee relationship. The main reason for not discussing this issue is that management and accounting research little insight into it for now. It seems to be a significant part of legal research (Hayes, 2020). Once the concept commences to spread across management and accounting research, it is possible to really address it. As of 2019, it may just be premature.

Tone at the top was not expressed as such and was explicitly discussed. But the idea of possible discrepancies between ethical guidelines issued at the top of the organisation and perception all along the hierarchy was discussed in Chap. 3 on the ontological construction of ethics. What can be known as tone at the top was presented here as a cascade of interpretations as well as an ethical cascade. Discussing tone at the top per se would have led to raise different questions not necessarily aligned with this volume's purpose, which was to understand the construction of the ethical management accountant.

Lastly, spirituality was not discussed either in this third volume. Quite a few prior publications have addressed the intertwining of management accounting and spirituality (Gallhofer & Haslam, 2011; Molisa, 2011). Even if spirituality was not explicitly discussed in this volume, these issues in the construction of management accounting's ethics were raised in two chapters. In Chap. 1, the management accounting's religious roots were briefly elicited, referring to their appearing as a divine revelation (Joannidès de Lautour, 2016). Management accounting as a spiritual practice was also developed in Chap. 2, as the notion of ethics as practice was discussed. The notion of practice was understood as an extension of practice theory with strong borrowings from the practice of everyday life (Certeau (de), 1984, 1986, 1988). This borrowing from Michel de Certeau, who was a philosopher and a Catholic priest, necessarily rested upon a notion that ethics is spiritually grounded.

Something that could appear as a surprise to numerous readers is to see that this volume borrows from many thinkers and philosophers belonging to different research traditions: Tocqueville, Bourdieu, Certeau, Foucault, Latour, Derrida, Lévinas, Badiou. It is true that some oppose each other, such as Badiou and Lévinas, especially on ethics. Whilst Lévinas sees ethics as an ontological construct and therefore as something very immanent (Lévinas, 1985, 1987), Badiou sees it as both immanent and transcendental: coming from within and imposed to the self at the same time (Badiou, 2001, 2003). Likewise, Foucault is a post-structuralist and Bourdieu is a structuralist-determinist, whilst Latour is perceived as a relativist. Far from being real inconsistencies, these various borrowings were aimed at highlighting different facets of ethics and at showing how critical accounting research has addressed these. Hopefully, these multiple borrowings would enable to shed light on what management accounting research can reveal when engaging in a discussion on ethics.

Given the paucity of management accounting publications addressing ethics, a research agenda can be envisaged. In the first place, it would be worthwhile further investigating how ethics is part of management accountants' professional identity. We know that their professional codes of conduct mention they must be ethical; albeit, not much else is known as to what this means and how this can be manifested in their profession (Preston, Cooper, Scarbrough, & Chilton, 1995; Reynolds, 2000; Velayutham, 2003). Outside of this, it would be pertinent to understand what this professional ethics encompasses and how it drives these professionals' actions. An extension of such a discussion would naturally consist in exploring the types of ethical dilemmas that could confront management accountants and how these are solved. In other words, management accountant's ethical decision-making needs further exploration and understanding. Otherwise, management accountants' work will remain a black box for a long time, as it has always been until the dirty work was unveiled (Morales & Lambert, 2013). In so doing, this would certainly clarify how management accountants conceive of good and evil, and how they include these notions into their own work. For this type of research, the traditional methodologies employed in critical management accounting research would be appropriate: auto-ethnography, ethnography or interviews. Theoretical frameworks that could be employed could borrow from all these thinkers mentioned in this third volume: Tocqueville, Bourdieu, Certeau, Foucault, Latour, Derrida, Lévinas, Badiou. Of course, this list is not exhaustive, other major thinkers being likely to help: Butler, Zizek, Agamben, Giddens, and Laclau & Mouffe.

Bibliography

Badiou, A. (2001). *Ethics: An essay on the understanding of Evil.* London: Verso.

Badiou, A. (2003). *Saint Paul: The foundation of universalism.* Stanford, CA: Stanford University Press.

Certeau (de), M. (1984). *The practice of everyday life, Volume 1.* Los Angeles: University of California Press.

Certeau (de), M. (1986). *Heterologies: Discourse on the other.* Minneapolis: University of Minnesota Press.

Certeau (de), M. (1988). *The practice of everyday life, Volume 2—Living and cooking.* Los Angeles: University of California Press.

Gallhofer, S., & Haslam, J. (2011). Emancipation, the spiritual and accounting. *Critical Perspectives on Accounting, 22*(5), 500–509.

Hayes, T. (2020). *The reliance paradigm: From Antiquity to modern law.* Doctorate of Business Administration, Grenoble École de Management, Grenoble.

Joannidès de Lautour, V. (2016). *Capitalism, accounting and the revealed religions—A study of Judaism, Christianity and Islam.* London: Palgrave Macmillan.

Lévinas, E. (1985). *Ethics and infinity.* Pittsburgh: Duquesne University Press.

Lévinas, E. (1987). *Time and the other* (R. A. Cohen, Trans.). Pittsburgh: Duquesne University Press.

Molisa, P. (2011). A spiritual reflection on emancipation and accounting. *Critical Perspectives on Accounting, 22*(5), 453–484.

Morales, J., & Lambert, C. (2013). Dirty work and the construction of identity. An ethnographic study of management accounting practices. *Accounting, Organizations & Society, 38*(3), 228–244.

Preston, A., Cooper, D., Scarbrough, D. P., & Chilton, R. C. (1995). Changes in the code of ethics of the US accounting profession, 1917 and 1988: The continual quest for legitimating. *Accounting, Organizations & Society, 20,* 507–546.

Reynolds, M. (2000). Professionalism, ethical codes and the internal auditor: A moral argument. *Journal of Business Ethics, 24,* 115–124.

Velayutham, S. (2003). The accounting profession's code of ethics: Is it code of ethics or a code of quality assurance? *Critical Perspectives on Accounting, 14*(4), 483–503.

Index[1]

[1] Note: Page numbers followed by 'n' refer to notes.

V. Joannidès de Lautour, *Strategic Management Accounting, Volume III*, https://doi.org/10.1007/978-3-030-20157-9

The manufacturer's authorised representative in the EU is Springer Nature Customer Service Centre GmbH, Europaplatz 3, 69115 Heidelberg, Germany. If you have any concerns regarding our products, please contact ProductSafety@springernature.com

Printed and bound by CPI Group (UK) Ltd, Croydon, CR0 4YY

30/09/2026

02225656-0006